Silence of the Songbirds

SILENCE OF THE SONGBIRDS

BRIDGET STUTCHBURY

Walker & Company
New York

Published by Walker Publishing Company, Inc., New York
Distributed to the trade by Holtzbrinck Publishers

All papers used by Walker & Company are natural, recyclable products made from
wood grown in well-managed forests. The manufacturing processes conform to the
environmental regulations of the country of origin.

Illustrations on pages iv, 1, 17, 34, 50, 78, 98, 129, 156, 190, and 214 by Julie Zickefoose
Designed by Sharon Kish

LIBRARY OF CONGRESS CATALOGING-IN-PUBLICATION DATA HAS BEEN APPLIED FOR.

ISBN-10: 0-8027-1609-1
ISBN-13: 978-0-8027-1609-5

Visit Walker & Company's Web site at www.walkerbooks.com

First U.S. edition 2007

1 3 5 7 9 10 8 6 4 2

Printed in the United States of America by Quebecor World Fairfield

For Douglas and Sarah
Who walk the green paths, lighted by fireflies

Contents

List of Songbird Illustrations
by Julie Zickefoose

Silence of the Songbirds

1 PARADISE NOT YET LOST
The Tanagers and Warblers of Gamboa, Panama

Birds were among nature's delights during my childhood, but they were not the stars of the show. Visits to the cottage were a kid's dream, filled with swimming, canoeing, and building makeshift forts in the woods. During games of hide-and-seek I shrank into the ground, breathing in the tangy scent of pine needles, and passed the time watching whirligig beetles clumsily rowing into each other, blue damselflies dancing an aerial ballet over the water, and spiders doing tightrope walks. My family would gather at the living-room window to admire the imposing figure of the great blue heron standing on his rock or when someone spotted a merganser duck and her fluffy brood bobbing in the waves along the shoreline. On crisp fall mornings, loud and insistent honking sparked a stampede to the dock, where we counted the low-flying geese as they headed south one squadron after another. I don't remember paying much attention to the little songbirds that nested in the blueberry bushes, cedars, and pine trees. The red-eyed vireos, song sparrows, and yellow-rumped warblers went about their business year after year despite three noisy kids and a dog that invaded on weekends and summer vacations.

Little did I know that songbirds would lead me on a life of discovery and adventure, from dodging surprised rattlesnakes in the desert of Arizona to dodging aerial bombardment by angry howler monkeys in the tropical rainforests of Panama. The gateway to my passion for these feathered jewels began with the graceful swallows, though my own interest was in their fierce battles for nesting cavities. As an undergraduate student, my summer home at a field station in southern Ontario was also home to dozens of nest boxes that were lined up row after row in several different hayfields, each one with a vigilant tree swallow perched atop or flying nearby. Shiny blue backs glittered in the sun as the bickering swallows circled their boxes like little fighter jets, scolding and chasing intruders that dared to come too close. The nest boxes are so valuable that both males and females have knock-down, drag-out fights with the desperate stragglers that arrive later in spring and have no place to breed. Once, during nest checks, I opened the door of a box to find two females fighting so intently they did not even notice the giant face peering in at them.

I studied the swallow battles for several years and earned a master's degree, but this was not enough for me. I was hooked for life on the challenge and satisfaction of posing questions of nature and devising ways to work out the answers. My Ph.D. at Yale University in the late 1980s was on another swallow, the purple martin, though this time I wanted to know how young males finesse their way to home ownership among older males who control all the nest cavities. Each spring I loaded up my pickup truck with most of my worldly belongings and drove across the country by myself to study colonies of martins in southern Oklahoma. This is where I saw my first roadrunner and spent many hours awestruck with the bright salmon-orange flashes and elegant tail streamers of scissor-tailed flycatchers as they did spectacular loop-the-loops in the air as females quietly looked on.

I got to know tree swallows and purple martins intimately after holding dozens in my hand and spending hundreds of hours watching them at their nesting houses. But until the end of my Ph.D., I had barely given a thought to what their lives were like *after* they left their breeding grounds. My outlook changed forever when I was invited along on a field trip to Brazil with the Purple Martin Conservation Association and Dr. Gene Morton, a senior scientist at the Smithsonian Institution's National Zoological Park—and, as it turned out, my future husband.

After a gruelling day of travel in early February, we ended up in southern Brazil at a small lodge in the Itatiaia National Park sipping a well-earned *caipirinha,* the national drink. The next morning I sat on the patio taking in my first look at wild toucans, parrots, and other exotic tropical birds. But we were there to study martins, not bird watch, so after breakfast we began the long drive to the busy town of Ribeirão Preto in the state of São Paulo. We needed to find the park in the centre of town where martins slept at night by the thousands, so our driver pulled up to a group of men standing by the side of the road.

In his rough Spanish, Gene told them we were looking for the swallows, or *golondrinas.* Amid wide smirks, winks, and knowing looks, they gave us the directions. Our Brazilian driver laughed and explained that *golondrina* was the local nickname for the prostitutes who, like the martins, congregated in the park at night. This seemed like such a foreign world to me, yet it was just as much a home for purple martins as the familiar nesting houses I had studied thousands of miles away.

The next year I worked with Gene at the National Zoo and began a study of hooded warblers on their wintering grounds in Mexico, and we married a few years later, after I took on a faculty position at York University, in Toronto. Over the past decade our family has lived a migratory lifestyle of our own while studying birds, dividing our time between our suburban home north of Toronto, our old farmhouse in northwestern Pennsylvania, and the tropical forests of Panama. Gene and I have spent many hours walking through the woods or sitting on the back porch at the farm, happily on the lookout for our daily fix of discoveries. These can be as simple as seeing chickadees stashing seeds under the bark of cedar trees, catching a parasitic wasp in the brutal act of laying her eggs inside a living caterpillar, or rare sightings like a male cowbird giving courtship displays to a rusty blackbird. Our children are growing up with parents who net and band birds in the back-yard, raise dozens of *Promethea* silk moths on the screened-in porch, and drive around town with an antenna on the roof of the minivan listening for radio-tagged purple martins. Their patience is sometimes pushed to the limit, for instance, when they run away from the picnic table yelling "Bee!" while I calmly explain that the offending creature is a *wasp,* not a bee.

I have spent my entire adult life studying and enjoying birds, taking for granted that they will be there for future generations to do the same. When I did my graduate work on tree swallows, the alarm bells were not yet ringing, and one heard very little about disappearing songbirds. Times have changed though, and now we have a long list of North American migratory songbirds that are disappearing at a frightening rate. Wood thrush, Kentucky warblers, bobolinks, and the eastern king-bird are among the victims. By some estimates, we may have already lost almost half the songbirds that filled the skies only forty years ago. The threats are almost too many to count: destruction of wintering habi-tat, pesticides, cowbirds and other predators, light pollution, and poor breeding habitat are among the problems birds face.

The early warning cries of the songbirds suggest that their enormous migration, even bigger in number and scale than that of the extinct pas-senger pigeons, is now at risk. If we could change the natural world enough to wipe out billions of passenger pigeons, it is not out of line to think that we are able to inadvertently cripple songbird migration. We can put a man on the moon and send an e-mail to the other side of the planet in a blink of an eye, but we can also burn a hole in the ozone layer, send our pollution across oceans and disrupt climates around the globe.

We are seeing dramatic songbird declines around the world, not just in North America. In Britain a wide variety of songbird species have suffered enormous losses in numbers since the 1960s, including a 95 percent drop in tree sparrows and an 80 percent decline in corn buntings. Other songbirds that have declined seriously include bullfinches, skylarks, pipits, and wagtails. Britain has little forest remaining and most open lands are used for agriculture, so many of the birds surveyed are open country and farmland birds. Woodland species are faring no better, however, as about a third of the species surveyed declined by over 50 percent from 1966 through 1999. The possible causes of the declines in Britain are as varied as for North America: loss of wintering habitat in the tropics, loss of breeding habitat, exposure to pesticides, climate change, and increased predation pressures. On the other side of the globe, extensive loss of woodlands in southern Australia has meant that once common songbirds, like the hooded robin and brown creeper, are now missing from whole regions. There is good evidence of population declines of many other species, and some ornithologists predict that unless drastic changes are made, the country will lose half its land birds over the next century.

Researchers from the Center of Conservation Biology, at Stanford University, published a formal analysis of the state of the world's birds, and ended with an ominous warning to all of us. They analyzed the current status of all bird species living today, almost ten thousand in all, as well as the hundred or so that have gone extinct in recent times. The International Union for Conservation of Nature and Natural Resources currently lists 1.3 percent of the world's birds as recently extinct and 12 percent as threatened with extinction in the near future. The Stanford group used different scenarios for the effect of climate change and habitat loss on birds to forecast what is likely to happen by the end of this century. If forest loss continues at its present pace, it is quite realistic to think that within a few human generations we will lose one quarter of the world's bird species.

Migrants, such as the purple martin, seamlessly switch from being tropical birds living somewhere in Central or South America to marathon flying machines that travel several thousand miles in a month. Just as easily, they become showy songsters obsessed with mating and breeding, and devoted parents tending eggs and caring for young. Each species has a different story to tell along the way, but the rhythm of the journey is shared among the migrants. We will unravel the mystery of the disappearing songbirds by taking a journey with them. Our trip begins in the tropics, where migrants spend more than half the year.

～⌒

Our students had arrived the night before at Tocumen airport, in Panama City, looking pale and shell-shocked, ready for a two-week reprieve from the northern winter. After hauling giant backpacks and suitcases off the baggage claim, they went through customs and stepped out into the main lobby of the airport where we were waiting for them. The airport was crowded with tourists, a few U.S. military personnel, and Panamanians returning from trips to Miami loaded down with gifts. Gene and I had already been in Panama for a month, but none of the students had ever been in a tropical country before, and we were about to introduce them to the wonders of tropical birds. As we walked out of the airport terminal we were enveloped in the warm, humid air of a Panama evening. Our visitors were giddy with delight as they stripped off their sweaters and jackets, and we all worked up a sweat doing the impossible task of somehow stuffing all the bags and bodies into the van.

Our van joined the cars, trucks, buses, and taxis on the busy airport road heading toward Panama City, weaving around buses and cars that suddenly slammed on their brakes. The buses in Panama are works of art, covered with detailed hand-drawn paintings of Jesus, Elvis, Britney Spears, alpine nature scenes, and inspirational messages that cover just about every square inch of the bus, including the bumper and at least half the windshield. The rush hour runs well into the evening, and the traffic was moving quickly amid the frequent honking of horns and heavy exhaust fumes. The students looked curiously at the stores flashing by. Many were simple small buildings made of cinder blocks with corrugated metal roofs advertising the local beer Cerveza Panama, or *llantas* (tires), and *ferretería* (hardware). There were also the all-too-familiar Toyota dealerships with gleaming SUVs parked out front, Sony electronics stores, Home Depot, Costco, and the equally ubiquitous Kentucky Fried Chicken, Pizza Hut, and McDonald's.

Our destination was the small town of Gamboa, on the shores of the Panama Canal, about twelve miles north of Panama City. This is not your typical Panamanian town because it is in the former Canal Zone, where American workmen and their families once lived in suburban-like surroundings complete with a small theatre, swimming pool, and tennis courts. Today Panama operates the canal, and Gamboa is home to the Dredging Division, which must constantly fight the silt that washes into the canal with the heavy tropical rains. The forest alongside the canal has been preserved for precisely this reason; it is an ecological safeguard against the heavy erosion that would otherwise bring the ships and economy to a halt.

Gamboa is literally at the end of the road and is encircled by the forest of the Soberania National Park. The Smithsonian Tropical Research Institute operates a research station in Gamboa, part of its extensive network of research facilities in Panama. We could tell when we were nearing Gamboa because the stores, gas stations, and chaotic traffic intersections were gradually left far behind as we entered the home stretch that passed through forest. There were few other cars on the road this late at night, and the students who were still awake could see only strobe-like glimpses of our headlights on the towering trees along the sides of the road. The last few hundred yards over the Chagres River was enough to wake the dead as the van's wheels thundered on the metal-topped wooden planks of the one-lane bridge that everyone driving to or from Gamboa must cross.

Nightfall cloaked the students' entrance to town, and they struggled up the stairs to the old schoolhouse, hauling their backpacks and suitcases, each intent on claiming a bed in the dorm room. It wasn't until they awoke at dawn that it really hit home that they were in the tropics. Tall royal palms lined the street in front of the schoolhouse, and our visitors were awed by their first looks at chestnut-mandibled toucans sitting proudly in the treetops calling loudly *Keeeer, kick-ik, kick-ik,* and red-lored parrots screaming overhead. The bird feeder outside the front of the school was stocked with bananas and papaya rinds, and there was a busy crowd of clay-coloured robins, blue-grey tanagers, and a red-fronted woodpecker having breakfast.

It was hard to persuade anyone to get into the van, but the day heats up quickly and the best birding is first thing in the morning. We drove the few miles to the forest where the Pipeline Road, a one-lane dirt road, runs far into the Soberania National Park. There actually was a working pipeline here once; it can still be seen here and there, rusted and out of place among the ornate heliconia flowers and erotic ruby red passion flowers that peep out from the forest by the side of the road.

The tropical forest is a showcase for evolution and the amazing and complex ways that plants and animals are adapted to their environment. As in any ecosystem, flowers need pollinators, fruits need dispersers, predators need prey, and prey need to hide. Part of what makes a tropical forest community so unique is the enormously high number of species that live there, creating endless possibilities for the number of ways species can be interconnected. This is where you can easily see acacia trees that house and feed their ant bodyguards, miniature wasps that never leave the confines of their home inside a small green fig fruit, flocks of birds that snap up insects fleeing from swarms of army ants, and strangler figs that have grown their roots down and around another tree's trunk to choke its host and steal its precious space in the sunlit canopy. The individual plants and animals are exciting to see, but the real reason the students were here was to learn how these complex relationships between species came to be and how very fragile they are.

Walking down Pipeline Road, binoculars and field guides in hand, it was hard to keep up with all the birds we were seeing and hearing. High up in the trees was a flock of insect eaters: tropical gnatcatchers, forest elaenias, white-winged tanagers, and a suite of migrants like the bay-breasted warbler, chestnut-sided warbler, and black-and-white warbler. These birds were all sticking close to the lead bird in the flock, the lesser greenlet that gave frequent *pit-sweet, pit-sweet* songs. Mixed-species flocks are a joint effort by birds to use their many eyes to spot dangerous vine snakes, owls, and hawks so each bird in the flock can spend more time looking for hiding insects. A little farther down the road we found a *Miconia* tree in full fruit, tens of thousands of tiny fruits up for grabs. Enjoying this feast was a flock of golden-masked tanagers, plain-coloured tanagers, honeycreepers, and migrants like the Tennessee warbler, Philadelphia vireo, and yellow-throated vireo.

In the 1970s ecologists believed that migratory birds were interlopers in the tropics, unwelcome visitors that descended en masse only to live under the shadow of permanent residents who were reluctant to give up their claim on the space and food. Standing with our students, watching these integrated and coordinated mixed-species flocks, it was impossible to guess from the birds' behaviour which were the migrants and which were the residents.

Our group stopped along the road, and Gene asked them to put down their binoculars, rest their necks, and simply listen. Gene has an uncanny memory for birdsong, and can remember the unique sounds of bird species years after he has heard them. Sounding a bit like an auctioneer, Gene started calling out the sounds he heard and quickly pointed in each direction. At first, the students could not pick out the sounds from the cocktail of voices in the forest, but one by one they began to isolate the songs. Gene started with the easy ones. A green shrike vireo, rarely seen but common in the canopy, was loud and conspicuous to the ears with its rhythmic *peer, peer, peer.* The tropical gnatcatcher was breathless with its incredibly long and descending trill, and the small tuxedo-dressed yellow-crowned euphonia barked out its *beam-beam.*

Not far to our right, in the dark of the forest away from the road edge, we heard a quiet *chiff . . . chiff . . . chiff.* Gene asked the students what the bird might be. New to the tropics, the students guessed wildly.

Manakin? Trogon? Continga? No, this was a run-of-the-mill Acadian flycatcher, a migrant from the eastern forests of the United States. In the winter individuals live alone in the tropical forest, quietly calling out their ownership of a small patch of forest to other Acadian flycatchers who might be nearby. These migrants come and go pretty much unnoticed by the shrike vireo, gnatcatcher, euphonia, and other residents who occupy the same land. The early idea that migrants must fight their way into the tropics each fall, always at the whim of competitively superior residents, was abandoned in the 1980s, once researchers began studying the behaviour of migrants during their southern stay.

The tropical forest is full of con artists of many species. The first that we found was a medium-sized ant running around on a leaf. The students gathered around to get a close look, and counted legs; yup, this critter had six legs, two antennae, and a narrow body and abdomen. Then we gave the leaf a poke with a stick and the ant disappeared into a tightly woven web on the underside of the leaf. This was actually a spider that walked on six legs and held her other two legs high over her head to make them look like antennae. Ants taste quite bad because they are loaded with formic acid, and few birds will eat an ant or an ant-mimicking spider. Next was a lump of bird droppings on a leaf that suddenly got up and ran away—another spider! We taught all our students the childish-sounding rhyme "Red beside yellow will kill a fellow" to help them identify the deadly coral snake, because harmless king snakes also have bold yellow, red, and black markings that give the look-alikes a kind of virtual armour from birds and mammals that instinctively know not to go near the real thing.

Crossing the road in front of us was a column of walking leaves. Well, the leaves weren't actually walking; a convoy of leaf-cutter ants was marching along in single file, each one carrying a freshly cut piece of leaf high over its head like a sail. We followed the trail of leaves and found where the ants were disappearing underground with their precious loads. Leaf-cutter ants are subterranean gardeners and use the leaves to grow a special fungus that they then eat. The ants carry the decomposed leaves back to the surface so that their colony does not get filled up with compost. One by one the ants come out of the ground, walk up a branch and drop a tiny brown load. This happens day after day, and before long there is a rich pile of compost. What is garbage to the ant is treasure to the tree. One researcher put tracer dye in the ants' garbage pile and found that trees several hundred yards away had roots that were tapping into this nutrient goldmine.

Nutrients are in short supply in the tropical forest despite the lush vegetation that is teeming with wildlife. There is very little leaf litter on the ground because it is broken down so quickly in the hot, humid environment. The nutrients are all tied up in the plants and animals, not lying around on the ground waiting to be used. Even the dung of animals doesn't last long around here. Long ago, one graduate student from the University of Maryland was studying dung beetles, insects that provision their eggs with a carefully rolled ball of dung for the kids to eat once they hatch. He had a three-month-old baby at the time, and used the convenient supply of the baby's dung to discover that some species of dung beetles pirate dung from smaller species rather than go to the trouble of finding their own. Dung is a scarce commodity, and it is said that even before the fresh dung from a howler monkey hits the ground a dung beetle has already claimed it, riding it down to the ground on its maiden voyage!

It takes a while for people to get used to the idea that the lush tropical forest is a place where nutrients are a precious commodity. We took the students down a trail that led into the forest and asked them to look at the forest floor. Large brown leaves of all shapes and sizes were scattered on the ground and crunched under our boots as we walked. The red soil underneath the leaves was as hard as rock, and the surface was scarred with deep cracks because it hadn't rained in about six weeks. Even though it was only eight o'clock in the morning, strong winds had already started their engines and every few minutes another leaf came floating down from the canopy to join the nutrient cycle. Late February is the peak of the dry season in this part of Panama, and it would be another month or so before the rains came. Though the trees are a banquet of flowers and fruit at this time of year, for insect-eating birds the dry season is when food is hardest to come by.

Migrant birds that eat primarily insects, like worm-eating warblers and Kentucky warblers, probably face their biggest food shortages while they are in the tropics. Far away on their breeding grounds, these migrants can gorge themselves on juicy caterpillars and other insect larvae that explode in numbers as fresh, succulent leaves grow on the shrubs and trees in spring. In the tropics, there is no massive flush of easy-to-catch insects; instead, most of the insect food comes in the form of large adult insects that hide from birds. Insects do not want to be eaten and hide in the leaf litter and under leaves to escape detection, or come out at night when birds are asleep. Insects are a scarce resource, so insect-eating birds typically stake out a territory and vigorously defend it from neighbours of the same species.

Gene had brought a mist net with him to demonstrate just how serious our migrants are about protecting their neck of the woods. With the help of two students he set up the short net along the trail in the forest and used a small speaker to play back a sharp staccato call: *chip-chup, chip-chup*. The students watched, holding their breath, but after a few minutes were disappointed with the still-empty net. "Keep watching," Gene whispered, as he pointed to the dark understory a few yards to the side of the net. The bushes were moving slightly, and a small shape darted from one branch to the next, gradually moving toward the raucous fake intruder. "When a bird is really mad, he doesn't give away his location to the intruder. He sneaks in quietly for the kill," explained Gene. Suddenly a Kentucky warbler was hanging in the net. He was surprisingly bright and boldly coloured, his black mask contrasting with the bright yellow throat and belly. Kentucky warblers are common along the Pipeline Road, heard more often than seen, maintaining invisible fences and living alone on their territories.

Some tropical forest birds have a lifestyle more akin to a bustling cocktail party; they gather to feast on insects flushed up by the ants. Army ants live in colonies of thousands of individuals, and when on a raid the ants swarm over the forest floor like an amber tide. Army ants build temporary bivouacs at night using live workers who link their legs together to make a nest the size of a basketball. Inside the writhing nest is the queen and thousands of hungry ant larvae. By day, streams of ants spread out over the forest floor in a blitz that leaves few places for their victims to hide. At the leading edge of the swarm the ants kill millipedes, katydids, cockroaches, frogs, lizards, baby birds, and everything else they can overpower. The best way to find an army ant swarm is to listen to the birds. Gene, as usual, heard the distinctive whinny *chirrrrr* before anyone else. It was a bicoloured antbird, which makes its living following army ant swarms and catching the many insects racing out of the way of the deadly ants. We saw dozens of birds crowding around the army ants, including the professional ant-followers like the bicoloured antbird, spotted antbird, and ocellated antbird. During migration, birds like the Swainson's thrush drop in for an easy meal and join the outskirts of the feeding frenzy.

As we walked farther down Pipeline Road, one student pointed to a wispy black strip hanging in a spider's web. Was this another mysterious case of mimicry, a spider's trick to catch unwary insects? After all we had seen that morning, anything was possible, and a circle of eager faces awaited our clever answer. I pointed up and asked them to watch. After a few moments, we saw a charcoal-black strip drifting down from the narrow gap in the canopy over the road, then another. The students were still puzzled. These were pieces of burned grass, carried here on the winds from nearby pastures that had been set aflame. The dry season in the tropics might as well be called the fire season. Pastures and roadside grasses are set afire in an annual ritual that chokes the air with smoke and ashes and covers such a large area it can be easily seen from space. The burning is done to control grass and weeds and replenish the tired soil with a short-lived dose of nutrients.

After spending our first few days immersed in the lowland tropical forest of Panama we set off on a road trip to Colón, a major port at the Atlantic end of the Panama Canal. As we left Gamboa, we drove slowly along the highway that passed through Soberania National Park so we could look for interesting birds in the forest. One student spotted a slaty-tailed trogon perched on a vine over the road; we laughed at the field guide's description of these birds as being "phlegmatic," after their habitat of sitting like statues for long periods. A little farther down the road someone found a huge spectacled owl staring back at us from the edge of the forest with its hauntingly large yellow eyes. Then, without warning, the forest was gone and the trees were replaced with mile after mile of open pasture, small houses, stores, and bus stops.

Gone was the excited conversation and frantic flipping through of field guides, replaced by stunned silence as civilization slapped our students squarely in the face. Impromptu piles of household garbage and wrecked cars were scattered along the roadside, and at dusty bus stops there were well-dressed ladies going off to work and groups of children in their neat school uniforms. One pasture was charred black right up to the road edge, still smoking in a few places, evidence of the previous day's burning. As we crested the next hill we asked the students to look far off to their left, and through the haze they could barely make out a forest edge along a distant ridge. That was the forested Canal Zone where we had spent the past few days, a narrow strip of forest that was preserved all along the length of the Panama Canal. Everywhere else, any forest without some kind of legal protection has been cut down. The students then realized that Gene and I were con artists too, allowing them to experience the joy of the rainforest before letting them in on the fact that they were actually in a forest remnant surrounded by a vast twentieth-century landscape.

~~~

It is almost impossible for a migratory bird to live out its short life without coming face to face with our modern civilization and all the changes this has brought to the lands we share with them. Tropical forests are being cleared at the highest rate in the history of mankind, and grassland birds have had their tropical homes plowed to grow foods that we can eat. Migrants are forced to dodge their way over and around farms, cities, and suburban sprawl as they leapfrog north to their breeding grounds. When we see a beautiful bird singing in the park on a spring day, it is easy to forget that many others did not survive the long journey.

At our farm in Pennsylvania, a male American redstart pirouettes among the fresh buds of the maple trees that line our driveway, flashing black and orange as he goes. He pauses several times a minute to belt out a high-pitched *tsee, tsee, see-see, see-you* challenge to the male across the road. Forgotten for the moment is his winter territory in a lush mangrove forest along the southern coast of Jamaica, though he will return there when the summer days get shorter and signal that it is time to travel. High in a cherry tree near the edge of the pond a female Baltimore oriole hangs upside down, her yellow-olive colours blending in subtly with the dried grasses she is busily weaving into her half-built nest. A few months earlier she was feeding on nectar from the bright orange flowers of an *Erythrina* tree in a coffee plantation in southern Mexico. The stunning colours of the male scarlet tanager singing in the giant oak tree back in the woods are purely for showing off. Earlier that year, he was in plain clothes as he gobbled down small fruits from a fig tree in the forested lowlands of Ecuador. Within the dark hemlocks that hug the stream a female Acadian flycatcher gives the same *chiff* calls that she used far away in Panama to defend her winter home.

Migratory songbirds lead an intriguing double life. The birds that we welcome to our backyards, meadows, and forests in spring have just completed a marathon flight after living for many months in their tropical homes. These migrants are vulnerable to environmental threats that occur thousands of miles away from where they breed, in places many of us have never had the chance to see for ourselves. Whether or not particular species are in harm's way depends entirely on the details of their natural history, including what they eat, where they live, and how

15

they compete for the essentials of life: space, food, and mates. This variety among songbirds is what makes them so interesting for naturalists, bird watchers, and ornithologists, but it also makes it a difficult task to keep track of bird numbers from year to year and to pinpoint the cause of their declines.

2 CANARIES IN THE MINE
Songbirds and Our Ecosystem

One hot summer evening in mid-August, I sat in my canoe by a marsh near the Presque Isle State Park in Pennsylvania, on the south shore of Lake Erie. The sun was sinking low on the horizon, and high above me tiny dark specks were visible against the clouds. Thousands upon thousands of purple martins swirled in huge clouds over the marsh and dotted the sky for as far as I could see. Hundreds more were skimming low across the waves, searching for a last meal before nightfall. As the sun dropped below the horizon, more and more martins flew in toward the marsh from every direction, and the swirling masses grew larger and larger. It was impossible to count them all, but there must have been more than forty thousand.

The purple martin is the word's largest swallow, yet it would fit comfortably in your hand. Its long, tapered wings are designed for fast flight and aerial acrobatics to pluck flying insects out of the air. The martins were here to sleep in the tall reeds of the marsh, protected from predators by the deeper water surrounding the large reed bed, nature's version of a bird hotel. Without warning, waves of birds dropped out of the sky in unison, forming a tornado-like funnel as they disappeared into the reeds. Once in a while a sudden gust of wind bent the reeds down like a giant hand shaking the bed, and hundreds of martins streamed out of the marsh flying low and right at me. They swooped over my head and around the canoe while they screeched indignant alarm calls. I felt as if I could reach out and grab them as they raced past, and wished I could spread imaginary wings and join them. This roost is one of many safe havens martins use as stepping stones on their journey south to Brazil. If I were to come back a few weeks later, in mid-September, I would be hard pressed to see even a single martin because the summer exodus would be complete.

A perfect full moon rose in the east as I paddled back to shore before it got dark, the martins safely tucked in for the night. Big storms had been brewing over land since late afternoon, and the towering thunderheads were backlit by the huge glowing disc emerging behind them. A distant lightning bolt lit up the bottom of the clouds briefly. I was tired and heading home at day's end, but as I paddled against a headwind I thought about the hundreds of thousands of songbirds that must be hidden in the forests and fields around me, only minutes away from taking to the sky. The warblers, tanagers, thrush, and countless others were about to begin their journey, making their own storm. The night travellers will head southward with uncanny navigation skills, not knowing exactly where they will land, driven by instinct born of the successful migration of their ancestors.

This living storm will not spark lightning or wake children with its window-rattling claps of thunder. The storm will pass by unnoticed by almost everyone in its path, even though it will rage for over six hours and cover several hundred miles. By the time children wake up after dawn, sleepily rubbing their eyes and padding downstairs in their fuzzy pyjamas, there will be little sign that the storm ever happened; no broken branches on the lawns, no raging torrents in the creeks, not even soggy leaves shedding old raindrops.

It is a storm of angels. This is what radar operators in the 1940s called the mysterious blips on their screen, angels, which they later discovered were the radar echoes of flying birds. On some nights in spring and fall, the night sky becomes choked with hundreds of millions of migratory birds making their way back and forth to their breeding grounds. The numbers are staggering and almost unbelievable because we are stuck here on the ground and cannot see the tiny birds passing high overhead under the cover of darkness.

Radar images give us a chance to fly with the angels and see for ourselves the huge numbers of birds that pour into our lands each spring. Radar has done for bird migration what telescopes did for the night sky and has opened up a whole new world that is otherwise masked to ordinary human eyes and ears. On the night of May 16, 1999, a spectacular bird super-cell was captured by weather radar near Buffalo, New York (figure 2.1). Around sunset that evening the radar was picking up ordinary ground clutter, the dust and smoke near the city of Buffalo. The birds were still on the ground hidden from the radar; each had spent its day gobbling up hundreds of insects. Within an hour of sunset, the birds took to the air, literally filling the night sky. Over the next few hours the radar screen showed millions of flying birds as a huge bright mass advancing over the northern shores of Lake Ontario and past the city of Toronto. Just as many birds were arriving in western New York from the south, replacing the ones that had left earlier that evening. Seemingly endless waves pushed north that night, riding a tail wind from the south. By daybreak most of the travellers were back on the ground, finding refuge somewhere among the houses, farms, and cities that blanket this region.

These are not isolated storms; bird migration happens on a continental scale in April and May, and again for the return trip in August and September. Sidney Gauthreaux, of Clemson State University in South

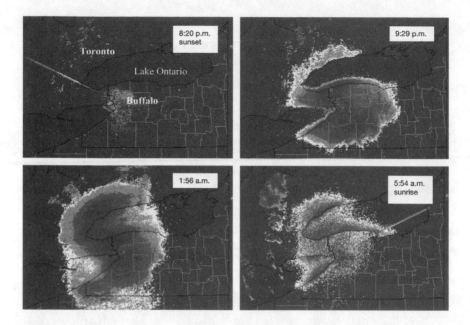

Figure 2.1. *Massive clouds of migrating birds show up as bright echoes on the Doppler weather radar station centred in Buffalo, NY. These images were taken on 16 May 1999, and show how birds suddenly fill the sky after sunset, then move north along the shores of Lake Ontario and over the city of Toronto. Sunset and sunrise are marked by long bright lines, formed by the sun's rays as they strike the narrow radar beam low on the horizon. (Images courtesy of John Black)*

Carolina, has used the network of weather surveillance radars across the United States to map all the hotspots of bird migration that spring up on a single night. The live Doppler image from each radar station can be viewed on and downloaded from the Internet, and shows the reflectance—how many objects are in the air—as well as the direction in which those objects are moving. Radar picks up birds for the same reason it picks up weather. Water is a tremendous reflector of radar energy; it bounces back the signal it receives and the radar picks up the echo and shows it on the radar screen. You can think of a bird as a very big raindrop. To screen out ground clutter from dust and smoke and echoes from insects and foraging bats, a computer program can remove objects that are not moving fast in a consistent direction, leaving only birds on the image. On rainy days the radar is doing the job it was designed for and bounces off rain, making it very difficult to get a clear picture of bird migration. The weather man curses the birds who clutter his radar and the ornithologist curses the raindrops that spoil his measurements of bird migration.

The big picture of spring migration shows bird super-cells forming all along the southern Mississippi River Valley and along the eastern coast of the United States from South Carolina up to Maine (figure 2.2). If our weather radios could be tuned to the bird channel, many people would be woken around 10 p.m. with the shrill *beeeep, beeeep, beeeep* of the weather alert that sets off the adrenalin for people living in the South, where spring outbreaks of tornadoes are all too common. This time they would hear the deep electronic voice announce, "This is NOAA Weather Radio. A severe bird warning has just been issued for counties in Texas, Louisiana, Arkansas, and Missouri. Please keep your weather radio tuned for further developments." Tens of millions of birds are on the move, pouring north from Texas and Louisiana into the heart of the continent. During the peak of spring migration, sixty thousand song-birds can arrive in a single day along just a short half-mile stretch of the Gulf coast; this adds up to tens of millions of birds who make landfall each day somewhere from Texas to Florida.

The radar migration map ends at the Canadian border simply because Canada does not have a comparable system of weather surveillance radar that is easily accessible by computer. The birds do not stop at the border, of course; one of the reasons so many light up U.S. radar screens is because billions are just passing through on their way to and from the vast boreal forest of Canada. The boreal forest, Canada's bird nursery, is so extensive it stretches from coast to coast and makes up a major por-tion of every province except New Brunswick, Nova Scotia, and Prince Edward Island in the southeastern part of the country.

The enormous clouds of birds are part of a phenomenal mass migra-tion. Billions of songbirds from dozens of different species pour into their breeding grounds in the spring. North America becomes a temporary home to migratory songbirds that otherwise live in the tropical regions

Figure 2.2. *Spring migration during 4–9 May 2000. Each arrow shows the average abundance of migrants detected by Doppler weather radar during the peak of nighttime movements. This map shows birds that were flying between about 300 ft. and 5,500 ft. above ground. The thickest arrows indicate major movements with over 600 birds per cubic mile. (Based on Gauthreaux and Belser, 2005)*

of Mexico, Central and South America, and the Caribbean islands. The migrants come north for the bonanza of insect food that goes hand in hand with the fresh lush leaves and warm days of spring, and spend a few hectic months finding mates, building nests, and feeding young. Their long and dangerous trip is made worthwhile because the rich food supply means that birds can raise many offspring in a single nest. As the summer comes to an end, migratory birds return en masse to their southern homes and resume their tropical lifestyles. The fields, marshes, and forests of a vast continent empty as if someone had let the air out of a giant balloon.

The billions of night travellers who come and go each year are not completely invisible to our senses, if we are willing to pause and listen to the whispers, murmurs, and cries from the heavens. Many migrants like thrush, warblers, and sparrows give distinct flight calls as they travel, the avian equivalent of a foghorn. A typical call note is a short, explosive sound and lacks the elegant musical qualities of the daytime song. The Swainson's thrush gives a short whistled note, the ovenbird a short, high *tzzp,* and the common yellowthroat a short, buzzy *tzzp.*

In 1896, Orin Libby, a recent Ph.D. graduate and a history instructor at the University of Wisconsin, sat in the darkness on a small hill near Madison, Wisconsin, in mid-September and heard more than three thousand birds fly overhead in only five hours. Libby wrote:

> More than once an entire flock, distinct by the unity of their calls, came into range and passed out of hearing, keep up with their regular formation with the precision of a swiftly moving but orderly body of horsemen. The great space of air above swarmed with life. Singly, or in groups, large or small, or more seldom in a great throng the hurrying myriads pressed southward. It was a marvel and a mystery enacted under the cover of night, and of which only fugitive tidings reached the listeners below.

For Bill Evans, now director of a non-profit organization to promote research and education on bird migration, listening to the angels as he camped one spring night on a bluff along the St. Croix River on the Minnesota–Wisconsin border changed his life. Lying in his sleeping bag, with nothing else on his mind, he was enthralled by the beauty of voices trickling down from the passing river of birds. One call he recognized as the distinctive nocturnal call of the black-billed cuckoo, a guttural *chuckle,* and he began to keep a mental tally. After an hour or so he had already counted one hundred cuckoos, and began to wonder whether there was a way to systematically count the invisible migrants by using tape recordings. Evans became a freelance scientist and spent the next ten years recording and listening to thousands of hours of audiotape recordings of the night sky.

A microphone on the ground, aimed at the sky, can record up to several thousand flight calls each night during the peak of migration. In early May, on the east coast of Florida, a recording from a single micro-phone unveiled the hidden passage of at least thirty migrants in only fifteen minutes. The travellers who could be recognized by their dis-tinctive voices included ovenbirds, common yellowthroats, American redstarts, black-throated blue warblers, northern waterthrush, and black-and-white warblers. These individual warblers had come from distant parts of Latin America, anywhere from Mexico to Panama, and were all heading to different breeding territories; the redstarts may very well end up in the forests of New Hampshire, the yellowthroats in a swamp in Wisconsin, and the waterthrush along a stream valley in Pennsylvania. Yet, on that evening, they shared a common sky and a common goal of finishing one leg of their long journey north to the rich breeding grounds that would soon be teeming with food.

We can catch a glimpse of the busy bird traffic in the night sky if we look carefully at a rising full moon during migration. Every few min-utes a tiny silhouette streaks across the brightly lit disc. In 1945, moon-watching provided some of the first evidence that migrating birds fly across the Gulf of Mexico on their way north. George Lowery, a pro-fessor at Louisiana State University, lined up his telescope on the full moon rising over Progreso, on the north coast of the Yucatán Peninsula, and saw birds flying northward out over the Gulf. On a good night, this celestial peephole might reveal four or five birds passing by every ten minutes. This doesn't sound very impressive, but keep in mind that moon-watching can sample only a tiny spot out of the entire night sky. Jeff Wells, an ornithologist with the Boreal Songbird Initiative, describes moon-watching as being like watching a baseball game through a paper towel tube pointed at first base.

The nocturnal cries heard from the ground, the shadows on the moon, and the bright dots on the radar screen spotlight the travels of individual birds. The hooded warbler that built her nest in the woods behind our Pennsylvania farmhouse in June will be one of the birds flying south on the late-night red-eye flight to Mexico sometime in late summer. She spent the last two weeks of July flitting around the thick tangle of raspberry bushes and razor-sharp wild roses near the edge of the pond, giving an occasional metallic *chip* call. Identified by her bright yellow breast, with an air-brushed thin black necklace, she dodged in and out of the dark recesses of the thick cover, rarely pausing for more than a second or two while she flashed her outer white tail feathers to flush insects from their hiding places. Over a few weeks, she gradually replaced all her worn and tattered feathers with brand-new ones and she put on so much weight that it would be comparable to my gaining thirty pounds in two weeks. This fat is the fuel that powers the bird's night flights, and she will fly sight unseen for a dozen nights over the lights of the cities and towns that blanket the East Coast of North America. By day, she will seek refuge and eat as much as she can, refuelling and waiting for a cold front to give her a tailwind for the next leg of her trip.

When she reaches the Gulf coast of the southern states, she will linger a little longer because the last leg of her trip is the most dangerous. A fourteen-hour non-stop flight across the Gulf of Mexico awaits her, and one storm could mean a quick and fatal end to her journey. If she survives, she will arrive in Mexico by mid-September and will settle down in one place for the rest of the fall and winter. Her winter home could be a sunlit tangle of shrubs and vines deep within a rainforest, a thin strip of trees separating cattle pastures, or someone's dense garden of banana plants and vegetables. She will have to keep a sharp eye out for predators like vine snakes and the small ferruginous pygmy owl, a notorious bird eater. The harsh dry season from January to March may not see a single drop of rain for weeks, if not months, and she will have to search long and hard to find enough insects to stay alive. Six months after her arrival, sometime in March, she will begin fattening up once again and head north to the woods behind my house for another chance to breed. It is amazing that a tiny bird can so matter-of-factly travel thousands of miles each year and return to exactly the same place.

The spectacular migration of songbirds is on a par with the immense flocks of passenger pigeons, seen until the late 1800s, that blocked out the sun for hours as they passed by. Today, it is hard to believe that at one time passenger pigeons formed flocks of billions of birds and were the most abundant bird in North America. John James Audubon, the premier bird authority of the day, described an unimaginably huge flock of pigeons that literally took three days to pass overhead and darkened the noon sky like a solar eclipse. In 1817 Audubon visited a nighttime roost of passenger pigeons in Kentucky that stretched for twenty-five miles. Though hundreds of men gathered at the roost nightly to hunt the pigeons, and took many thousands each night, even this slaughter barely made a dent in the flock. Pigeons also nested in massive colonies that could stretch for twenty miles in one direction and ten in the other, with a dozen nests in almost every tree. This was the bird version of the huge buffalo herds that once roamed the prairies, and if it still existed today would bring throngs of curious visitors to stand in awe of one of nature's amazing spectacles. It was inconceivable at that time that this superabundant bird could become extinct in an evolutionary blink of an eye. The pigeons disappeared when the forests that once blanketed their breeding range were reduced to small patches that were too small to house and feed their large colonies.

The demise of the passenger pigeon has taught us not to take our abundant birds for granted. The world under the wings of our migratory songbirds is not the same landscape that their ancestors flew over. From one end of the journey to the other, forests have been logged, marshes drained, prairies plowed, and natural habitats of all kinds have been replaced with millions of square miles of fields of corn, rice, and hundreds of other crops that feed an exploding human population. There is good reason to believe that the angels are slowly falling from the sky, dwindling in numbers year after year. The bird migration system that is the heart of our northern lands is slowly but steadily eroding. By some estimates, we may have already lost almost half the songbirds that filled the skies only forty years ago. We have learned the hard way that when birds begin disappearing, we may be next.

Figure 2.3. *R. Thornburg, foreman, U.S. Bureau of Mines Rescue Car No. 3, holding a mine canary. 1928 Hollier Mine fire, Timmins, Ontario. (U.S. Bureau of Mines, photo TICL-00203)*

In the 1800s and early 1900s, coal miners in the United States and Europe took caged canaries down into the mines to test if the air was safe to breathe (figure 2.3). If carbon monoxide was present in the tunnel, the canary would pass out and sometimes even die, long before any of the miners felt the ill effects of the poisonous gas. Carbon monoxide is odourless, tasteless, colourless, and deadly, a threat that humans could not detect without canaries or the manmade but more expensive safety lamps of that era. Canaries are highly sensitive to the poisonous gas because they have a much higher heart rate (five hundred beats per minute) than humans and take two hundred breaths every minute. The canaries that fell off their perches were clear signals to the miners that their own environment was unsafe, yet the miners still had time to escape from the tunnels before they too passed out.

Wild birds are powerful indicators of the health of our outdoor environment, too. In the 1960s and 1970s the mighty bald eagle, so powerful and symbolic, was rapidly dwindling in numbers because of the heavy use of DDT and other pesticides. DDT and its main breakdown product, DDE, disrupt the reproductive hormones in birds, making it hard for them to put calcium into their eggs. Eagles and other raptors that were contaminated with these chemicals laid eggs with thin shells, and few, or none, of these eggs could hatch. With breeding shut down by the pesticides, raptor numbers in North America and Europe fell catastrophically from the late 1940s until the early 1970s, the period when DDT was in wide use. When DDT was finally banned in the United States in 1972, birds of prey began producing young, and their populations grew rapidly, evidence that the toxins had indeed caused the population crash.

The environment that affects our health today is much larger in size than a coal mine or even a country; for better or worse we live in a global society. Global climate change and ozone holes are not local, isolated problems, and pesticides sprayed on crops in Chile or Mexico could very well end up on your dinner table. The individual lives of migrants who travel thousands of miles every year between the tropics and North America are affected by environmental changes on the same huge geographic scale that our own lives are.

Although songbirds can occasionally be found dead on the ground by the thousands, it is their chronic and long-term decline in numbers that have sparked alarm among naturalists and scientists. Ecologists measure the health of wild animal populations by counting heads and tracking changes in population size. In most years the number of young birds joining the population roughly balances the number of deaths among the adults, so the population remains roughly the same size over time. A bad year or two will mean that the population drops, but usually this is temporary, and in good years the population size will bounce back up. Small changes in the size of a wild bird population are a natural and healthy part of a species' ecology, but a population that is declining

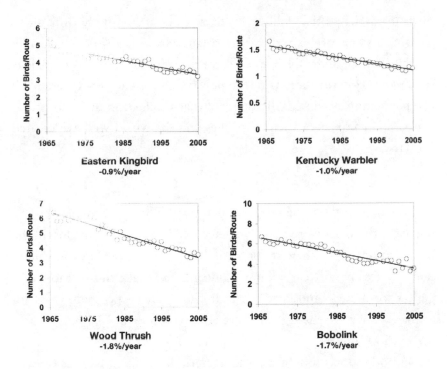

Figure 2.4. *Population trends of neotropical migrant songbirds, based on survey-wide estimates from the North American Breeding Bird Survey, 1966–2005. (Based on data from Sauer et al., 2005)*

steadily year after year is one that has been knocked off balance and is in trouble.

The songbirds that are fading away from our world include birds as diverse as the eastern kingbird, Kentucky warbler, wood thrush, and bobolink, all of whom have experienced a serious drop in numbers since the 1960s (figure 2.4). These birds each tell us something important about different parts of our shared environment. These four species are all neotropical migrants—that is, birds that move seasonally between the New World tropics and the temperate zone in North America. They have all experienced long-term population declines, yet in other respects they are as different from each other as apples and oranges. They live in different habitats, eat different foods, and spend their winters in different tropical countries. As you read about the lives and habits of these birds in the pages that follow, it will become increasingly difficult to imagine a single problem that can explain why so many of them are in trouble. Unlike in the DDT era, where the smoking gun was pesticides, for migratory birds there is no single, straightforward explanation for the population declines. The dangers that threaten these birds are as varied and complex as their own lives and the world we have created for ourselves.

~

The canaries in the mine were gas detectors. The declining eagles and falcons in the 1960s were chemical detectors. In both cases, the loss of the birds did not make the environmental problem worse. A dead canary does not create more carbon monoxide gas and make the air more dangerous for miners, and dead eagles do not increase pesticide loads for humans. They are passive detectors of environmental health, a bioindicator whose job could be done by a machine.

Our migratory songbirds, the eastern kingbirds, Kentucky warblers, wood thrush, bobolinks, and many others, go far beyond being simple detectors of environmental problems. Yes, their populations are very sensitive to the sweeping changes we have made to our environment, a warning that we have gone too far already. The important difference is that migratory birds do, in fact, directly affect the quality of our environment. Songbirds provide many important functions in our ecosystem, ranging from insect control to seed and fruit dispersal. They are not simple indicators of environmental problems, but rather their populations help to sustain a healthy and productive environment for our societies.

Gretchen Daily, in her book *Nature's Services,* asks the reader to think about all the animals and plants that would be needed to support a simple human community, for example if you were to move to a new planet that had only air and water but no life. We would pack the foods we like to eat, fruits, vegetables, grains, and spices, and also trees that we use for building materials. Some medicines come from plants, so we would need those too. Cows, pigs, sheep, and chickens would come along, of course. These are the goods that humans typically consume directly, born of our agricultural way of life. Would this shopping list make a healthy and self-sustaining new world? The answer is no, because plants and animals do not grow in a vacuum independent of the world around them. The natural resources we use directly are supported by tens of thousands of species that we pay little attention to. Strawberries, apples, and squash will not set fruit unless a bee moves pollen from one plant to another. Plants need fertile soil, and soil is not made fertile by itself; the soil is teeming with millions of microscopic organisms that are crucial for breaking down organic matter and recycling nutrients. The human population's biggest competitor for food is insects, which eat up to 20 percent of our crops before and after harvest; this loss would be much higher without birds and predatory insects that provide natural pest control.

The "services" that natural ecosystems provide for humans are many and include cleaning our air and water, reducing the severity of floods and droughts, detoxifying soil and water, decomposing waste, maintaining soil fertility, pollinating crops and wild plants, non-toxic control of insect pests, dispersing seeds, moving nutrients through the food web, providing raw material for genetically improving crops, and so on. Human society cannot live without bees, roundworms, and predatory wasps—or songbirds; they are the unsung heroes of our modern world. They, however, can live perfectly well without us.

The 2005 U.N. Millennium Ecosystem Assessment report estimates that 60 percent of the ecosystem services of the world are being degraded or used unsustainably. When it comes to our dangerous experiments with ecosystems, the impact of losing a species, or set of species like our migratory birds, depends on whether their role in the environment can be filled by other animals. This is the concept of ecological redundancy; if one warbler species disappears it usually won't trigger a serious loss in ecosystem services because other insect-eating songbirds in the community can take up the slack. In my Toronto suburb there are a dozen different doughnut stores within a five-minute drive of our house. If one chain went out of business, there would still be lots of other places to buy chocolate-glazed treats. Parents rely on redundancy too; if I have to work late, my husband can pick up the kids from the daycare before the six o'clock penalty hour. One of the best ways to appreciate redundancy is to have to live without it. What if all the grocery stores for twenty miles around closed for a week, or there was no family member or friend who could pick up the kids? When we lose a critical piece of our ecosystem machinery, and there are no spare parts, the natural processes we take for granted quickly unravel.

One of the least admired and unappreciated cogs in our environmental machinery are the scavengers that clean up dead animals—nature's sanitation workers. Try living without them. In the 1990s, three kinds of vultures in India and Pakistan suddenly experienced a catastrophic collapse: their population dropped by 95 percent in just ten years. The vulture crash was caused by a drug commonly used in human medicine, diclofenac, that was being given to cattle and happened to cause kidney failure in vultures that ate treated animals. Carcasses of buffalo and cattle that once swarmed with large naked-headed vultures who made short work of the flesh now sat rotting in the sun for weeks. Livestock diseases such as anthrax and foot-and-mouth disease increased after the vultures disappeared. Other scavengers, like foxes and feral dogs, boomed in numbers, spreading rabies to themselves and creating a rabies epidemic among the human population.

Our songbirds are disappearing, and I am convinced that our natural world will be shaken to the core if their numbers drop so far that they can no longer play their traditional and crucial ecological roles in our natural communities. Birds have been such an important part of the world around us for so long that they are irreplaceable. Plants depend on them to pollinate flowers and to carry their seeds and fruits away from the parent plant. Plants are also counting on birds to keep leaf- and seed-eating insects under control (though the insects would be perfectly happy to see the birds disappear). For tens of thousands of years insects have been falling prey to billions of hungry mouths as the birds move north and gorge themselves each spring and summer. The world around us is already in a very fragile state, barely hanging on by a thread as we continue to cut forests and plow under grasslands, pour pesticides on the land, and expand our cities to accommodate the millions of people that join our world every year. We cannot afford to lose our birds; they are part of the complex web of life that sustains life on our planet.

3 THE BREEDING BIRD SURVEY
Taking a Census of Migrating Birds

Songbirds are a closely related group of birds that have diversified into an impressive kaleidoscope of colours and song. All the colours of the rainbow are represented among the warblers, tanagers, thrush, buntings, orioles, and sparrows, and their voices range from simple whistles and single notes to long musical songs that no human can possibly imitate. Less obvious are their equally diverse lifestyles. The forest near our farmhouse is filled with the symphony of wood thrush, hooded warblers, and scarlet tanagers, while the bobolink, meadowlark, and field sparrow make up the orchestra in the fields that line the road. While planting lettuce and carrot seeds in the garden I can lift my head to watch the eastern kingbird twittering and fluttering toward its perch in the sumacs at the garden's edge, but I have never seen an Acadian flycatcher from that vantage point. Some songbirds eat seeds, some eat fruit, some eat insects, and some switch diets as the seasons change. Their homes range from dark, lush forests to hot, open grasslands. Birders know this all too well, and half the battle in identifying a bird is to become familiar with who is likely to be found skulking in a thorny raspberry bush at forest's edge as opposed to hopping from branch to branch and peeking out from behind the leaves high in a maple tree.

There is no "one size fits all" solution to helping songbirds. The eastern kingbird, Kentucky warbler, wood thrush, and bobolink span the entire range of songbird lifestyles and give us a taste of the challenge we face in trying to unravel why each of these species is in decline.

During summer, eastern kingbirds nest across much of North America in open habitats like orchards, wooded edges of fields, and narrow strips of forest along rivers. Kingbirds are named for their disposition and not their size; their scientific name, *Tyrannus,* means "tyrant, despot, or king." Eastern kingbirds are renowned for their attacks on hawks and crows who dare to fly near the nesting territory; high in the sky the kingbirds repeatedly dive-bomb the predators to drive them away. Despite these daredevils' tenacity and pluck, their populations have declined by roughly 30 percent since the 1960s. Kingbirds are members of the flycatcher family; in spring and early summer, kingbirds are easy to see as they feed on insects that they catch in mid-air. In late summer they eat fruit from dogwood and wild cherry that ripen in July and August, a sign of things to come. Kingbirds are not "fly catchers" during the many months they spend in the tropics during winter; they switch to a fruit diet because so many tropical trees are loaded with food. During winter, kingbirds form flocks of dozens of birds and start the winter in South America, where it is the dry season and their favourite fruit, *Panax moro-totoni,* is already ripe. As the winter progresses the dry season moves farther to the north, and the kingbirds move into Panama and Costa Rica, following the ripening wave of fruit.

While kingbirds are nomadic during winter and live socially in flocks, many other migrants live a more lonely, sedentary life. The Kentucky warbler is a forest bird, both on its breeding grounds in the southeastern

U.S. and on its wintering grounds in Central America. This small bird sports a yellow throat and jet black mask and is often seen hopping on the forest floor as it searches for insects to eat. During the non-breeding season, each bird sets up its own small territory in a tropical forest to protect its precious share of hard-to-find insect food. Here, there is no chivalry. Females compete with males to get their own territory, and each bird lives by itself for eight months. Territories are hotly defended using call notes (*chip-chup*), and some individuals return year after year to defend the same small patch of tropical forest.

Kentucky warblers breed throughout the eastern United States, not just in Kentucky. My husband, Gene, and his colleague Vickie MacDonald studied Kentucky warblers for many years at the Smithsonian Conservation and Research Center's 1,200-acre property in Virginia. They caught males by setting up a short net and playing back the male song, which is reminiscent of a bugled cavalry charge. The territory owner is duped into believing an intruder is in his territory, hits the net, and is safely released a few minutes later wearing colourful leg bands with unique identification numbers. In the first years of their study, Gene and Vickie noticed that even though the number of territories was holding steady, few of the banded males ever came back the next year. They began to suspect that males were not surviving their journey to Central America. Within a few years many territories were not claimed by anyone; good habitat sat empty because populations were dropping fast, not just in Virginia but across the breeding range.

The wood thrush is a forest bird too, feeding on or near the forest floor for insects, but it also snacks on fruit late in summer and during winter. Wood thrush numbers have gone down at a much faster pace than either the eastern kingbird's or the Kentucky warbler's. The wood thrush is a favourite of many birders, even though it has drab colours, because its song is so beautiful, complex, and haunting. The wood thrush, like most songbirds, can sing two songs at once. The syrinx of birds, the equivalent of our voice box, is deep down the throat in the upside-down Y where the trachea splits into the two air tunnels that lead to each of

36

the lungs. Each side of the Y has its own sound-producing membranes and sets of muscles to control them, so a bird can produce its own duet and sing two songs at once. Just as the call of the common loon on a northern lake evokes a sense of wilderness and a strong connection with nature, the wood thrush song does the same for visitors to the forest. Wood thrush pairs stick close together during the breeding season, and for good reason. Neotropical migrants are renowned for their sneaky copulations with neighbours, and DNA testing has shown that up to half of the females produce illegitimate young. Male wood thrush have got around this problem by closely following their mates, even when the female leaves her territory to visit other males. Males are also good fathers and stay close to the nest while females are incubating eggs, probably to defend the nest from such predators as chipmunks, squirrels, blue jays, and crows. Wood thrush spend the winter in Central America, where they live in the ever-dwindling remnants of tropical forest. Researchers studied wood thrush in Mexico by attaching tiny transmitters to their backs and following their movements for several months. Adults lived alone on territories in the forest, but young birds who were trying to survive their first winter could not get territories in prime habitat and instead were forced into a wandering existence, eking out a living along the hot and dry forest edges.

The bobolink looks like a blackbird that has put its clothes on backwards; the male is jet black below and has a large buff patch on the back of his head and a wide white stripe on his back. In some places it is called the skunk blackbird. Bobolinks decorate the hayfields and grasslands of North America as they perch boldly on top of tall grass stalks before launching off in a low display flight, wings whirring madly while singing their name over and over in what Arthur Bent, a renowned ornithologist, described long ago as a bubbling delirium of ecstatic music. Bobolinks are greedy when it comes to romance and males routinely attract several mates to live with them on their territory. The nests are often destroyed when the hayfields are cut midway through the breeding season. Although the breeding range of bobolinks stretches in a wide swath across the middle of the continent, all the birds migrate to a much smaller wintering area in South America in the grasslands, or pampas, of Bolivia, Paraguay, and Argentina. Here, though, the grasslands have recently met the plow, which gives bobolinks little choice but to consume seed crops instead of native grasses, bringing their hungry flocks face to face with angry farmers and modern pesticides.

How do we know that kingbirds, wood thrush, Kentucky warblers, and bobolinks are all on a long downhill slide? Plenty of older bird enthusiasts, amateurs and scientists, have been paying close attention to birds since the 1950s. They remember the good old days of spring migration, when they could see dozens of migrants in tree after tree, rather than just a handful at a time. They believe in their hearts that the birds are disappearing. Scientists, though, are charged with gathering proof and evidence and putting reliable numbers on such observations.

In the early 1960s, the United States Fish and Wildlife Service designed a nationwide bird monitoring program called the Breeding Bird Survey, or BBS. After the dramatic population crashes of the bald eagles, peregrine falcons, and other raptors, the nation needed an early warning system to monitor the health of all bird populations. The Breeding Bird Survey gives us some real numbers to work with, and provides convincing evidence that our birds are facing serious problems. I was born in 1962, just a few years before the BBS monitoring began. If the BBS results are to be taken literally, then in my modest lifetime the world has lost 30 to 40 percent of the wood thrush that it had when I was born. Wood thrush are still a common bird—at least for now. At bedtime on spring nights my children can hear the male wood thrush in the woods across the road giving his nightly dusk chorus. I take it for granted that I will hear wood thrush when hiking along trails, riding along bike paths, and sitting on the porch in the summer waiting for the fireflies to start their show. If the BBS is any sign of the future, by the time my children are parents it will be a rare treat to hear the nightly yodel of the wood thrush.

~

Although it is pretty obvious to a miner when a canary has fallen off its perch, it is not so easy to track the health of our wild birds. To know if a population is increasing or decreasing in size, or holding steady, ecologists have to first count the birds each year. Songbird populations contain millions of birds and span a geographic distance that measures in the thousands of square miles. To make matters more difficult, dozens of different species need to be counted, and they live in such widely different places as marshes, fields, and forests. The BBS, done once a year like an annual physical, was designed to track overall changes in the numbers of breeding birds in North America. To really believe that birds are in trouble, we have to understand how the counting is done.

Forget about birds for the moment and imagine that you have been asked to count the number of people in the city nearest to where you live. Your tools are a car, binoculars, a watch, and a notebook. You have a day job, so this has to be done on a weekend or a day off. You've been given a few volunteers to help you. How would you design a counting system that is simple, can be done in a reasonable amount of time, and doesn't cost too much money? You could sit by a highway for a set amount of time—let's say three minutes—and count the number of people passing by in cars. By sampling twenty or so different highway locations scattered around the city, you would start to get a picture of the relative size of your local population. Of course you wouldn't even come close to estimating the actual population size of the city, but you would get an estimate of the number of people seen during a set amount of time. An observer near Chicago would surely count many more people than someone stationed in rural Virginia. The population near our suburban neighbourhood in Toronto has grown in the past decades from a quiet farming community to wall-to-wall homes; a simple roadside count done over the years would certainly register large increases in population size.

The BBS survey uses a similar approach by asking volunteers to count all the birds they see on a predetermined route during the peak of the breeding season. Volunteers make fifty stops, each three minutes long and around a half-mile apart, along a 24.5-mile-long route. The original route, first assigned in the 1960s, was chosen in a rural area with a decent amount of natural habitat, and these routes have been re-surveyed each year. Sometime in late May or early June, you get up before dawn and drive to the starting point of your BBS route, armed with notebook and binoculars. At each of the fifty stops you get out and record every bird you see or hear within fifteen hundred feet of the stop. The total count for each bird species over the whole route will reflect to some degree the number of birds that actually live there. Each year, volunteers survey two thousand BBS routes, drive nearly 50,000 miles of road, and make 100,000 different census stops to count the migrants who have spread across the continent.

The BBS army of volunteers is no geriatric squad. People not familiar with the birding culture might mistakenly imagine birders to be elderly, neatly dressed in outdoorsy clothes with pants tucked into socks, lightly worn hiking boots, wide-brimmed hats, binoculars hanging around the neck, and a bird guide tucked into a wide pocket of their vest. BBS volunteers come in all shapes and sizes, just like the birds they are counting. Men and women, twentysomethings and retirees, teachers and lawyers—you name it and they are out there watching, listening, and helping with BBS data collection.

The key to the BBS is being able to identify birds by sound alone, because most birds are heard but not seen. This takes plenty of practice and a brain that automatically recognizes sounds without even thinking about it.

As I drove into the entrance of my daughter's Girl Scout camp on a hot day in June, I unconsciously tallied the steady stream of voices: Acadian flycatcher, red-eyed vireo, American robin, scarlet tanager, hooded warbler, black-throated green warbler, eastern wood peewee. This was all during the one minute before I had to stop and let my daughter hop out of the car. A gang of girls assembled in neat, numbered rows was being led by camp counsellors in a chorus of "Tarzan, jungle man, swinging from a rubber band." As I pulled away the girls' voices faded and were replaced by the other chorus, and I added wood thrush, dark-eyed junco, blue-headed vireo, and American redstart to my mental list. I can't go anywhere without looking for and listening to birds; my ears are always open for the songs and whispers of nature's language.

Just as with someone learning Spanish, or any language, learning bird language begins with memorization. *Desayuno* is breakfast, *gato* is cat, and *cabeza* is head, and with practice these words become so familiar that their meaning is understood without having to think about it. Birders do the same thing with the sounds of birds, which are unintelligible at first. *Zee zee zee zoo-zee* is the black-throated green warbler; *See me, up here, aren't I pretty* is the human rendition of the red-eyed vireo. A male hooded warbler sounds something like *weeta, weeta, weet-ee-o*, but this species has about five different song types. You have to learn them all; some males sound more like *weea, weea, weeah,* and others *chee, chee, chawup, chawup.* A sharp metallic *chip* from the wild raspberry bushes that crowd a small gap in the forest is the call note of a hooded warbler, probably a nesting female. The louder but very similar *chink* from the same patch is a northern cardinal scolding me because I am too close to her nest of young. A good birder can count birds with her eyes closed, by listening for the dozens of bold songs and sharp call notes that fill the morning air during early summer.

The strength of the BBS lies in its massive geographic scale, and not in its precision in counting the birds at each and every stop. What are the odds that a wood thrush in the forest will happen to sing during the three minutes you are standing by the side of the road? The BBS counts only a small sub-sample of the birds that actually live in a given place. I have been studying forest birds at our summer home in northwestern Pennsylvania for fifteen years, so I know the residents well. My students and I have done intensive studies of birds living on this tract of land, among them the wood thrush, hooded warbler, Acadian flycatcher, and scarlet tanager. I know exactly how many pairs of each species live in this large patch of forest because we have mapped out all the territory boundaries; in a typical year, there are several dozen pairs of each of these birds.

To find out how well a Breeding Bird Survey does at counting birds, I simulated an official BBS on the paved road that runs along the edge of the forest. On my first stop, I saw several birds in the field on the other side of the road: red-winged blackbird, barn swallow, Baltimore oriole, and American crow. I heard, but did not see, quite a few forest birds: yellow-throated vireo, American redstart, American robin, veery, scarlet tanager, northern cardinal, and red-eyed vireo. Hmmm, no wood thrush, hooded warbler, or Acadian flycatcher, even though I knew they were all abundant in that forest. I tried again, but at my second BBS stop a little farther down the road I didn't hear any of the four forest birds that I was expecting to hear. On my third try I finally heard a hooded warbler and a wood thrush.

The BBS was never designed to count birds accurately in one particular place; to do this you would have to spend many days carefully mapping out all the singing birds, as my students and I do. Our roadside survey of the people passing by in cars also would not come close to the detail and accuracy of a door-to-door census. There aren't enough days in the summer to count all the birds that live along a 25-mile stretch of road, and one would be hard pressed to find any volunteers willing to devote their entire summer to the task. It certainly would be impossible to survey two thousand routes in that level of detail unless one had a few million dollars to spend to hire helpers and pay for their travel. The BBS is not precise and was never meant to be. But it does a good job as a continental health test for breeding birds because it gives us a rough estimate of the overall abundance of a bird species averaged over hundreds of BBS routes. If a forest bird such as the wood thrush has really declined over the past forty years, then a volunteer standing by the side of a road today will be less likely to hear a wood thrush.

If a single route shows a dramatic crash in one type of bird, it is not necessarily cause for panic. The routes that are surveyed every year were first chosen forty years ago. What may have started as a quiet country road could now be a busy two-lane highway. Trees have grown older, abandoned farm fields may be cluttered with bushes and saplings, and woodlots and meadows may have disappeared altogether and been replaced with rows of houses. For a single BBS route it can be hard to know whether a drop in one species is strictly a local event or a sign of a serious and more widespread problem. A tiny drop in numbers from a local event will not even register on the overall BBS results because hundreds of routes are combined over many states. Local events can add up to become large-scale problems if habitat change is happening over a wide enough area and affects huge portions of a species' breeding range. One housing development will not bring Kentucky warblers to their knees, but the loss of thousands of woodlots throughout their range may very well decrease the numbers of breeders so much that our listeners along the roadside begin to notice a drop in numbers. The BBS allows us to stand back and see the big picture of what is happening to our birds.

The results from the first twenty years of the BBS sent out a shock wave that made headlines around the world and rattled university professors, government biologists, and conservation groups. Neotropical migratory songbird populations were in a tailspin, reported Chandler Robbins, a biologist with the U.S. Fish and Wildlife Service at the Patuxent Wildlife Research Center, and his colleagues. During the decade from 1978 through 1987, almost one third of the migratory songbirds showed a decline in numbers along BBS routes. In all, eighteen migratory songbird species had lost significant numbers. Only four species had increased in abundance. Songbird species that live within North America all year round fared better, suggesting that neotropical migrants could be running into problems during migration or on their wintering grounds in the tropics. This discovery sparked a stampede of research articles, symposia, conferences, and popular books all trying to dissect the BBS data to uncover what might be causing such a dramatic downturn in migratory songbird numbers. In 1990, the U.S. National Fish and Wildlife Foundation created a special group called Partners in Flight in response to these songbird declines, and the Smithsonian's Migratory Bird Center was hatched. Despite this massive response to understand the problem, there are no signs yet that the declines have been halted.

Eastern kingbird	Prothonotary warbler
Olive-sided flycatcher	Cerulean warbler
Least flycatcher	Kentucky warbler
Western wood-peewee	Canada warbler
Eastern wood-peewee	Golden-winged warbler
Barn swallow	Chestnut-sided warbler
Bell's vireo	Prairie warbler
Wood thrush	Mourning warbler
Swainson's thrush	Common yellowthroat
Veery	Wilson's warbler
Baltimore oriole	Bobolink
Bullock's oriole	Dickcissel
Orchard oriole	Indigo bunting
Rose-breasted grosbeak	Painted bunting

Table 3.1. *Neotropical migrants that show an overall continent-wide decline since 1966. (Data from the Breeding Bird Survey http://www.mbr-pwr.usgs.gov./bbs/)*

Since 1966, more than two dozen species of migratory songbirds have suffered continent-wide decreases in population size (table 3.1).

The BBS cannot predict the distant future any more than the weatherman can. How can we know whether the declines we have seen up to now are going to continue? We have the advantage of 20/20 hindsight if we travel back in time to the early 1990s, when some of the pivotal papers on songbird declines were published. In a leading article published in the 1992 book *Ecology and Conservation of Neotropical Migrant Landbirds,* a total of thirteen neotropical migrant songbirds were reported to be suffering highly significant declines based on BBS data collected up to 1988. What would the future hold for these species? Was this just a temporary and normal period of decline that would be followed by better times? Perhaps it was premature to cry wolf and pour money into saving migrant birds. Today we can look into our crystal ball using the BBS results from 1989 through 2005 and see the future as it unfolded. Eight species continued their gradual downhill slide, and not a single one of the original species that were declining in the 1970s and 1980s enjoyed a subsequent increase in abundance. This was no temporary dip in numbers. To make matters worse, today even more species show long-term declines.

⁓

One of the biggest limitations of the BBS is that it needs people and roads. This is not a problem in most parts of the United States and southern Canada, where there are plenty of both. The BBS does not survey northern Canada, yet the boreal forest that stretches from coast to coast is home to billions of songbirds. The boreal forest of North America is one of the largest intact ecosystems left in the world, even bigger than the Amazon rainforest, with almost 2.5 million square miles of forests, wetlands, and peat bogs. For some neotropical migrants, such as the palm warbler, Tennessee warbler, and Connecticut warbler, more than 90 percent of their entire breeding population lives in the boreal forest.

Although these northern breeding grounds are not easily accessible, we can count the migrants as they pass by us twice a year. This is like trying to estimate how the population of Ontario is changing over time by doing our roadside survey on the I-81 highway in Winchester, Virginia. In November we would see plenty of Ontario licence plates zipping by us as older Canadians head south for the winter. We could count the number of occupants in those cars and repeat this again in March in the northbound lanes to get an independent count. Not all drivers will even use the I-81; some may drive south on I-95 along the east coast but then return home on I-81. Despite these important details, counting the travellers en route would help us track, albeit in a very rough way, whether there are more or fewer people from Ontario heading to Florida each winter.

My daughter Sarah, six years old at the time, banded her first bird in early May 2005 at our farm in Pennsylvania. We had stocked a bird feeder in our backyard with sunflower seeds and put mist nets near the feeders. The mist net is the most important tool for a bird bander. It is made of fine nylon mesh, forming a seemingly infinite number of tiny squares that make up its forty-foot length, and it has four or five long panels. A bird who hits this nearly invisible wall gently drops into a "pocket" and is enclosed by the netting; it hangs there waiting to be taken out. Sarah enjoyed hiding by the house, watching the birds hit the net. Sarah's first bird was a chubby white-crowned sparrow who had been enticed to the feeder by an easy meal. I gently removed the bird from the net and showed Sarah how to hold the bird in the "bander's grip." She fit his neck snugly between her first two fingers and wrapped her hand gently around his body. The bands are numbered aluminum rings issued by the U.S. Fish and Wildlife Service, and you need a federal permit before you can band wild birds. I took the next band off the string and loaded it into a special pair of pliers that close without crushing the band around the bird's leg. I helped Sarah carefully position the pliers so the band was around the lower leg, just above the foot, then we gently closed the band. The sparrow was now banded 1761–16066, for life, and no other bird in the world will ever have the same number. This bird would not be breeding anywhere in our neighbourhood; he was on his way to the tundra somewhere near Hudson Bay, in northern Canada. He was in good shape, plump from the layers of fat he had stored under his skin; he was ready to fly north that evening as soon as it got dark. Sarah couldn't resist petting his white-and-black-striped head before she slowly opened her hand. The bird hesitated and then flew across the lawn toward the safe cover of thick bushes, giving a harsh *pink* to let us know what he thought about our interruption in his busy day.

Migration monitoring stations do bird banding on a grand scale by setting up dozens of nets and counting birds during the two migration seasons: March to May and August to October. The banding stations are positioned where migrants are funnelled by the land around them: peninsulas that stick out into lakes, lakeshores, and coasts. Several banding stations have been running since the 1960s, so they can look at year-to-year changes in the numbers of birds that have been caught over forty years. Bird Studies Canada oversees a network of sixteen banding stations strung across southern Canada that monitor populations of boreal forest birds. As well, dozens of banding stations intercept migrating birds in the United States along the coasts and Great Lakes, as well as some inland sites.

The Manomet Center for Conservation Sciences is on the west side of Cape Cod Bay in Massachusetts, on an exposed coastal bluff with lots of brush and small trees—perfect habitat for weary migrants. Since 1970, about forty-five to fifty nets have been used to intercept migrants during the peak migration periods. During wet weather the nets have to be closed, and banders keep meticulous notes on how many hours each day the nets are open so that they can make fair comparisons between years. Over thirty-two years of banding, a total of 205,545 individuals were banded, which is more than 6,000 birds each year. By looking at the number of nets used and how many days and hours they are open, we can compare how many individuals of a given species are caught each spring or fall. If the number caught each season goes down consistently over the decades, this suggests there could be a large-scale, across-the-board population decline.

The migration counts at Manomet did a good job of detecting the sharp peak in warblers in the mid-1970s during a spruce budworm outbreak. The spruce budworm is a native insect that occasionally undergoes an explosion in numbers, carpeting the spruce forests of eastern Canada and the northeastern United States with millions of caterpillars that devour coniferous leaves. This is bad news for the trees and foresters but good news for insect eating-birds. Bay-breasted warblers, Tennessee warblers, Cape May warblers, and blackpoll warblers rush into infested areas and breed at very high density; there is ample food for everyone and territories are small, females lay more eggs, and well-fed nestlings thrive. Nova Scotia and New Brunswick experienced a huge spruce budworm outbreak in the mid-1970s, and both the migration counts at Manomet and the regional Breeding Bird Surveys showed a boost in numbers. This is a good sign that the counting works.

The bad news is that the banding station also showed many species in sharp decline, which is consistent with the BBS results. Almost half of all the songbird species captured during migration, about three dozen in all, had lower capture rates in the past two decades than during the first years of banding in the 1960s and 1970s. The banding station caught more than two dozen species of migratory songbirds that are not reliably counted by the BBS because of their northern breeding ranges, such as the white-crowned sparrow. The migration counts at Manomet found that more than half of these northern breeders were experiencing significant declines. Our list of declining neotropical migrants grows when we add boreal forest breeders, and now would include birds like the grey-cheeked thrush, Tennessee warbler, and Connecticut warbler.

Thousands of miles from the roads that criss-cross the Breeding Bird Survey area and the neat rows of mist nets that intercept boreal forest songbirds, researchers have also been counting birds on the wintering grounds. John Faaborg, a professor of biology at the University of Missouri and author of *Saving Migrant Birds,* has netted songbirds in the Guánica forest along the coast of southwestern Puerto Rico since 1972. By 1992 it was already clear that many species were quickly falling in numbers. The prairie warbler and the northern parula had virtually disappeared from the site, and several other warblers were showing signs of erosion. The hopes that this was a temporarily problem have vanished. The three most common species, black-and-white warbler, ovenbird, and American redstart, have all declined sharply since the first net lanes were set up decades ago. Exceptionally low numbers of wintering migrants have been caught for the past five years in a row (2002 to 2006), a frightening and depressing pattern that does not bode well for the future.

No counting method will be accurate and fail-safe because it is virtually impossible to keep track of so many birds over such enormous distances. The best we can do is to get a glimpse of the true numbers through radar and breeding surveys and by eavesdropping on and banding migrants. Each counting method has its own pros and cons but together they form a patchwork of best estimates that tells us there are fewer songbirds in today's world than yesterday's. I imagine that in forty years, I'll be sitting on the back porch in my rocking chair, clutching at my old pair of Leica binoculars, telling stories about our woods once being full of tanagers, thrush, and warblers as my teenage grandchildren listen politely though not really believing a word the old lady says.

4 BIRDS IN THE RAINFOREST
The Effects of Deforestation and Fragmentation

One February I got a short reprieve from another northern winter and flew south to catch up with the migrants who were sensibly living in their winter homes in Costa Rica. The first night I stayed in a hotel in the hills outside San José, away from the hustle and bustle of the city. The Bougainvillea is well known for its large eco-friendly gardens that feature orchids, bird feeders, lush flowering trees and shrubs, and even frog ponds. After a day of taxis, airport terminals, and cramped seats on airplanes I was anxious for my first look at a neotropical migrant since the last time I had seen one in late October, when the stragglers left.

On either side of the main path though the garden I heard a chorus of incessant high-pitched *chip, chip, chip, chip* coming from the trees. These were small yellow warblers, migrants that are territorial in the winter, with each bird laying claim to a handful of trees where it can feed on insects all winter. While admiring the orchids I heard a distinctive *spit-a-check* and looked up to see a red songbird in the tree overhead, a male summer tanager. In the large flowering *Erythrina* tree in the back of the garden, a female rose-breasted grosbeak was delicately sipping nectar from one of the big orange blossoms, an unlikely sight for a bird with a thick, powerful beak. She usually uses this tool for eating insects and fruit and for crushing seeds. The warblers, tanager, and grosbeak had probably spent their entire winter in this garden. These migrants live side by side with birds that seem exotic to us but who are run-of-the-mill neighbours for our migrants. The blue-crowned motmot is on the "must see" list for birders; one was sitting low on a branch near the orchid garden, switching its long pendulum tail from one side to the other in a clock-like rhythm and saying his name in a low haunting voice: *mot-mot, mot-mot.* Nearby, a large and awkward-looking squirrel cuckoo let out a startlingly loud *chik-burr,* then hopped on quietly through the branches looking for small lizards to eat.

The next morning we drove through the mountains on our way to San Isidro in southern Costa Rica. The road twists and climbs to more than six thousand feet in elevation before dropping down into a valley on the other side of the continental divide. We were told not to drive the road at night, and now I knew why. An endless stream of semi-trucks ground slowly uphill, and impatient drivers of cars, buses, and other trucks thought nothing of pulling out to pass, even at blind corners. The road was wet and visibility was poor because we were literally in the clouds, windshield wipers going at a furious pace. During a brief sunny break, we pulled over to do some bird watching. As the traffic roared past, I saw a little bird creeping in the bushes beside the car. The small black crown and bright yellow body made it instantly recognizable as a Wilson's warbler, a migrant from western North America.

When we finally arrived in San Isidro we stayed at the Talari Lodge, a favourite spot for bird watchers. I got up before daybreak to hear the dawn chorus. The songsters were all tropical residents, not migrants.

Migrants defend their winter territories with simple call notes, like the *chip* of the yellow warbler, and save their singing for the breeding season far to the north. It was still dark as I listened to yellow-bellied elaenia males singing back and forth with their loud, rollicking dawn song *we-do, we-do, we-do . . . weeee do!* Just before breakfast I found my first migrants, in the trees near the swimming pool. This was a mixed-species flock, in which dozens of birds of different species stick together for safety, feeding on insects in the trees. Flocks are safe places to spend the winter because there are more eyes to spot vine snakes, hawks, and other predators. Bird watchers love to find a mixed-species flock, since you can see so many different birds in only a few minutes. There in the flock was a black-and-white warbler, a migrant that often joins a mixed-species flock. There were also the opportunists, a Blackburnian warbler and mourning warbler, both insect-eating migrants who join flocks when they get the chance.

Later that morning we drove to one of the few remaining patches of rainforest in this agricultural community. As I was walking down a narrow dirt road through the small forest I heard two flycatchers, one on each side of the road. One was a tropical resident, the other a migrant. The resident was a male ochre-bellied flycatcher who was perched in the shrub understory. His song was a repetitive *whip wit whip wit chip chip,* and every thirty seconds or so he would suddenly raise and open one wing high over his back in a quick snapping motion, as though he were waving to someone in the forest. Males display on small territories to attract females for mating, but do not help with any of the domestic duties of building nests or raising young. When they aren't busy waving to females, males travel through the forest eating fruit and getting ready for their next session of showing off.

The migrant across the road, a least flycatcher, was also defending its territory but in a more modest way. Every ten seconds or so the least flycatcher called out a quiet *wheesht;* it took me almost ten minutes to finally see the dull-coloured bird perched in a low branch of a tree. Least flycatchers are insect eaters and defend feeding territories during the

winter. They are not on the "must see" list for birders, but these incon-
spicuous migrants are there if you look for them.

During this week-long trip, I saw eighteen species of migrants representing most of the groups of songbirds that I'd expect to see breeding
in the forests and fields near my summer home in Pennsylvania. There
were flycatchers, vireos, swallows, warblers, grosbeaks, and tanagers;
some were living in people's backyards and gardens, others by roadsides,
and others inside patches of rainforest. For many migrants, the future of
their species may very well depend on how well they can make do living
outside the forest, which is shrinking as every year passes.

In 1863, renowned English naturalist and explorer Henry Bates, who
travelled the Amazon, wrote, "There is something in a tropical forest
akin to the ocean in its effect on the mind. Man feels completely his
insignificance, and the vastness of nature." The almost endless forests
of the New World that greeted the first European explorers were not
untouched by man, though it must have seemed so at the time. There
probably is no such thing as a truly virgin forest, unless you travel over
two million years back in time to when strange upright-walking pri-
mates with oversized heads had not yet evolved. The New World once
held a large and thriving population of native people, many living in
sprawling cities surrounded by miles and miles of corn fields, beans,
and other crops. In many places the landscape had been physically engi-
neered with extensive networks of irrigation and drainage canals and
intricately terraced hillsides.

Charles Mann, in his book *1491*, takes us on an imaginary airplane
ride over Latin America to see what the landscape would have looked
like one thousand years ago. Our trip would take us over the Mayan
city of Kaan, the Kingdom of the Snake, at the base of the Yucatán
Peninsula. For several miles in each direction we would see hundreds
of pyramids, temples, palaces, and homes among a network of canals.
As many as fifty thousand people would be living in the city itself, sur-

rounded by a sixteen-foot wall to ward off enemies. Around the city we would see thousands of hectares of land cleared of its forest to grow food for the perhaps half million people that lived in the area. Over what is now the Peru–Bolivia border in the highlands of the Andes, where it is too high and dry for tropical forests, we would look down on the city of Tiwanaku along the shores of the 125-mile-long Lake Titicaca. Dozens of pyramids and monuments would fill the city, and several stone piers would stretch far out into the lake. Tens of thousands of people would be living in the city and the surrounding countryside. Flying northwest over the territory of their war-loving neighbours, the Wari, we would see small fortresses dotted for nine hundred miles along the spine of the Andes. In the capital city of Wari would be as many as seventy thousand people living among the gleaming white walls of temples, royal tombs, six-story apartment buildings, and courtyards.

If we wanted to visit all the major societies of that time we would have to fly from Canada to southern Chile, and from coast to coast. Before Columbus, the New World was, as Mann puts it, "a thriving, stunningly diverse place, a tumult of languages, trade, and culture, a region where tens of millions of people loved and hated and worshipped as people do everywhere. Much of this world vanished after Columbus, swept away by disease and subjugation." By the time hordes of Europeans arrived on ships to claim the New World, most of its original inhabitants had been wiped out by European diseases, and the evidence of their complex culture and extensive management of the land had been largely erased.

Humans have always manipulated their environment to their own benefit, and one of the first and most potent tools was fire. Beginning thousands of years ago, the undergrowth in the forests of the New World was routinely burned to make travelling and hunting easier and safer. Forest was cleared and burned to grow such crops as maize, potatoes, manioc, beans, squash, and dozens of other New World inventions. Classic slash-and-burn agriculture was practised by the Maya and others, with individual sections of tropical forest going through a cycle of cutting and burning, rotation of crops like maize and beans for a number of years, then abandonment of the now-depleted site, followed by regrowth of the forest. As local populations swelled into the tens of thousands, more pressure was put on the forests to supply food and firewood. Larger areas of forest were cleared, hillsides were terraced, and wetlands were drained to expand the lands devoted to growing food. After these great societies collapsed, the lands were left untended and the forest gradually grew back and reclaimed the land. The evidence of the region's cultural wealth became hidden under a thick green blanket, to be found only when the forest was cleared again by the new inhabitants at a pace and scale that has never before been seen by the world.

An enormous wave of tropical deforestation began as soon as Europeans repopulated Central and South America. From 1700 to 1850, about 25 million hectares* of forest were cleared. This clearing accelerated as the population grew rapidly, and by 1920 another 50 million hectares of tropical forest was gone. The forests were being cut to grow food, build homes, and cook food for the millions of people who flooded into the region. Trees were also cut as a commercial enterprise, and valuable timber and crops were shipped to the ballooning cities in Europe. In these early years of colonization a few countries like Cuba and Brazil underwent large-scale deforestation, but for most other countries the forest remained largely intact because it took time for local populations to increase and for them to develop an infrastructure for efficient and profitable export of goods. Pacific-facing countries and regions had trouble getting their goods to ports on the Atlantic side that served the lucrative trade to Europe and eastern North America.

Brazil's early devastation of its forests was largely a result of a well-developed caste system in which the elite received land rights and grants from Portugal, entitling people to do what they liked with four-thousand-hectare parcels of primary forest. At that time, land had no value itself because it was so endless in quantity. Landowners cleared forest, burned

*A hectare is about 2.5 acres, slightly less than the area of a baseball field.

it, and grew crops for a few years on the ashes of former giants until the soil was exhausted of its few precious nutrients. Then a new land grant was requested and the cycle started over again somewhere else. Landowners had armies of slaves who made short work of turning forests into huge profits. The abandoned fields soon were filled with herds of unfenced goats, sheep, and cattle that multiplied freely and grazed the recovering vegetation. These four-legged, heavy-footed lawn mowers were a new addition to the landscape. The great agricultural pre-Columbian societies did not have livestock, and their few domesticated animals were limited mainly to geese, turkeys, and dogs. The natural regeneration of the forest that had occurred for hundreds of years before came to a screeching halt as the soil was trampled and young seedlings were grazed. Pastures were burned in the dry season to encourage fresh and succulent grasses for the animals, killing seedling trees and keeping the area open and vulnerable to heavy erosion.

The population of southeastern Brazil exploded from about one million in 1800 to more than six million people by 1890. Forests were cleared to produce food locally and for export, and the wood was used as fuel for cooking and industrial uses like iron forges. Coffee became an extremely lucrative export crop and was thought to grow best on ridges freshly cleared of forest. Roughly 14 million hectares of primary forest in this region was lost to coffee plantations by about 1930. The deforestation continued unabated throughout the twentieth century as the population reached 22 million people by 1950, leaving only a few fragments of what was once a vast forest ecosystem (figure 4.1).

For the rest of Latin America, this great onslaught came later, in the second half of the twentieth century. From 1950 to 1980 a vast area of forest was cleared; indeed, more forest was cleared in those few decades than during the preceding two hundred years. This was only the beginning; since the 1980s, Latin American countries have been clearing about four million hectares of forest *per year*. This sweeping deforestation has not slowed despite huge outcries about biodiversity losses and dire warnings of global warming. During the twentieth century we

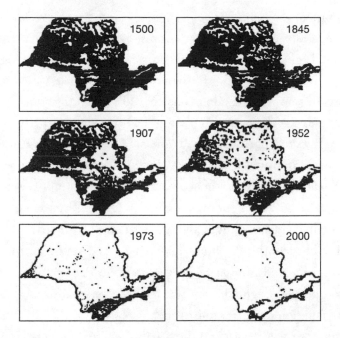

Figure 4.1 *Clearing of tropical forest (black) in São Paulo State, Brazil. (Images courtesy of Williams, 2003)*

have lost roughly 300 million hectares of tropical forest, an area about a third of the size of Canada or the United States.

Tropical forests are being destroyed even though they are one of the most important natural resources on the planet. Tropical forests cover only 6 percent of the land surface but receive half of the rainfall. For this reason, they play a critical role in protecting the watershed and all that lives there. The canopy cover acts like an umbrella, physically intercepting heavy rain during downpours, which protects and stabilizes the soil and keeps nutrients within the watershed. Deforestation causes massive soil erosion, washing away nutrient-rich topsoil, eventually dumping it in estuaries and contaminating fisheries near coastlines. Forests are giant sponges, soaking up heavy rains and releasing the water gradually. Flooding is less severe and the rivers run clear and clean, providing a regular and safe water supply. Tropical forests also make their own rain. In some places of the Amazon forest, up to 80 percent of rain is recycled;

the water that evaporates from the plant rises into the sky, condenses into clouds, then falls back down to the forest as rain. When forests are cut, this cycle is broken, and communities suffer less rainfall and a higher frequency of droughts. The forests that are cleared to make way for agriculture were the source of the rain that is needed to grow the crops in the first place; the perceived benefits of clearing the forest are short-lived indeed.

Now let's take Charles Mann's plane ride over Latin America as it is today. Our flight might take us over the hotel strip in Cancún at the tip of the Yucatán Peninsula, then over the impressive but deserted pyramids of Kaan, then to sprawling Mexico City and its almost 20 million residents. Then we might swing south and see the narrow strip of green that borders the Panama Canal, then head southeast over Lima, Peru, with almost 8 million residents, and São Paulo, Brazil, with its 18 million people. Even Charles Mann's generous estimate of the New World population just prior to European colonization is only in the tens of millions. Latin America and the Caribbean currently are home to an incredible 560 million people, and this is projected to climb to 710 million by 2030. These extra 150 million people will need homes, food, and a livelihood, so we can expect that tropical deforestation will carry on like a runaway train until the primary forest is all but gone.

This satellite view of our destruction conceals the tragedy of what is happening at the level of individual populations of trees and animals as the forest disappears. At first, the cutting begins at one or many edges of a vast forest that stretches for tens if not hundreds of miles. As the chainsaws and bulldozers eat away at the boundaries of the forest like a cancer, gaping holes and corridors penetrate the forest and split it into smaller patches. The trees and other plants are prisoners of their roots, and are killed outright by the axes, chainsaws, bulldozers, and fire. Less mobile animals like tree frogs and sloths cannot easily flee from the falling trees and fires and die in large numbers at the time forests are cleared. More mobile animals can flee the advancing line of fallen forest, but as fragmentation continues they eventually end up in islands of forest.

What happens to the survivors as the remaining forest becomes an archipelago of islands among a sea of pastures and fields? The ever-widening gaps make it increasingly difficult for individuals to move between forest patches, isolating small populations in their respective fragments. Trees can move only via their seed-bound offspring. When deforestation is extensive, seeds are likely to drop into pastures or banana plantations and die. Army ants need large home ranges to feed their huge colonies and disappear quickly from small forest fragments. The professional ant-following birds lose their meal ticket and they too disappear from forest fragments soon after the ants. One study in Colombia found that one third of the bird species that lived in the forest in 1911 when most of the forest was still intact were now locally extinct in the scattered patches of forest that remained after extensive clearing.

The size of the remaining forest fragment has a huge impact on how many species can persist there over the long run. A tiny patch will support only small populations of any one species, especially if those individuals are cut off from other surviving members who may be trapped in forest fragments half a mile or more away. Small populations are prone to extinction because they cannot ride out the normal losses in the population that happen during food shortages, disease, or high predation. Their genetic diversity drops too, as relatives are forced to breed with each other from lack of other options. Local extinction can also happen through direct persecution and damage by humans. Spider monkeys and jaguars are among the first animals to go locally extinct from forest fragments because they have nowhere to hide from human hunters. Dry-season fires in the adjacent pastures burn into the forest edges, killing trees and exposing others to the strong drying winds of the desert next door. The individuals living in a small forest patch are under siege even if the forest is never completely cut to the ground. A study of forest fragments in the central Amazon region of Brazil found that one-hundred-hectare patches of tropical forest lost half of their understory bird species in under fifteen years. That is why protected areas, to be useful for conserving biodiversity, should measure in the thousands of hectares to provide healthy homes for large populations.

Tropical forests hold more than half of the world's plant and animal species and hundreds of thousands of species that have not yet been described. Many species are highly specialized so live in only a small, confined region within the tropics. A tropical forest in the highlands of Costa Rica will contain a different set of species than a tropical forest in lowland Panama, which will have different species than a forest far away in the Brazilian Amazon. Mexico has already lost 95 percent of its original forest, and the species and populations that once lived in that forest most certainly did not simply move to the Amazon forest in Brazil. As Mexico was cleared, individuals died and populations of thousands of species withered as the forest disappeared.

When a forest is lost, we do not lose just the plants and animals that once made up the complex community. We also lose history. The evolutionary forces that led to these unique species are an irreplaceable piece of the history of our planet, and will never again be repeated. Alive, these species give us a glimpse into the distant past and help us to unravel the mysteries of life on earth. Extinct, we have lost not just one but dozens of pieces of the puzzle. If someone were to bulldoze Stonehenge we would not lose just a puzzling array of large rocks; we would lose our ability to figure out why the rocks were arranged in that particular pattern. Our children would never be able to visit this historic site and ponder the mysteries of the human mind. With the tropical forests vanishing, children, whether they live in Latin America or North America, will not be able to easily visit our ecological jewels and ponder the mysteries of leaf-cutter ants, strangler figs, and ant-following birds.

The dramatic decline of neotropical migrants has happened during the same decades that tropical forests have been cleared faster than ever before. Many migrants live in tropical forests during the winter, including the Acadian flycatcher, Kentucky warbler, black-and-white warbler, Tennessee warbler, Philadelphia vireo, yellow-throated vireo, bay-breasted warbler, chestnut-sided warbler, and many more. We can expect that the drastic changes to the landscape have had a big impact on these birds, but how big exactly? After all, migrants are not stuck in a shrinking tropical forest patch like sloths and tree frogs. Even migratory birds can only go so far in search of a new home. Migrants travel thousands of miles a year but many have a narrow and well-defined winter range; they are born with a mental map of what part of Latin America constitutes a bull's eye for their final stop on fall migration. Individuals are genetically programmed to head for a particular region, a flight plan that is the result of thousands of years of evolutionary fine tuning. Forest birds like the wood thrush and Kentucky warbler both zero in on Central America, while others, like the black-throated blue warbler, head to the forests of the Caribbean islands and the veery flies all the way to Brazil (figure 4.2). Kentucky warblers do not have the option of spending the winter in Brazil, and the veery cannot seek refuge in a Biosphere Reserve on the Yucatán Peninsula.

The example of the veery has taught us not to let our guard down even when winter ranges appear to be well forested. Until recently, the veery was thought to have a large wintering range that coincided nicely with the biggest tropical forest wilderness remaining in the world, the western Amazon. Since it was one of the few migrants to enjoy a largely intact wintering habitat, the cause of its steep population decline must lie in the breeding grounds or somewhere en route. A careful look at museum specimens that were collected in South America showed that in fact all the veery collected during the winter were from the woodlands of south-central Brazil. The specimens from the western Amazon and northern South America were birds that were passing through on migration in early fall or early spring. The true size of the veery's winter range is as little as 10 percent of the earlier estimate and is much farther to the south, in a heavily populated and agricultural region of southern Brazil. The conservation compass that once pointed north suddenly did an about-face, and now efforts are focused on the wintering grounds.

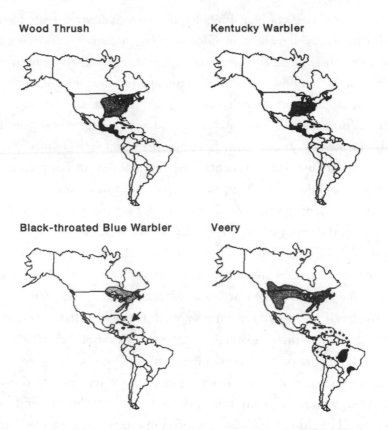

Figure 4.2 *Breeding (grey) and wintering (black) ranges of typical neotropical migrants. The dashed line for the veery indicates early but incorrect estimates of the winter range. (Based on Rappole et al., 1983, and Remsen, 2001)*

For many migrants the wintering range was already a crowded place a thousand years ago, before such vast amounts of habitat were lost. The funnel-like geography of Central America forces migrants into an area just a fraction of the size of the breeding range. All the breeding populations of wood thrush that are spread over some 300 million hectares have to fit into an area one fifth the size during the wintering season. Young birds, born just a few months earlier, have always had to compete with older, more experienced birds to find food and a safe haven during the winter. Their adaptations for surviving the winter were shaped on an ecological stage where tropical forest blanketed the Caribbean islands and much of Central and South America. In an evolutionary blink of an eye, this life-supporting habitat has been swept away and replaced with pastures, crops, and cities. With tropical deforestation proceeding at a breakneck pace, we have to ask if enough good quality habitat remains within the small wintering ranges to provide a decent home for migrants.

Kentucky warblers and wood thrush are both forest birds that have declined dramatically in the past few decades. Their entire wintering range in Central America has undergone extreme deforestation during this same period. Both species are territorial, so they cannot simply crowd into remaining forests and share what little habitat is left. In areas with extensive agriculture and forest clearing, both species are common only in the remaining forest fragments or coffee and cacao plantations that have large trees and a forest canopy.

Pioneering studies of the wood thrush in the 1980s show exactly what can happen to individual birds when the forest is in short supply. John Rappole, from the Conservation and Research Center of the Smithsonian, followed wintering wood thrush in southern Mexico by outfitting them with tiny radiotransmitter backpacks. At that time there were several large patches of undisturbed forest and selectively logged forest in the region. Wood thrush that lived in the forest were sedentary, defended a small territory and ate insects on the forest floor. The surprise for Rappole and his students was that half the birds that they radiotagged did not even own territories at all. These birds were non-territorial wanderers that lived in high density along the forest edges where the habitat was marginal. Wanderers were skittish and wary, moved long distances every day and often made secretive trips into the forest where they were sometimes chased away by territory owners. Wanderers were four times more likely to be killed by predators than were the sedentary birds living in the forest.

The Sierra Santa Marta region where this study was done lost an estimated 40 percent of its original forest cover between 1950 and 1986, leaving less than 10 percent of the area forested (figure 4.3). Although wood thrush are still common in the remaining forest patches, almost half the

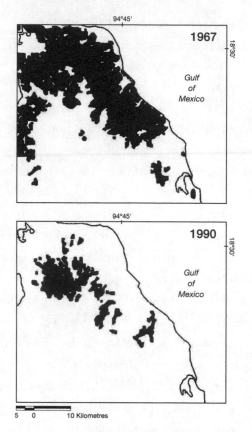

Figure 4.3. *Loss of tropical forest (black) in the Sierra Santa Marta region, southern Mexico. (Images courtesy of Durand and Lazos, 2004)*

wintering population exists as nomads, reducing their chance of surviving the winter. This pattern of extreme forest loss has been repeated countless times throughout the winter range of the wood thrush, and there is every reason to think tropical deforestation is driving the strong population declines seen on the breeding grounds.

Other forest migrants are in the same sinking boat as the wood thrush and Kentucky warbler. Worm-eating warblers live in mixed-species flocks with other insect-eating birds, and together defend a vast communal territory in the tropical forest. Worm-eating warblers are highly specialized foragers and search the branches for curled-up dead leaves, peering and poking inside the leaves to find insects and larvae that are hiding from birds. They are obligate flock joiners because they spend so much time upside down sticking their heads into leaves that they cannot keep a sharp eye out for predators. With a dozen or more flock mates to give alarm calls at any sign of danger, the warbler can focus its attention on foraging. Within the flock the worm-eating warbler defends its valuable coalition from others of its kind. This species is highly vulnerable to forest fragmentation because mixed-species flocks defend such large territories that they can persist only in large patches of forest. A small fragment cannot support the tropical birds that make up the core of the mixed-species flock, and the worm-eating warblers cannot use the forest fragment if its watchdogs are not there. In southern Mexico researchers studied a forest patch before and after it was severely degraded by logging and clearing, and found that the worm-eating warbler disappeared from the patch soon after disturbance.

Many other migrants are found in the forest but also use a wide range of other habitats. For instance, the hooded warbler, American redstart, black-and-white warbler, and summer tanager are commonly found outside the forest in strips of trees near streams, scrubby field edges, and secondary forest in abandoned fields. Cattle pastures can be a refuge for some birds if the farmer has left scattered trees to provide shade for livestock. In heavily agricultural areas there may be strips of scrub and trees along rivers and streams and along the edges of fields. Birds may also find some refuge in living fences made from cuttings of *Bursera* trees that sprout leaves, flowers, and fruit. The amount of scrubby habitat and secondary growth is increasing rapidly across the winter range of many species because cleared land that was abandoned when it was no longer productive has been left to grow back. We know many of our migrants do live in such places, but is it by choice or are they forced there for lack of real forest?

There is good evidence that our migrants are paying a big price by living in lousy, second-rate accommodation and that these alternative habitats are not good enough to support healthy populations of wintering birds. Young and inexperienced birds may be crowded out of high-quality habitat and do very poorly in secondary habitat. As we have learned with wood thrush, high abundance in a marginal habitat does not necessarily mean that the birds are in good condition or surviving well. Following the fate of individual birds for weeks or months is difficult because it requires intensive banding and hundreds of hours of observing birds. Researchers have used an impressive tool box of ecological experiments and laboratory tests to find out just how badly birds are doing in secondary habitat.

The region encompassing the Yucatán Peninsula, Belize, and southern Mexico is the winter heartland for the hooded warbler. In the early 1990s I stayed in a small town, Puerto Morelos, on the southeast side of the Yucatán Peninsula, which consisted of a few dozen homes, one motel, a fancier hotel for tourists, some beach houses, a small tienda, and a very popular tortilleria. After a long, hot morning in the field I would go back to town and join the lineup for steaming fresh tortillas. Inside the tiny store, a heavy-set older man operated a large contraption that spat out a steady stream of tortillas while a young boy, about nine years old, carefully wrapped stacks of them in brown paper and weighed them on a rickety old scale. Puerto Morelos was far enough away from Cancún to be off the beaten path, and its beaches were almost empty.

A few miles inland a road that was battered and potholed from the heavy rains of the wet season stretched for miles northward across the peninsula. This was my twice-daily commute, driving four or so miles to the forested areas inland as though I was a toddler at the steering wheel, pulling and turning with exaggerated and frantic turns. It was impossible to miss all the holes in the road, and I went through two rental cars during my stay. Inspired by the wood thrush study of John Rappole, I was there to study how hooded warblers duke it out for a winter territory.

The area where I worked had forest stretching down one side of the road and scrubby second growth on the other. Hooded warblers lived

on both sides of the road, but the sexes disagreed on which was better habitat. Males were partial to the forest, with its tall, straight tree
trunks, while females were more often found in dense vegetation where
branches and stems criss-cross in crazy patterns. Hooded warblers are
born with built-in habitat preferences, the result of a long evolutionary
history of avoiding competition with each other. Males are larger and
more brightly coloured so have the upper hand when going head-to-head
with females. Females, by specializing on second-growth habitat and
natural gaps in the forest, can defend territories without being severely
harassed by males who may try to kick them out. Historically, there has
always been plenty of habitat for females. Violent storms blow down big
trees in the forest to create gaps that fill in gradually over time, and hur-
ricanes and forest fires create plenty of large-scale scrubby habitat.

By the time I arrived in late September, most of the habitat had been
filled with hooded warblers who had already staked out a territory. The
first week I concentrated on catching and banding territory owners with
individual coloured bands so I could tell them apart and figure out who
owned which territory. Hooded warblers patrol their territories, always
on the lookout for skulking intruders who sneak around and steal the
precious supply of insects. Males and females both use the same vocali-
zation for territory defence, a metallic *chip* call that is also used by both
sexes on the breeding grounds. I caught birds by playing back a recording
of the *chip* call under a mist net or by attracting a mob of birds (hopefully
including the hooded warbler) by whistling *hoo hoo hoo hoo,* in imitation
of the ferruginous pygmy owl, which likes to eat warblers for lunch.

My experiment involved kidnapping territory owners to find out
what would happen when they weren't home to defend their territory.
If good-quality habitat was in short supply because it was already full of
hooded warblers, then wandering non-territorial birds should move in
quickly and claim vacant territories. By banding all the territory owners
in the neighbourhood, I would be able to tell if the vacant territory was
taken over by a neighbour looking for better habitat or by a wandering
bird à la wood thrush. I drove my unwilling collaborators, the captured

territory owners, about an hour away down the main highway south of Puerto Morelos and let them go, figuring either it would take them a few days to find their way back or they would simply find a new territory along the way.

Empty space was quickly claimed, and most of the replacement birds were wanderers who did not, until then, own a territory. Most of the original territory owners were older birds that had already spent at least one winter in the tropics. On the other hand, almost all the wanderers were young birds trying to get a winter territory for the very first time. Wanderers were equally likely to be male or female, meaning that for both sexes many young birds have trouble securing a territory when they arrive on the wintering grounds in fall. Even the scrub habitat was full and quickly attracted wanderers, suggesting that these young birds are in a desperate situation. If wood thrush are any example, the survival of these wanderers is likely low.

My Ph.D. student Francisco De los Santos used radiotelemetry and blood tests to measure how the health of hooded warblers is affected by the habitat they live in during the winter. His first study site was the Chiquibul Forest Reserve, in Belize, part of a vast continuous forest that measures in the hundreds of thousands of hectares. Francisco regularly saw jaguars on the trails in the forest, an experience only possible in large forest tracts. Male hooded warblers defended territories cheek by jowl in the forest, while females defended the scattered scrubby gaps where trees had recently crashed to the ground. This is the way much of the hooded warbler's winter range would have looked two hundred years ago. Francisco's second study site was at the other extreme of habitat disturbance, an agricultural area in southeastern Mexico that had extensive pastures, citrus plantations, and small patches of secondary forest that bordered the fields. Here, hooded warblers were also common but they were mostly females who occupied the scrubby habitat along field edges. Francisco radiotagged birds at both study sites and found that birds occupying the pristine forest in Belize had smaller territories and spent less time foraging each day, a sign that more food was available.

These forest birds were also heavier and better fed than their counterparts in the fragmented landscape of Mexico.

Next, Francisco asked the birds which habitat was best for them. He took blood samples from all the birds he caught and froze the blood until he could get it to the lab in Mexico City. In the lab he measured levels of the hormone corticosterone, which is an indicator of chronic stress. Birds will become stressed out if they are chronically short of food, living under the constant threat of predation, or frequently chased and harassed by other birds. Corticosterone helps the bird cope with stress by raising its activity level and increasing its desire to find food. Mammals have the same kind of physiological stress response. Parents of young children and people who commute in heavy traffic every day have high levels of corticosterone, while retirees who spend their time on photography and golf likely have low levels of the stress hormone. The birds in the Chiquibul Forest in Belize were laid back and had very low levels of corticosterone in their blood. The birds living in the scrubby field edges in Mexico had very high stress levels, a result of the daily challenges of finding food and staying alive in a poor habitat.

Together, these studies on hooded warblers show that all is not well on the wintering grounds. This migrant is often found outside the tropical forest in scrubby habitat, but the birds who live in these places are struggling to stay healthy. Given the large amount of forest loss in the tropics, it is probably true that most hooded warblers heading south for the first time will find themselves in a hot, dry patch of scrub looking at cattle all winter rather than flitting among the branches of a towering mahogany tree while jaguars pass by below them. Where a bird spends the winter can affect not only its food supply and body condition, but also its ability to migrate north and breed.

⁓

Peter Marra of the Smithsonian Institution and his colleagues have found a long list of short-term and long-terms costs of living outside the forest, using an elaborate set of experiments on the American redstart. These studies were done in Jamaica, where redstarts prefer black mangrove forest over scrubby second growth. The mangrove is a coastal forest with an open understory and trees that are adapted for salty conditions when the high tide floods the forest floor. Mangrove is worth fighting for because the insect supply there is three times higher than in hot, dry scrub habitat. This big difference in insect food has a cascade of effects on the individual bird and the population health of this species. Like hooded warblers, males and females are usually found in different habitats; older males dominate the mangrove forest and the competitively inferior females and young males are relegated to the scrub. Stress tests confirmed that during the dry season, when food is scarce, scrub-living birds had higher stress hormone levels than birds in the mangrove.

Colin Studds, a Ph.D. student at the University of Maryland, did an experiment to find out whether the scrub birds would be in better shape if they *could* live in the mangrove. He allowed scrub birds to move to better accommodations by removing the older males who owned nice territories in mangrove. He then compared the success of the females and young males who suddenly found themselves in a good home with the fate of their unlucky counterparts who were stuck back in the scrubby second growth. Birds that moved into the mangrove maintained a normal body weight through the dry season, but the birds in the scrub lost weight. The poor food supply for the scrub birds did not kill them outright during the winter but had other serious consequences. Living in scrub habitat delayed their departure for spring migration by almost a week because these birds were in bad shape and needed more time to get ready for their marathon journey north. An amazing 59 percent of the mangrove birds returned the next winter to reclaim their good territories, but only 33 percent of the scrub birds survived the round trip. Living in scrub habitat has bad effects on redstarts long after they leave their wintering grounds.

Birds carry part of their winter habitat with them when they fly north, not on their backs but deep inside their bodies. The tissues and blood of a bird are continuously being replenished with new cells that are made from the universal building blocks of life: carbon, oxygen, hydrogen. Birds get individual carbon atoms from eating an insect, which in turn got those same carbon atoms from eating a plant. So the carbon in the redstart who has just arrived on its territory in New Hampshire actually entered the bird a few weeks beforehand while it was eating insects on its winter territory. Moist habitat like tropical forest and mangrove forest produces a different carbon isotope signature than do grasses and many other plants found in shrubby second growth. Researchers can catch a redstart who has just arrived on the breeding grounds and, by measuring the type of isotopes in the bird's tissue or blood, figure out what kind of habitat it lived in thousands of miles away during the winter.

Stable isotope analysis has shown that not only do scrub birds leave later on spring migration but they also arrive later on the breeding grounds. Ryan Norris, now a professor of biology at the University of Guelph, found that a late-arriving male could find himself getting last pick of a breeding territory and suffering poor reproduction. Ryan's study in Ontario showed that the late spring arrival triggered a domino effect; males who had been in scrub during winter ended up having mates who nested later in the spring and suffered higher predation on their eggs and young. The result was that they produced 20 to 50 percent fewer young than males who had overwintered in the mangrove. The males who had lost out in the competition for winter territories were still paying the price six months later and a few thousand miles away. Clearly, even if winter habitat does not affect the immediate survival of birds, it can still have a huge impact on their long-term survival and breeding success.

We set out with a question: How well do forest birds survive in alternative habitats like scrub and secondary forest? A diverse set of migrants do very poorly outside the forest. Not a single study has found that neotropical migrants do equally well in scrubby secondary habitat. Young birds cannot get good winter territories, and those who occupy crummy habitat may pay with their lives. Even for those individuals that can survive in poor habitat, late arrival in spring and a poor breeding territory means that the trip may have largely been in vain because their reproductive success is so low. We should not feel so pleased to see dozens of neotropical migrants occupying the scrubby habitat along field edges and streams, because these birds are really just buying time.

~

Migratory songbirds are not on vacation while in the tropics; every day they are busy at their ecological jobs of being insect predators, pollen movers, and fruit dispersers. Although some work alone, others join flocks of other birds, both migrants and residents, whom they work alongside. Migrants have been doing these jobs for tens of thousands of years, and the tropical ecosystem that is their home many months of the year has come to depend on them.

Birds play a critical role in maintaining healthy tropical forests because about three quarters of the trees depend on them to eat fruit. Being stuck in one place, one way a tree can have its seeds leave home is if they hitchhike inside the body of an animal. Trees have good reason to want their seeds to escape from their own shadow. Plants compete for soil nutrients and sunshine, so a tiny seedling stands little chance of growing well underneath its own towering parent. In the mountains of Costa Rica, only a handful of birds regularly eat the fruit of an avocado-like tree called *Ocotea endresiana,* and of those, only one, the three-wattled bellbird, is an especially useful seed disperser because it reliably moves the seeds more than 130 feet from the parent plant. Daniel Wenny, a Ph.D. student at the University of Florida in Gainesville, watched birds eating fruit from the tree, and then followed them closely until they spat out the seed or simply defecated.

Wenny found that bellbirds "planted" the seeds in an ideal place for seedling growth: a forest gap. Male bellbirds, for several months of the year, defend perches above forest gaps as their display sites. (They lure in females with a display that would turn most of us off. Hanging from the edges of his mouth are three worm-like sacs of skin that engorge and extend three times in length when he displays; he waggles his head silently to show off his dangling ornaments. If a female visits his perch, he leans over and puts his beak near her ear, then lets out a thundering bell-like roar that nearly knocks her off her feet, literally.) The tree benefits tremendously from the exotic mating behaviour of one particular bird in the forest because the seeds moved by bellbirds are half as likely to die from a fungal disease when they are planted in a sunny gap within the forest. Large fruit-eating birds like the bellbird are very sensitive to forest fragmentation; when areas are logged the bellbird disappears, and then the trees are left without anyone to move their seeds.

Forest fragmentation can break up routine fruit dispersal even for common tree species in the tropics. In Africa, the tree called *zonozono* in Swahili has a large group of unspecialized forest birds that move its fruits through the forest. The region was heavily deforested a few centuries ago to grow coffee, and today is a major producer of tea. In small patches of tropical forest, many of the key fruit-eating forest birds are rare or uncommon, and relatively few of the fruits are taken away by birds. From the tree's point of view, this means trouble. In fragments, young seedlings are packed in high numbers underneath the parent tree, where they die from lack of sun and nutrients before they reach a decent size. The trees are helpless; there is no way they can move the seeds themselves. Although the forest fragments do have other birds, especially those that like scrubby forest and edges, these do not take the place of the forest fruit eaters. Fragmentation severs the long and successful evolutionary relationship between the fruit-eating birds and the trees that depend on them.

Throughout the tropics, forests that become islands surrounded by open land slowly but steadily lose their biodiversity. The remaining patches of Atlantic tropical forest in Brazil are suffering from a shortage of birds. Less than 10 percent of the original forest remains as scattered fragments (figure 4.1), the largest only about two thousand hectares. About half of the trees in these forest fragments depend on large fruit-eating forest birds for seed dispersal, though these birds are relatively uncommon in the bird community. Many of these large birds are rare or absent in fragments because they are heavily hunted or live only in large tracts of forest. In tropical forests, resident forest birds rarely fly more than 650 feet over open space, so will be unable to reach isolated fragments. We can expect that many tree species will become locally extinct within their forest patches and will be replaced by a different set of trees that do not depend on large birds. This unique tropical forest is expected to change dramatically over the next few decades and lose much of its biodiversity; some trees will go extinct altogether. Though the trees are not cut down by chainsaws, their genetic future is cut off because they cannot reproduce.

During the winter, billions of migrants pour into Central and South America, and almost a quarter of them are species that switch from a summer diet of insects to a winter diet of fruit. The migrants that gorge mostly, or exclusively, on fruit include the eastern kingbird, Tennessee warbler, Philadelphia vireo, white-eyed vireo, yellow-throated vireo, scarlet tanager, and rose-breasted grosbeak. It is hard to watch a fruiting tree in the tropics and *not* see a migrant. Many migrants are generalists and are happy eating a wide variety of fruit, so no single tree depends on a particular migrant species. This ecological redundancy means that if the numbers of one migrant species plummet, their job as disperser may be filled by other migrants or even one of the many resident fruit-eating birds like euphonias, tanagers, and manakins. This backup system has led many researchers to believe that migrants do not play an important ecological role compared with tropical residents. This may be true for individual migrant species, but if migrants as a whole are declining then even the tropical residents may not be able to keep up with moving the fruit.

Tight specializations between trees and migrants do occur, and may be much more common than we realize. In the Yucatán Peninsula, the gumbo-limbo tree (*Bursera*) is dispersed mainly by one neotropical migrant, the white-eyed vireo. In Panama, locals sarcastically call this tree the "tourist tree" because of the thin sheets of red bark that hang off the trunk, making it resemble a sunburned gringo. Vireos defend territories that include gumbo-limbo trees, and almost all the fruit they eat comes only from this kind of tree. The small seeds are not hidden in a juicy fleshy fruit; rather, the plant uses a waxy nutritious coating around the seed, an aril, to entice avian visitors. White-eyed vireos eat the aril but not the seed itself; holding the seed in the tip of its bill, the vireo squeezes hard, shooting the seed out of its mouth, just like a kid spitting watermelon seeds at a picnic. From the tree's point of view, the white-eyed vireo is its most frequent visitor and it has several adaptations that appear specialized for this disperser. The aril is covered with a rosy green capsule, hiding the bright red aril that in other plants attracts the attention of passing birds from far away. The vireos are already living near the tree, so there is no need to advertise. *Bursera* trees fruit gradually over the winter season, providing a rich and steady reward a little bit at a time that allows the bird to remain on its territory and specialize on the fruit.

Migrant birds, with their long-distance movements in spring, play a special role in tropical ecosystems because they have the potential to spread seeds into forest patches where a tree has gone locally extinct, reseeding the patch with restored biodiversity. The eastern kingbird is a fruit eater during winter and follows the ripening wave of *Panax* fruit as it moves north from South America into Central America. Their entire winter ecology revolves around the timing of fruiting of this tree.

Scarlet tanagers are also important seed dispersers as they head north through the tropics from their wintering grounds in the forests of South America. As they move through the narrow land bridge of Panama they are often seen feeding at *Tetracera* vines along the forest edge. Its small black seeds are surrounded by a brilliant red aril that is especially attractive to tanagers because male scarlet tanagers are not scarlet at all during winter. They moult back into their stunning colours while they travel north and need the carotenoid pigments in the aril to make their red feathers. Many tropical trees in Central America fruit during the dry season, usually February or March, so they too likely benefit from the huge numbers of hungry migrants on the move at that time of year.

At the same time that millions of hectares of primary rainforest are being cut, other lands that have been denuded and degraded are abandoned. Fruit-eating birds speed up the healing of the land because they restore biodiversity when they deposit seeds that have hitchhiked from elsewhere. Remaining forest fragments, even if they are low in biodiversity, are important sources of seeds for nearby land that is regenerating. Expensive and labour-intensive human efforts to restore land can take advantage of the free services that birds provide. Perch sites give birds a place to land, and defecate, and forested corridors may encourage the movement of forest birds out into areas they would not otherwise visit. Planting of different native fruiting trees attracts fruit eaters who may be carrying rare species of seeds in their gut. Natural seed dispersal is much cheaper than growing seedlings in nurseries and planting them by the hundreds.

Seeds come from flowers and will not grow unless the flower is pollinated. Most tropical trees rely on animals to bring pollen to their flowers, so forest fragmentation can interfere with making seeds as well as with moving seeds. Many plants and trees use bird pollinators, most notably the hundreds of species of hummingbirds that occur in the tropics. Although many migrating birds are fruit eaters, some migrants, such as Tennessee warblers, Baltimore orioles, and orchard orioles, drink the nectar from flowers, so may be important pollinators for some trees and vines. *Erythrina* trees grow along rivers and flower in the dry season, after losing all their leaves. Each tree is covered in bright orange flowers and attracts more than a dozen species of birds looking for a sweet drink. The orchard oriole is a good pollinator because it has a strong pointy beak that can pry open the flowers. The orioles descend in flocks, chattering noisily, and with a flick of their sharp beak pop open the closed *Erythrina* flower to reveal the sweet nectar within. When an oriole pokes its head inside to get the nectar, the pollen at the tip of the flower rubs off on the bird's forehead, ready to hitchhike to a flower on the next tree. The oriole greedily sucks up the nectar, then moves on to other branches and nearby trees for more goodies and inadvertently pollinates those flowers. Other birds, like parrotlets, woodpeckers, and even native orioles, just steal the nectar by poking a hole in the side of the flower; they go away full but do the plant no good at all because they are not carrying pollen.

Tropical forests also depend on birds that are professional exterminators of large leaf-eating insects. The best way to show the predatory prowess of insect-eating birds is to put up netting and stop them from reaching the insects. In Panama, researchers went high into the tops of the tropical forest using the Smithsonian's canopy crane and put small cages around branches to keep birds out. During the wet season, when insects were at their highest, the birdless branches had twice as many insects as unprotected branches. Similar experiments in coffee plantations in Mexico and Guatemala also show that birds make a big dent in the local population of leaf-eating insects, reducing insect numbers by as much as half.

In many tropical regions, neotropical migrants make up more than a third of the bird population during the winter months; they are not benign visitors but key players in the tropical communities where they live. They are more mobile than tropical residents so play an important role restoring diversity both to forest fragments and to lands that are gradually regenerating back into forest. We are stuck in a downward spiral; deforestation forces birds into poor habitat where they suffer lower survival and, eventually, poor reproduction. As migrant populations shrink, there will be fewer birds to keep forests healthy and to help build new forests.

There is a simple way to help migrant birds and tropical forests at the same time: drink shade-grown coffee. In the next chapter we will see how consumers can make a difference.

5 COFFEE WITH A CONSCIENCE
Preserving Bird Habitats, One Cup of Coffee at a Time

A traditional shade-grown-coffee farm is a mini ecosystem with more than two dozen different species of trees that shade the coffee plants below and provide a surrogate home for plants and animals that are normally found in tropical forest. Shade-coffee farms are teeming with resident birds that are joined by migrants from the north from September through March. The birds are attracted not to the coffee itself but rather to the food that the shade trees provide. Many birds are insect eaters, like the worm-eating warblers that prefer the canopy of shade trees, where they hang upside down on dead leaves searching for insects that are hiding inside. Most insect eaters feed in the canopy rather than on the coffee plants because few insects can stomach coffee leaves, which are tough and full of chemicals. Kentucky warblers and wood thrush prefer the forest floor, where they search for insects under the fallen leaves. Small, drab Tennessee warblers flit among the treetops, pausing to stick their beak into tree blossoms to sip nectar as we might sip an exotic tropical drink decorated with cherries and a gaudy umbrella. The stunningly bright orange Baltimore orioles almost blend in with the large orange flowers of the *Erythrina* tree, a favourite among coffee farmers since it grows quickly and adds nitrogen to the soil. Other migrants are there for the fruit that is abundant all winter, like the rose-breasted grosbeaks who gobble up tiny *Miconia* fruits in the dense canopy of the shade trees.

Shade-coffee plantations, like a natural forest, are a tapestry of relationships between the thousands of species that make up the living community. The tree branches in a tropical forest are laden with special plants called epiphytes that use other plants as a platform for their roots. The epiphytes include bromeliads with thick, wide leaves that project dagger-like out from the base, delicate orchids, and thick mats of mosses and lichens. Sometimes it is hard to tell the branch from its freeloaders! These gardens in the canopy are avian fast-food restaurants teeming with a smorgasbord of insects, flowers, and fruit. The centre of a bromeliad forms a well that can hold water for weeks after a rainfall, an important resource for birds during the long dry season. There is fast food on the forest floor too, but this kind is mobile and unpredictable in where and when it can be found. Army ants flush up and attack insects and small lizards in their path. Some birds routinely follow the army ant swarms, darting in to snatch up their fair share of the desperate insects. Migrants like wood thrush, Wilson's warblers, mourning warblers, and yellow-bellied flycatchers opportunistically join the ant-following flock of birds. When the ants are not swarming, these migrants have to go back to searching for food the hard way, looking for insects that are hiding in and under leaves.

Coffee can be a bird's best friend, but in the past few decades modern farming has swept the coffee industry in Latin America and has also swept away some of the last forest refuges for birds. In the swirling steam that rises from your coffee cup could be the ghosts of warblers flitting among the orchids, orioles sipping nectar from spectacular bouquets in the treetops, and thrush flipping up leaves on the forest floor.

~✦~

For many of us our first stop in the morning, after a quick trip to the bathroom, is the coffee pot. I religiously down two cups of coffee before breakfast, a habit that began when I was in graduate school. North Americans are coffee addicts and can barely make it through a day without a cup or two (or more!) of coffee; we drink 300 million cups of coffee a day and import more than 3.3 billion pounds of coffee beans each year. This huge thirst for coffee has fuelled the economies and shaped the lands and peoples of Latin America for two hundred years. We take for granted our mugs of coffee whether they come from our own kitchen, an office coffee pot or a drive-through window. We don't think twice about how the coffee was grown, or even whether that matters; we know in some vague way that the beans were picked in some faraway tropical country. Coffee drinkers have been slow to wake up to the environmental and social damage that their habit is causing, but they also hold the key to the survival of many neotropical migrants.

The coffee plant (*Coffea arabica*) originated in the highland forests of southeastern Ethiopia, where it still grows wild as an evergreen shrub beneath the towering tropical forest. The leaves are thick and waxy, and the dozens of small bushy white flowers along the branches are pollinated by bees. Coffee plants produce small red berries that hold two seeds each. The fruits ripen asynchronously, so the plant can have both unripe green fruits and brilliant crimson berries at the same time. In a natural setting this trick allows the plant plenty of time to attract birds and other animals who will eat the ripe fruit and serve the plant's interests by carrying the seeds harmlessly in their gut to be deposited far from the parent plant. While fruits are meant to be eaten, the seeds are the reproductive future of the plant and must be protected. The plant stocks its seeds with an alkaloid called caffeine, a chemical bodyguard against animals who might otherwise try to eat the seed itself for its nutritional benefits. What we drink so eagerly in the morning is the ground-up roasted seeds of the coffee berry that is full of a "poison" that the plant puts there to stop seed predators like us.

Coffee was first consumed as a food, not a drink. The whole berries were mixed with animal fats and shaped into balls that were easily carried on long journeys. Commercial production of coffee as a beverage began around the twelfth or thirteenth centuries in the Arabian Peninsula, in the rugged inland mountains of what we now call Yemen. This was the birthplace of the prized "mocha" bean, originally grown on hillside terraces under the shade of bananas. In the early 1700s European colonists introduced coffee into their tropical territories, beginning with the Dutch, who took coffee to Ceylon, Timor, and Sumatra as well as other holdings in southeast Asia. Coffee arrived in the New World soon after, when the French began growing it on the Caribbean islands, and the Dutch introduced coffee to Surinam, French Guiana, and Brazil.

In Latin America, coffee production geared up slowly during the early 1800s, in part because so few people had experience with this new crop and the arabica seeds grew well only in very specific growing conditions, with just the right kind of soil, elevation, temperature and rainfall. A big capital investment was needed to grow coffee in large quantities because seedlings had to be tended for years before the first crop was produced; processing the berries required expensive new equipment. Without a well-developed system of roads and railways, coffee growers had a difficult time transporting their coffee beans to export markets. Once the coffee trade and transportation systems became established in the mid-1800s, though, coffee quickly became a popular cash crop, and plantations spread rapidly across the countryside as tropical forest was cleared (figure 5.1) and lands already producing other crops were converted to coffee production. Brazil quickly established itself as the number-one coffee producer in Latin America, largely on the backs of its slave population. Large coffee plantations had dozens of slaves to clear land, tend the trees, and harvest the crops.

Figure 5.1. *Workers planting coffee seedlings on a finca in Guatemala where the tropical forest had recently been cleared to expand the coffee plantation. (Photo by Eadweard Muybridge, 1875. Stanford University, Special Collections)*

Up until the late 1800s, world production and the price of coffee were dominated by coffee growers in Southeast Asia. This changed suddenly when a fungal disease called coffee leaf rust decimated coffee production in the Old World, spreading quickly from coffee farms in India and Ceylon (now Sri Lanka) to Indonesia. The shortage of coffee sparked high prices; coffee tripled in value between 1883 and 1893. With a gold rush mentality, coffee production increased more than 350 percent in Guatemala, El Salvador, and Nicaragua over the few decades following the coffee collapse in the Old World. During this era, Latin America produced about 90 percent of the world's supply of coffee, compared with only about 30 percent today.

Steven Topik, a professor of history at the University of California in Irvine, describes arabica coffee as the umbilical cord that tied much of Latin America to the world economy. Coffee fuelled an export boom that saw the tropical forests fall to the axe, cities swell, and factories rise. Although coffee production caused the clearing of millions of hectares of tropical forest, ironically coffee plantations today can be safe havens for thousands of tropical birds and plants.

~

Russell Greenberg, director of the Smithsonian Migratory Bird Center, studied the biodiversity in traditional shade-coffee farms in the southern state of Chiapas, Mexico. Land use is heavy here; the valley floors are covered with open cattle pasture and the hills made up of corn fields, degraded woodlands, and coffee plantations. Most of the coffee plantations in this region are heavily shaded by a tall and well-developed canopy that shields the coffee plants. Using systematic bird surveys, Greenberg found forty-six species of neotropical migrants living in shade-coffee farms, including twenty-two species of warbler. The diversity of resident tropical birds was also high, with more than a hundred bird species making use of this semi-natural forest. Similar studies have been done in other parts of Mexico and Panama with similar results: shade coffee is home to a high diversity of birds, including dozens of species of neotropical migrants.

Shade coffee makes a good home for migrants, almost as good as a real forest. Joe Wunderle, wildlife biologist at the U.S.D.A. Forest Service in Puerto Rico, and Steve Latta banded birds in shade coffee and natural forest in the Dominican Republic to find out how well birds survived. For three species of migrants—the American redstart, black-and-white warbler, and black-throated blue warbler—about 70 percent of the banded birds in the shade coffee were still alive by the end of their winter stay. A third of the migrants who lived in the shade-coffee plantation returned the next year to make it their home once again. This semi-natural forest provided security and food that was comparable to natural forest. Another indicator of habitat quality is the number of males living there. Males are more likely than females to defend territories in high-quality forest habitat (and females end up in scrubby second-growth habitat). In the Dominican shade-coffee plantations, about 80 percent of the redstarts and black-throated blue warblers were males, suggesting that the birds viewed this habitat as similar to forest.

If we travel back in time two hundred years, we can see a stark example of how shade coffee can save birds. In 1770, Puerto Rico was almost completely covered in tropical forest. Over the next century, almost all the forest was cut down to make way for an exploding export industry of tropical crops like sugar cane and coffee. Virgin forest shrank to only a few thousand hectares; shade-coffee plantations, however, covered almost 10 percent of the island, providing an extra eighty thousand hectares of semi-forested habitat at the western end of the island. Puerto Rico, like many of the Caribbean islands, is home to unique species of birds that are found nowhere else in the world. Birds like the Puerto Rican woodpecker, tanager, screech owl, and tody are frequently seen in coffee plantations today and likely could not have survived if it were not for the coffee plantations that sheltered them during the wave of deforestation on the island. Puerto Rico still has very little virgin forest, but it now has extensive secondary forest; when the sugar cane industry collapsed in the 1940s, cultivated lands were abandoned and allowed to grow back. Many of the birds that could hold on through the worst times are now quite common on the island, thanks to shade coffee.

Joe Wunderle did not have to travel back in time to see the same thing happening in the Dominican Republic, which is the eastern half of the island of Hispaniola. Joe believes that many species endemic to this island are surviving today because there is shade coffee. His studies of coffee plantations in the Dominican Republic occurred in a heavily deforested region that mimicked the conditions on Puerto Rico during the deforestation period. In the absence of those shade-coffee plantations, many of the forest-dwelling species would disappear from the agricultural region of the Cordillera Central where he worked. There is little doubt that if the shade-coffee plantations in this region were lost we would see sharp declines of species like the Hispaniolan parrot, parakeet, emerald woodpecker, and lizard cuckoo.

Shade-coffee plantations are crucial for sustaining biodiversity because the coffee-growing regions in Central America are global biodiversity hotspots. Many species have small geographic ranges, sometimes restricted to single mountain chains or islands, and occur nowhere else on the planet. Heavy deforestation in one area can wipe out most of their natural habitat and threaten an entire species. There is so little natural forest in many coffee-growing regions that shade-coffee plantations are the best habitat for miles around. Shade coffee has given many forest-loving species a chance to survive deforestation.

Shade coffee is biodiversity friendly, not just bird friendly. In one study in Costa Rica, Ivette Perfecto, a professor at the School of Natural Resources and Environment, University of Michigan, used an insecticidal fog to collect all the insects from single shade trees. The canopy of one *Erythrina* tree contained twenty-seven species of ants, sixty-one species of bees and wasps, and one hundred species of beetles. She also studied butterfly diversity in Mexico, and found that heavily shaded coffee plantations were home to more than twenty species of butterflies, similar to the natural forest nearby. Surveys of shade-coffee plantations in Veracruz, Mexico, have found about ten different species of frogs, half a dozen species of bats, and two dozen species of mammals such as opossums, rabbits, and the threatened nutria.

Although shade-coffee houses high biodiversity, it should not be thought of as a complete substitute for preserving large tracts of natural forest. Many forest species are so specialized they occupy only mature forest and won't touch even a heavily shaded coffee plantation. Several species of birds did not survive the drastic habitat loss in Puerto Rico and are extinct: the lesser Puerto Rican crow, Puerto Rican barn owl and quail dove. Bird censuses in the extensive El Triunfo Biosphere Reserve in southern Mexico found many forest birds that are highly sensitive to forest disturbance, like the singing quail, blue-throated motmot, scaly-throated foliage-gleaner, and tawny-throated leaf-tosser. These birds were never seen in the shade-coffee plantations nearby. Shade-coffee plantations are also not a good home for many forest frogs, among them the variegated tree frog, Berkenbusch's robber frog, and the globally threatened Mexican tree frog and lesser bromeliad tree frog. Many large mammals like tapirs, spider monkeys, and jaguars might well venture into shade-coffee plantations, but would not last very long there because of hunting pressure.

The trees in a shade-coffee farm are important for sustainable farming, not just providing a home for biodiversity. The trees are a source of food and timber for the farmer, and the shade provides cool temperatures and high humidity for the coffee plants. The berries ripen slowly, producing premium-quality coffee. The shade trees shelter the soil from wind and rain and help to prevent soil erosion during downpours. The leaves from deciduous shade trees fall to the ground, adding nutrients to the soil and helping to keep the soil moist. Many of the shade trees are an underground lifeline for the coffee plants because they have special nodules on their roots that allow them to capture atmospheric nitrogen. Coffee, like many other plants, cannot "fix" nitrogen and is totally dependent on the nitrogen already in the soil. Corn is in this category too, and must be rotated with other nitrogen-fixing crops like soy beans or, if grown year after year in the same field, requires large doses of fertilizer. In a traditional coffee plantation the nitrogen-fixing roots of shade trees are grown alongside the coffee plants, meaning that coffee can be grown continuously without depleting the nitrogen supply in the soil. Shade-coffee plantations are a model example of sustainable agriculture, a win-win arrangement for farmers and wildlife that far surpasses other agricultural landscapes like rice, sugar cane, and pasture in its ability to support biodiversity.

Bob Rice, a geographer at the Smithsonian Migratory Bird Center in Washington, D.C., describes a traditional coffee plantation as more akin to gardening than to farming. Farms are typically small, a couple of hectares or less, and most of the work is done by one family. Berries are picked carefully by hand, and each plant is visited several times during harvest season because only the ripe berries are picked. After harvest the coffee plants are individually inspected and pruned, much like a gardener dotes on each and every plant. Weeds are pulled by hand and then used as green fertilizer along with manure from cattle and sometimes the mashed pulp from the coffee berries that is left over after extracting the seeds. Shade-grown-coffee plantations provide farmers with more goods than just coffee. The shade trees are farmed too, for their supply of fruit, nuts, construction materials, fence posts, and firewood. These crops, like bananas, mangoes, avocados, oranges, and lemons, can be harvested at different times of year from the intense coffee harvest, spreading out the workload and marketable produce over a longer period. These products give small coffee producers an economic safety net that helps them ride out the ups and downs of international coffee prices that, in a bad year, can mean they don't break even on their coffee crop.

~

A shade-coffee plantation is a lifeboat for thousands of species of plants and animals in Latin America, including our migrants who spend their winters in tropical forests. But the lifeboats are sinking. Latin America has suffered a second wave of deforestation as the shade trees in coffee plantations have been cut down to make way for "sun" coffee.

The catalyst for these sweeping changes to how coffee is grown in Latin America was an old nemesis of the coffee industry, the coffee leaf rust. The disease finally arrived in the New World in the early 1970s, making landfall on the east coast of Brazil. Only a few years later there was an outbreak in southern Nicaraguan coffee plantations. This sparked panic among coffee growers, who feared that history would repeat itself and their coffee production would collapse the same way it had in Southeast Asia almost one hundred years earlier. Shade-grown arabica coffee was thought to be highly susceptible to the fungus because of the high humidity under the shade of trees. To avert an economic crisis in the region, many countries launched large-scale government initiatives, often sponsored by the U.S. Agency for International Development, to convert farms from shade-grown coffee to sun-tolerant coffee. The belief was that without shade trees, the leaf rust would not be able to thrive and destroy the precious coffee plants.

Shade trees were ripped out, and a completely different variety of coffee was planted, one that grew well in full sun. Most sun coffee is derived from a different species of coffee, *Coffea canephora* (*robusta* variety), that was discovered in the late 1800s growing in the equatorial forests of the Congo. This species is a hardier plant (hence the name robusta) as it has greater resistance to disease and insect pests than its cousin arabica. Sun-coffee varieties grow quickly and can be harvested after three or four years, rather than the four to six years required for traditional shade-coffee varieties. Sun coffee can also be planted at over triple the density of shade-coffee plants, resulting in a 30 percent increase in coffee production. Robusta grows at lower elevations, where temperatures are warmer, produces more fruits and hence more beans, and contains twice as much caffeine as arabica. The downside for coffee drinkers is that robusta is rather bitter, so it is used mainly for instant coffee and mass-produced supermarket coffee.

The downside for farmers is that sun coffee degrades the land it is grown on and pollutes the environment. Sun coffee can only work its miracle of high production with heavy inputs of fertilizer, and lots of herbicides, fungicides, and insecticides. Petroleum-based fertilizers are added in huge quantities because there is no rain of leaves from shade trees to provide a natural source of nutrients. Plantations completely lacking in shade trees must provide the nitrogen that would otherwise be added naturally by nitrogen-fixing tree roots. Estimates of annual fertilizer use range from about 830 pounds per hectare in Colombia to more than 2,500 pounds per hectare in Costa Rica. The absence of a protective tree canopy means that heavy rains during the wet season leach the nitrogen and other nutrients out of the soil, and the nutrients are carried away in streams. Heavy rains also wash away the soil itself, particularly on the steep slopes where much coffee is grown. The high productivity of sun coffee can be sustained only as long as the farmer can keep doling out fertilizers to make up for the ever-worsening soil quality, and as long as he can use pesticides to eliminate the insect pests and weeds that thrive in the open sun.

Although shade- and sun-coffee plantations sound as different as day and night, in reality coffee farms range from traditional heavily shaded farms with a high diversity of trees, to partially shaded farms with one or a handful of shade-tree species, all the way to coffee farms

Heavy Shade: Rustic and Traditional Polyculture

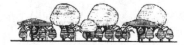

Moderate/Low Shade: Commercial Polyculture and Shaded Monoculture

Sun: Unshaded Monoculture

Figure 5.2. *Range of coffee-farming methods, showing the extreme differences in height and canopy cover of the shade trees and the complexity of the vegetation layers. The coffee plants (lowest shrub layer) in "sun" plantations are grown in much higher density compared with shade coffee. (Based on Moguel and Toledo, 1999)*

with little or no shade at all (figure 5.2). Traditional rustic plantations most resemble natural forests because some of the original forest canopy is left intact and the understory is removed to make way for coffee shrubs. More common are traditional "polyculture" farms, where the shade trees themselves are chosen and managed to provide nutrients for coffee and a suite of other crops for the farmer. At the other extreme are the modern sun-coffee plantations that have a monoculture of coffee that may have few or no shade trees. Some of these coffee plantations have scattered trees, but those trees often provide virtually no functional shade. The trees are often there for their roots rather than their shade; they are nitrogen-fixing trees that are heavily pruned and have a messy jumble of small branches protruding from the thick amputated trunk that is rarely more than ten feet in height.

The numbers of plants and animals that can live a healthy life in a coffee plantation depends on the size and number of the shade trees. The rustic shade plantations in Chiapas that Russell Greenberg studied supported bird biodiversity similar to natural forest because there were tall trees, extensive canopy cover, and many types of vegetation, just like a real forest. In Guatemala, heavily shaded coffee plantations are almost non-existent; most coffee farms have just a few species of small shade trees that are heavily pruned. Not surprisingly, these ecologically simple coffee farms support much lower bird diversity than the rustic shaded coffee plantations in Mexico. Even a modest number of shade trees can increase bird biodiversity. Greenberg found that many species of neotropical migrants that specialize on forest were more common in a partially shaded coffee plantation compared with sun coffee. Tennessee warblers were seven times more abundant in partially shade coffee than in sun coffee, while other forest migrants like wood thrush, blue-grey gnatcatchers, and yellow-bellied flycatchers were never seen in sun-coffee plantations.

Sun coffee has triggered an ecological disaster because the shade trees, and the communities they harbour, have been lost on such a large scale. The combined allure of growing more coffee and sidestepping the coffee leaf rust disaster led to wholesale conversion from shade-grown coffee to sun coffee. By the early 1990s about 40 percent of the lands used for growing coffee in northern Latin America had been converted from shade coffee to sun coffee. Birds, frogs, bats, insects, and countless other forest creatures suddenly lost their homes. Some countries, such as Mexico, have retained much of their coffee production in traditional shaded farms, but other major producers like Colombia now grow almost two thirds of their coffee in open sun. Overall, more than a million hectares of shade coffee in northern Latin America have been lost to sun-coffee plantations.

The Smithsonian Migratory Bird Center thinks that this massive loss of shade-coffee habitat might have triggered declines of migratory songbirds that are frequent visitors to shade-coffee plantations. The population declines of Baltimore orioles and Tennessee warblers on their breeding grounds coincide with the dramatic conversion of shade to sun coffee. There is precious little natural forest left on the wintering grounds in the many regions where coffee is grown, so shade coffee may be the only hope for forest birds like wood thrush and Kentucky warblers. Now, even the shade coffee is hard to find in some regions. Losing a million hectares of shade coffee has forced generations of migrants into poor habitats where it is hard for them to stay alive and build up enough energy reserves to migrate north in spring.

Coffee drinkers, the hundreds of millions of us, are a powerful force for saving biodiversity in tropical countries and giving our migrants a safe haven for the winter. We cannot give up our coffee, but we can insist that it be grown under trees. Shade coffee tastes great, but most people buy it because it is good for birds and good for farmers. Many conservation groups, like Audubon, are now selling their own brands of environmentally friendly coffee. Paul Tolme, in an article on sustainable coffee in *Audubon* magazine, quotes the coffee farmer in Mexico who produces much of Audubon's line of shade coffee: "We don't just sell coffee. We sell the opportunity for the consumer to buy a concept: a fair, organic, bird-friendly, and sustainable product. That is what we sell in every cup." Buying ecologically friendly coffee can help migrant birds, tropical wildlife and plants, and even the communities for whom coffee has been a lifeline for generations.

Las Nubes coffee is the brainchild of Howard Daugherty, a colleague of mine in Environmental Studies at York University. The coffee beans come from farms that the Ministry of Agriculture of the Costa Rican government has certified as sustainable, and the coffee is marketed throughout Canada by Timothy's World Coffee. The coffee farms are sustainable because farmers plant trees in their coffee farms, conserve soil, stabilize stream banks, and minimize pesticide use. More trees means a better environment for farmers and birds, and today more than sixty farms in the region are certified as sustainable, compared with none only a few years ago. Timothy's World Coffee guarantees good prices for the local coffee cooperative, COOPEAGRI, to make sure that farmers can make a reasonable profit from their hard work. Nursery projects that provide seedling shade trees for farmers were started by York University in collaboration with a Costa Rican community group, and the nurseries are run with the help of student volunteers. More forest will mean better soil, less erosion, increased biodiversity, and better prices and lives for coffee growers.

Las Nubes coffee is grown at about thirty-six hundred feet above sea level in southern Costa Rica's Alexander Skutch Biological Corridor, named after the grandfather of tropical ornithology. During his lifetime Skutch wrote dozens of articles and books about the birds who lived in his backyard. His home, Los Cusingos, is now a neotropical bird sanctuary run by a Costa Rican environmental group, the Tropical Science Center. The biological corridor links the small, isolated forest at Los Cusingos to the large uncut forests that are far up the valley in the Chirripó National Park and adjacent Las Nubes Biological Reserve. The corridor from Los Cusingos to the highlands is a natural one, framed around the watershed of Río Peñas Blancas. There are coffee plantations just about everywhere, and with more trees being planted, Skutch's forest island may one day be connected by a natural green bridge to the highlands.

On my visit to this biological corridor a few years ago, the highlight of the trip was a shade-coffee plantation owned by Luis Angel Rojas Gonzalez, an avid bird lover who has a small house across the river from Los Cusingos. He became interested in birds when binocular-toting students began visiting the forest reserve and he saw his first field guide to the birds of Costa Rica. Luis now has several bird feeders near his house, which he stocks with bananas that he grows in his garden. His feeder was swarming with gaudy tropical fruit-eating birds: speckled tanager, bay-headed tanager, golden-masked tanager, scarlet-rumped tanager, shining honeycreeper, and green honeycreeper. I was surprised to see that "our"

Baltimore orioles and Tennessee warblers were banana-holics. At any one time, I could count four or five warblers and half a dozen orioles eating the bananas. Luis would probably be just as astonished to watch the Baltimore oriole in my backyard in June, carrying juicy green caterpillars into its long pendulous nest hanging from a high tree branch.

Luis began his shade-coffee farm for practical reasons, not really to save birds—he thought he would use the wood to build himself a new house. He has not cut down the trees, though, and proudly grows his coffee in the shade and without pesticides. He works closely with the sustainability project, and many York students have lived at his home. On his balcony that enjoys a spectacular view of the valley hangs a small Costa Rican flag beside a Canadian flag.

For every pound of Las Nubes coffee sold, Timothy's World Coffee donates one dollar to the Fisher Fund for Neotropical Conservation, which supports research and conservation within the corridor. York students travel to Costa Rica to work in local schools and teach environmental education programs to students and farmers; others study the biodiversity of insects and birds in natural habitats and coffee farms. Far away, on the York University campus in Toronto, the tens of thousands of students who attend classes have a chance to help farmers and birds in Costa Rica. Las Nubes coffee is sold at kiosks in several of the busiest buildings on campus. Some of the profits from the coffee sales on campus go directly to education, research, and promoting sustainable farming practices in Costa Rica. The mood at the kiosk is set by lively tropical music and photos of white-faced monkeys and a *cusingo,* the fiery-billed aracari, a colourful toucan that is the namesake of Skutch's forest island. A handsome sign advertises what they are really selling: "Coffee with a Conscience."

❧

My morning ritual includes grinding whole coffee beans (shade grown, of course!) amid a loud whirring of blades. The roasted beans are dark and shiny, and I can imagine a cool morning under the shade of tropical trees, mist slowly rising above the treetops, the rich, moist smell of the leaves on the ground, and the chattering of orioles as they jostle for position in the *Erythrina* trees. Whose hands picked these beans off the plant? The weathered hands of a sixty-five-year-old grandfather who has been picking his whole life? A Panamanian migrant worker who travelled for four days to reach a coffee plantation in Costa Rica? A twelve-year-old girl who is out of school for the two-month summer break, and is picking alongside her parents and aunt?

Coffee growing is a way of life for thousands of farmers and the workers they depend on for the harvest. Workers begin at dawn, picking the ripe berries off the coffee plants under the cool shade, filling wicker baskets carried around their waists. They work until mid-afternoon, their fingers turning black and sticky from the sap on the berries. Late in the afternoon, pickers carefully sort through their berries in the baskets, taking out the green unripe ones. Workers are paid by the quantity of ripe berries they pick, and a family might pick about thirty bins of coffee a day and earn just under a dollar per bin. For a family working all day, this means they would go home with less than $30 for their efforts. The ripe berries are trucked to the local *beneficio,* the mill where the pulp of the fruit is removed and the beans are dried in the sun. Here, workers who make perhaps $15 a day spread the beans out in long rows on large sun-drying patios, regularly turning the piles of beans with a shovel to ensure even drying.

The proliferation of sun coffee has not just hurt birds and other wildlife; it has been a disaster for many rural coffee farmers in Latin America. The financial gains from increased productivity of sun coffee are offset by the cost of fertilizers and pesticides, and the increased labour needed for the intensive maintenance of sun coffee, which requires year-round attention. The farmers who decided to switch to high-yield sun coffee were initially subsidized by government programs, but were then left to fend for themselves and were at the mercy of international coffee prices. Coffee prices are notorious for their wild fluctuations, bringing profits one year and ruin the next. Meanwhile, sun coffee has made gigantic profits for large multinational companies that are happy to supply North Americans and Europeans with cheap coffee to guzzle.

Birds may have a reason to cheer because the pot of gold at the end of the sun-coffee rainbow was short-lived. The International Coffee Association, which regulated production to ensure high coffee prices, dissolved in 1989, resulting in coffee chaos and a sudden drop in prices for producers. In the late 1990s, a glut of coffee on the world market resulted from increased production in Southeast Asia, particularly when Vietnam suddenly became a major global producer of cheap sun coffee. Prices dropped to such low levels that many small producers could no longer afford to grow intensively managed sun coffee. Between 1999 and 2001, coffee bean prices fell by 57 percent, too short a period for farmers to substantially downsize their production. It is hard for coffee farmers to fine-tune their production from year to year to match the volatile coffee prices because there is a three- to five-year time lag between the time when young plants are sown and their first harvest. Mature coffee plants produce for many years in row, oblivious to international coffee prices, so farmers may find themselves with a bumper crop in years when prices are low.

The winter homes of cerulean warblers, Swainson's thrush and Baltimore orioles have been saved by a recent boom in the specialty coffee market. Thousands of small farmers survived the international coffee crisis by growing shade-grown specialty coffee because it commands a higher price. The coffee industry serves two markets that differ dramatically in the quality of coffee demanded and consumer tolerance for higher prices. Mass-produced canned or instant coffees are cheap robusta varieties that are sun grown. Specialty coffee, on the other hand, uses high-quality coffee beans like arabica, and consumers are already prepared to pay premium prices for the best coffee. (Americans spend over $10 billion annually on specialty coffee.) Specialty coffee puts taste first, not quantity—and most of the best coffees are shade grown. Shade coffee can be ordered from many distributors on the Internet and is sold at specialty coffee shops and many major grocery stores.

My favourite shade coffee, Café Oro, is grown on Ometepe Island, a double volcano that sits in Lake Nicaragua, its two peaks rising high out of the water. The island's thirty thousand residents are mostly farmers who grow plantain, sesame, fruit, and coffee under the shadow of Volcán Concepción, which still spits out smoke and ash from time to time. Volcán Maderas is smaller and has been dormant for thousands of years, so it is covered with lush cloud forest. The volcanic soil is rich, but most residents of Ometepe live at or below the poverty line.

For over fifteen years, a coffee cooperative of almost thirty families has grown organic, shade, and fair-trade coffee that is sold in the U.S. by their sister island, Bainbridge Island, near Seattle. The Bainbridge-Ometepe Sister Islands Association, or BOSIA, was established in the mid-1980s by Kim and Ela Esterberg, long-time residents of Bainbridge Island. In the first few years, volunteers from Bainbridge came home from Ometepe with suitcases filled with hundreds of pounds of "green" unroasted coffee beans to sell to local coffee shops, including Pegasus Coffee, which now roasts Café Oro. When the Sandinista government was ousted in the early 1990s, BOSIA began importing coffee in a container shipment rather than a suitcase. Most of the Café Oro coffee is grown on Finca Magdelena, a classic—and organic—rustic shade-coffee plantation, where it is hard to even tell that you are in a plantation rather than a natural forest. Today BOSIA imports about 15,000 pounds of Ometepe-grown coffee annually to sell to coffee shops throughout the Puget Sound region and to customers all over the United States through mail order and online sales.

BOSIA raises about $40,000 a year that is returned to Ometepe to improve the communities where the coffee was grown. Although you couldn't possibly buy even half of a house on Bainbridge Island for that amount of money, it is a small fortune for the residents of Ometepe. The residents of Ometepe select their own projects to undertake, and they put their own sweat and blood into the construction.

Café Oro is pure gold for this community. The first project funded from Café Oro piped in clean spring water to communities that had no safe water supply and where kids and adults alike were plagued with intestinal worms and infections. Volcán Maderas has a pristine lagoon in its dormant crater, and in many places on the forested slopes down below fresh spring water shoots out from the ground. By tapping this water supply and piping it down to the small towns, the residents finally had safe, clean water to drink. Funds have also been used to build public health clinics and to provide much-needed medical supplies. In one community a new high school was constructed for $14,000, which meant the local children did not have to make the gruelling two-hour trip to the nearest school every day. A church on Bainbridge Island sponsors a free literacy program for young children on Ometepe so they can learn to read and write. Some families cannot afford to send their children to school, but this literacy program means that many kids now have a chance for an education.

It is not just Ometepe residents whose lives are enriched by Café Oro. On Thursday afternoons, Bainbridge volunteers eagerly gather at Pegasus Coffee to bag the beans that are roasted once a week and to ship the one-pound bags to customers across the country. Residents of a seniors' centre and special-needs children stick the labels on the shiny gold bags. Third-graders at the Bainbridge elementary school sell calendars to buy school supplies for classrooms on Ometepe. Each year during spring break, high-school students travel to Ometepe to help with construction projects and live with local families. The Bainbridge soccer team raises money to send soccer shoes, uniforms, nets, and balls to their counterparts on Ometepe. From children to seniors, residents of this wealthy Bainbridge community experience an intimate connection and friendships with ordinary people thousands of miles away in Nicaragua.

Wood thrush, Kentucky warblers, and other migrants who winter in shade-coffee farms connect our lives with those of the coffee farmers. Ask for shade-grown or sustainable coffee the next time you visit your favourite café, and look for it in the grocery store. Give your friends and neighbours a pound of shade coffee next holiday season; I have yet to meet anyone who does not love the message (and taste!) of shade coffee.

6 FALLING FROM THE SKY
The Ongoing Scourge of Pesticides

As the mid-morning sun lit up its pale belly, the Swainson's hawk soared in large, slow circles, one of thousands in the flock. The day was heating up quickly in the hot sun, and the hawk was riding a thermal of hot air rising up from the ground, getting higher with each turn of this invisible spiral staircase. After spending the night in a nearby grove of eucalyptus trees, the hawk was hungry and ready to eat his first meal of the day. The flock was heading for a large sunflower field a few miles from the nighttime roost. The hawk dropped down to fly low over the sunflowers. Within seconds his sharp eyes caught some movement, and with talons outstretched he snatched up a flying grasshopper. He repeated this manoeuvre over and over, and gobbled down two dozen grasshoppers in half an hour. The grasshoppers were slow in their escape and were easy pickings that day.

By noon the hawk was feeling dizzy and his wings felt heavy. He landed awkwardly on the ground and sat there dazed and trembling. The shaking got worse and he began rapidly opening his sharp beak, desperately trying to get air into his lungs. A few minutes later he was dead, and lay amongst the tall sunflowers. Beneath the sea of yellow lay hundreds of dead hawks.

That afternoon a farmer pushed his way through the field to see if the spraying had worked. The sunflowers had not grown well this year, probably because of the drought, and to make matters worse the crop was being attacked by millions of grasshoppers. If the crop was lost, he could be out of a job. The day before, the plane had come with its chemical clouds, spraying *plaguicidas* over the fields to kill the grasshoppers. There were still some grasshoppers in the field, but he was pleased to see that hordes had been killed. He almost stepped on the dead hawk; he had already found twenty dead hawks in the fields. This one caught his eye; there was a silver bracelet on its leg. He looked closely and saw that it had a number stamped on it; perhaps it had been someone's pet? Although he was curious, he walked on to check the other fields. When he returned to the worker's quarters of the ranch that evening he had a headache and felt sick to his stomach. He did not tell his wife and hoped that he would not miss any days of work, as he did last season when the plane came. He put his dusty clothes on the pile with the others; water was scarce and his wife washed the family's clothes only once a week. As he watched his children play outside he thought about all the dead birds and the chemicals; he hoped they would not have to spray the fields again the following week.

A few weeks later a car came down the road toward the ranch, a trail of dust flying out behind it as though it was on fire. As the car passed through the eucalyptus grove near the main house it stopped suddenly, and three Americans got out. Brian Woodbridge, who had been driving, was stunned. The road was littered with dead Swainson's hawks, hundreds of them, and many of the carcasses had been run over repeatedly by trucks and cars. There were more carcasses off in the woods. What could cause so much death? Brian and his two assistants met with the ranch owner the next day, and learned that the hawks had died a day after a nearby sunflower field had been sprayed with a pesticide. The hawks must have eaten poisoned grasshoppers in the fields and then flown back to the roost only to die later in the night.

The biologists picked through the rotting birds among the trees, looking for the legs. One of the hawks Brian found was banded with a white band marked "05" on the left leg, and a metal U.S. Fish and Wildlife Service numbered band on the other. The world suddenly seemed a smaller place. Brian had actually banded this bird himself, the year before in northern California. The first time he had held this magnificent hawk it was an adult male who had been caught at his nest, and Brian had added the white "05" band so he could recognize him from a distance. The second time he held him, the bird was dead in Argentina, more than six thousand miles from his breeding territory.

The team found three banded hawks in all, but they did not find the banded male that the farmer had come across or the thousands of other hawks hidden among the sunflowers. They had counted a shocking seven hundred bodies, and guessed that the total kill in that area alone had been more like three thousand. They later learned that the hawks were being killed by a highly toxic pesticide called monocrotophos that many farmers in the region were using to combat the grasshoppers. Most of North America's Swainson's hawks concentrate in Argentina's grasslands for the winter. How many had been killed that year alone?

The grisly discovery of thousands of dead migratory Swainson's hawks in Argentina was a wake-up call to North American ornithologists. Since the 1960s the Swainson's hawk had declined dramatically across many parts of its breeding range, but no one knew why. Many breeding adults that were individually banded never came back in spring, suggesting a problem during migration or on the wintering grounds somewhere in South America. No one was sure exactly where Swainson's hawks spent the winter, only that it was somewhere in South America. In 1994, Brian Woodbridge attached a radiotransmitter to a hawk in California and used satellites to track the bird's movements. The bird spent the winter far south in Argentina, just west of Buenos Aires.

In January, Woodbridge and two other researchers flew south to look for their bird but had no idea of the horrors that awaited them. No one at that time would have guessed that lethal pesticides were killing thousands of hawks on their wintering grounds. Driving around the vast countryside in the general area where their satellite-tracked bird was located, they found Swainson's hawks congregating in flocks of thousands, feeding on grasshoppers in fields of alfalfa and sunflower. For the first time ever, they could describe the winter habitat and behaviour of the Swainson's hawk. It was pure luck that someone suggested that they visit a ranch where very large flocks of hawks had been seen. They did not know that a mass kill had happened at that ranch until they drove up the driveway that fateful day.

Brian Woodbridge returned to Argentina the next year with a larger research team, including toxicologists who would test the blood and tissues of live and dead hawks for pesticides. They worked closely with Argentine government wildlife researchers to find out how widespread the pesticide poisoning was, and how many hawks were being killed. That year ranchers suffered another grasshopper outbreak and once again the hawks fell like stones from the sky. The recovery teams found five thousand dead birds but estimated that twenty thousand had probably been killed. This catastrophic killing led to unprecedented cooperation among conservation groups, federal agencies of the United States, Canada, and Argentina, the local ranchers and even the manufacturers of monocrotophos. They worked together in a public-education campaign to persuade ranchers not to use this pesticide when hawks and other birds were near the fields. Argentina first restricted the use of the pesticide and then cancelled its registration altogether.

In the mid-1980s, the U.S. Environmental Protection Agency began requiring manufacturers to conduct field tests on birds to measure how toxic their pesticides were for birds' survival and breeding. This tough regulation was expensive to comply with, and early studies suggested that even a low amount of monocrotophos that would barely make a dent on insects would nevertheless cause high bird mortality. Seeing a lost cause, the manufacturer with the U.S. rights (DuPont at that time) simply withdrew the product from the U.S. market in 1988. For the next decade monocrotophos had the dubious honour of being the second-most popular organophosphate in the world. In the mid-1990s about 15 million pounds were imported each year into South America alone. Although Argentina has banned its use, many other Latin American countries still import monocrotophos in large quantities. Some manufacturers (DowAgrosciences and Syngenta) have been steadily phasing out monocrotophos from the world market. But these two producers account for only 20 percent of the world supply—an estimated 66 million pounds of monocrotophos are produced annually—so other producers can easily make up the difference. If hawks are being killed by the thousands, then many other migrants who use the same grasslands must be falling victim to the same fate.

Scott Weidensaul describes the discovery of the Swainson's hawk poisonings in his book *Living on the Wind: Across the Hemispheres with Migratory Birds.* He suggests that the monocrotophos disaster is not the first time Swainson's hawk populations have crashed as a result of pesticide use. Weidensaul writes, "Until the 1940s, the Swainson's probably fed most heavily on a species of migratory locust, which the Argentines call the *langosta.* This insect bred in relatively small areas of subtropical northern Argentina, then swarmed by the billions across the pampas in hordes that looked like black thunderclouds—a bonanza of food for bug-eating hawks but a nightmare for farmers." In the 1950s the langostas were virtually eliminated with DDT and other powerful pesticides; that was the same time that North American scientists first noticed declines in hawk numbers.

～⌒

We are as hooked on pesticides today as we were in the 1960s, when, in her seminal book *Silent Spring,* Rachel Carson warned us of the rain of poison that was bringing death to our waters and killing thousands of birds. DDT (dichlorodiphenyltrichloroethane) was first used heavily in World War II to wipe out mosquito larvae in the Pacific to protect soldiers from malaria and typhus. Eradication of malaria in many areas of the globe was so beneficial to human health that the inventor of DDT won a Nobel Prize in 1948. Towns sprayed DDT from airplanes to control insect outbreaks like gypsy moths, tent caterpillars, and the beetles that spread the Dutch elm disease that killed the stately trees that lined so many streets. For a time, DDT was a household chemical and was found under many kitchen sinks. One advertisement from *Time* magazine in 1947 shows a cartoon of a happy housewife singing with her farm animals and vegetables, extolling the benefits of DDT (figure 6.1).

We still have a cavalier attitude about the massive pesticide use that dominates agriculture around the world. The United States applies in excess of 660 million pounds of active ingredients of pesticides each year. Central America, a small area by comparison, imports 100 million pounds of active ingredients of pesticides each year. Migratory songbirds live in both worlds and have to run a chemical gauntlet in their yearly travels. There is growing evidence that they, too, fall victim to dangerous pesticides on their wintering grounds.

Although we are using more pesticides than ever, at least the types of pesticides have changed dramatically in response to environmental concerns. The pesticides of choice in the 1950s and 1960s were DDT, dieldrin, and heptachlor, and other similar chemicals known as organochlorines (OC, for short). These OC pesticides are fat soluble, which means they are stored in the fatty tissues of animals. This property, as well as the fact that the chemicals are hard to metabolize, means that they accumulate in the food chain. Plants and small animals at the bottom of the food chain may contain barely detectable traces of DDT, but a top predator who eats hundreds of tainted prey will build up DDT concentrations that are ten thousand times higher or more.

DDT and other similar chemicals have been banned or restricted by most countries, but they are not gone. In their glory years OC pesticides

Figure 6.1. *A 1947 advertisement for the pesticide DDT.*

were valued for the length of time they stayed in the soil and on the leaves of crops and forests; more bang for the buck. An estimated 1.4 billion pounds of DDT were applied in the U.S. before it was banned, and decades later the chemical and its breakdown product DDE linger in the environment. One study of apple orchards that were heavily sprayed with DDT in the early 1970s found that the soil was still contaminated twenty years later and robins nesting in the orchard carried high levels of DDE in their bodies. All major OC pesticides are still found worldwide in water, plants, animals, and people. In 1999–2000, the U.S. Centers for Disease Control tested the "body burden" of pesticides in more than nine thousand people of all ages across the United States. The study found that almost everyone has DDE in their bloodstream; you probably do, so do I, and even our children do.

In many ways, birds are in greater danger today than in the 1950s because modern pesticides are more lethal. The older OC pesticides were replaced in the 1970s and 1980s by "safer" pesticides like organophosphates and carbamates. These pesticides are safer because they break down within a few days and are not stored in the body, and so do not accumulate in the food chain. But many, like monocrotophos, are vastly more toxic to birds (and people) than were the OC pesticides.

Modern insecticides are designed to kill their target swiftly and then break down before "non-target" animals come into contact with the poison. This is easier said than done. Birds can be exposed to these insecticides via direct contact with sprayed plants, by eating insects and fruits in areas that have been recently sprayed, or by eating pesticides that are applied to the ground in the form of granules. Birds can also breathe in the insecticide, or get it on their skin and feathers during aerial spraying and drift from spraying. Contact with these pesticides during and soon after application can kill large numbers of birds. If not used carefully, these pesticides can also cause serious illness and death in the farmers who mix and apply the pesticides. We have traded persistence for toxicity.

Many insecticides are lethal to birds because they are neurotoxins and interfere with the nerve impulses inside the bodies of animals. Our nervous system is not wired the same way as a house is. If you flick the light switch on the wall, an electrical current runs along a continuous wire to the light fixture that holds the light bulb. Inside our bodies, the electrical signals pass along a series of tiny "wires," the neurons, which are physically separated from each other like a dashed line. The signal must jump from neuron to neuron via chemical messengers. When a nerve fires, the far end of its nerve fibre releases a chemical messenger, acetylcholine, into the gap between the neurons. When the acetylcholine hits the next nerve in the line, it signals that nerve to fire. Once the signal has been sent, the body needs to get rid of the acetylcholine so that the nerve stops firing. A second chemical, cholinesterase, is released into the gap to remove the acetylcholine; it's a kind of molecular sanitation worker. Many pesticides are designed to attach to the cholinesterase and prevent it from doing its job. The chemical garbage piles up and the nerves remain in the "on" position, causing severe shaking, then paralysis and asphyxiation. Our nervous system depends critically on the chemical on/off switch, and all animals have the same basic system to control nerve impulses. This is why many of the pesticides that are so effective in killing insects also are so toxic to birds and people.

The deadly yardstick by which the toxicity of pesticides is measured is the lethal dose at which half the animals in a sample will die. Toxicologists call this the LD_{50}, the lethal dose that kills 50 percent of the test subjects. Rachel Carson described neighbourhood streets littered with dead robins; relatively high doses of DDT are needed to kill a bird outright. The LD_{50} of DDT for birds is 1330 milligrams per kilogram of body weight. Other organochlorines, like dieldrin and heptachlor epoxide, have a lower LD_{50} (35 mg/kg and 125 mg/kg, respectively), meaning it takes a lower dose to kill the same number of birds. All these OC pesticides are neurotoxins and at lethal doses interfere with the nervous system. There are dozens of accounts of OC pesticide overdoses that killed thousands of birds in a matter of days, though most of these date back to the era when OCs were still in wide use.

Although OC pesticides can be lethal, many of the modern organophosphates and carbamates are up to a hundred or a thousand times deadlier in the same dose. The LD_{50} for monocrotophos is 0.2 mg/kg in golden eagles, making it one of the most lethal pesticides for birds. Some of the Swainson's hawks that Brian Woodbridge found dead still had grasshoppers in their mouths, and must have died very quickly. In the early 1970s, monocrotophos killed an estimated ten thousand wintering robins in Florida that were feeding in two fields that had recently been sprayed. Carbofuran and methamidophos are not much better, with an LD_{50} in red-winged blackbirds of 0.4 and 2.0 mg/kg, respectively. Carbofuran is responsible for the most reports of bird kills in the United States; for instance, one incident in a vineyard in California in the fall of 1993 killed at least 1 blackbird, 12 finches, 11 western bluebirds, 133 yellow-rumped warblers, 34 mourning doves, 22 northern flickers, and 1 sharp-shinned hawk. In 1999, an even bigger kill happened after carbofuran was applied illegally on a farm in Illinois; thousands of blackbirds, cowbirds, grackles, and horned larks were found dead.

Modern pesticides affect birds at concentrations so low it defies belief. In my day-to-day life, I am used to measuring small amounts in the scale of millimetres and millilitres. One milligram per kilogram of pesticide ingested is a quantity equivalent to one millionth of the bird's body weight. In the book *Our Stolen Future,* Theo Colborn and his co-authors use the analogy of the weakest gin and tonic ever made to explain the tiny concentrations of pesticides that can circulate in the body yet cause great harm. One part per million is equivalent to one shot of gin in 250,000 glasses of tonic water.

Many modern pesticides are highly toxic to birds and kill them frequently, yet are used widely in North America and other countries. Most developed countries established strict regulations in the 1970s for pesticide use, including toxicity tests on birds that had to be completed before the chemical could be registered for use. The irony is that the registration and use of a pesticide in the United States is determined on a cost-benefit basis. Pesticides that are known to be harmful to wildlife, or even people, are often used widely because the economic benefits from increased food production are thought to outweigh the costs. Ethyl parathion was known to readily kill birds soon after it was registered in the United States, yet it took some forty-seven years before the product was withdrawn. Granular carbofuran is a notorious bird killer, yet its use was virtually eliminated in the United States only after a twenty-year struggle by environmental groups and scientists. There is good evidence that historical use of carbofuran contributed to the population declines of grassland birds such as horned larks and western meadowlarks. Until recently, rice farmers in Louisiana routinely applied for "emergency" exemptions to use carbofuran on thousands of hectares, which sparked an outcry and legal action by conservation groups.

Many pesticides that are acutely toxic to birds, like chlorpyrifos and diazinon, are still used widely on vegetable and fruit crops in the United States and Canada. The U.S. Department of Agriculture keeps statistics on pesticide use for most crops in the country, giving the gory details of which pesticides are used, how much is applied, and how often (*www.pestmanagement.info/nass*). The pesticide list for most crops is surprisingly long, with many of types of pesticides, fungicides, and herbicides used routinely to grow a single crop.

As bad as this sounds, and is, some of the worst problems for birds lie on their wintering grounds. In Latin American countries, regulations controlling pesticide use are much looser, and many chemicals that are restricted in use or not even registered in the United States are widely used in Latin America. These pesticides are popular because they are so much cheaper than alternative less toxic pesticides. Most government agencies are underfunded and understaffed, and have trouble enforcing the regulations that do exist. Pesticides that are banned for use in one country are often used freely next door, and food from neighbouring countries is imported and consumed with little or no testing for pesticide residues. The sheer quantity and dangerous types of pesticides use in Latin America are downright scary and may be to blame for the declines of many of our migratory songbirds.

Almolonga is perched high at the end of a long narrow valley in western Guatemala, 7,520 feet above sea level. The town proudly calls itself the vegetable garden of the Americas. Volcanic soils provide fertile ground, and the cool temperatures and 60 inches of rainfall every year allow the Almolongueños to grow crops year round. Truckloads of potatoes, onions, carrots, beets, cabbage, celery, lettuce, and radishes leave town daily for the local markets in western Guatemala and more distant markets in Mexico, Honduras, Costa Rica, and El Salvador. Just about everyone in Almolonga is involved with growing vegetables, selling agricultural supplies, or transporting produce to market. Land is expensive because it is so fertile and so many people live in the area. A family typically owns or rents only a half hectare of land. Crops are planted, tended, sprayed, and harvested by hand, and this hard labour is carried out by the whole family.

Sonia Arbona, a geographer, describes the heavy human and environmental toll from excessive pesticide use in this community. The farmers of Almolonga spray their crops heavily with pesticides, sometimes daily, and apply much more pesticide than is recommended by the manufacturers. The pesticides that are favoured include methamido-phos, which is highly toxic and a restricted-use pesticide in the United States. Pesticide containers are routinely washed out in irrigation canals, and empty containers are often dumped at the edges of fields. Farmers typically mix and apply highly toxic pesticides without even wearing gloves. Many falsely believe that many years of exposure to pesticides actually makes them immune to any ill effects. The horrible Catch-22 is that the abundant crops of Almolonga cannot be shipped to the lucrative North American market. The U.S. Food and Drug Administration regularly rejects shipments from Guatemala because pesticide residues on the vegetables are too high. Nearby countries, however, do not have strict pesticide-residue regulations and provide a steady demand for the poisoned food of Almolonga.

The chemical culture of Almolonga is typical of most parts of Latin America. Douglas Murray, in his book *Cultivating Crisis: The Human Cost of Pesticides in Latin America,* paints a bleak picture of an ecological nightmare. Latin American countries have vastly expanded their production and export of cash crops over the past decades to support their economies. These cash crops include traditional crops like bananas, coffee, and cotton as well as diverse new non-traditional crops that have become popular exports only since the 1980s: cantaloupes, pineapples, strawberries, broccoli, snow peas, and more. Costa Rica increased its exports of non-traditional crops from $14.5 million U.S. in 1983 to more than $100 million by 1991. Guatemala increased these exports from $16 million to $53 million in the same period. Many of the non-traditional crops had not been grown in tropical regions before, and farmers quickly encountered pest problems. The solution: dump on the pesticides. Pesticide use has increased dramatically in Latin America since the 1960s, hand in hand with the rise in non-traditional export crops (figure 6.2).

Pesticide use is heavy because farmers spray pesticides according to a regular schedule, rather than as needed when pest outbreaks occur. The export crops are so valuable that most growers feel they cannot risk a

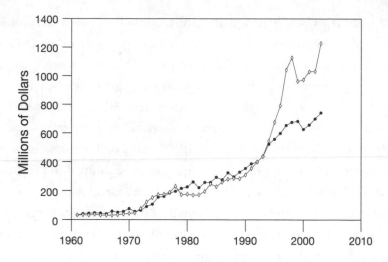

Figure 6.2. *Pesticide imports in millions of dollars (USD) per year for Central America and the Caribbean (solid circles) and South America (open diamonds). (Data from U.N. Food and Agriculture Organization)*

pest outbreak and would rather spray pesticides as a pre-emptive strike. Most advice on what pesticides to spray, and how often to spray them, comes from the pesticide vendors, who clearly have an interest in seeing wide and frequent use of pesticides. To minimize the labour costs involved in repeated spraying, farmers typically combine many different pesticides into one deadly cocktail, and make a single pass through a field. During the late 1980s, in a desperate attempt to stay ahead of the pest outbreaks, melon growers in Honduras sprayed each melon crop eleven to nineteen times with various highly toxic insecticides and fungicides. Most of these pesticides are supposed to be used alone, and the chemical and toxic effects of haphazardly mixing pesticides together can create an ecological bomb.

The export market demands high-quality produce. Pesticides are used not only to increase production but also to meet the standards of picky consumers in North America and Europe. By some estimates, 10 to 20 percent of pesticide use is for cosmetic purposes only. Few shoppers at supermarkets will buy fruits or vegetables that are blemished, even if they are otherwise perfectly tasty, nutritious, and safe to eat. For farmers, the extra pesticide applications needed to ensure a high-grade rating may be well worth it, at least in terms of the price they get for their crops.

This pattern of repeated spraying of crops adds up to a large pesticide load on any given piece of land. In Costa Rica, banana plantations typically apply one hundred pounds of active ingredients of pesticides per hectare. "Only" forty-four pounds of pesticides per hectare are used for most vegetables and fruits, and twenty-two pounds per hectare for rice production. By comparison, similar fruits and vegetables grown in the United States typically apply eleven pounds per hectare, or less, of pesticides. Farmers in Latin America often unknowingly mix together several different pesticides that actually contain the same active ingredient, so may apply well over ten times the recommended amount of a particular toxic ingredient to their crops.

What are these pesticides that are being sprayed so often and so heavily on crops in Central America? The monocrotophos that killed Swainson's hawks is only one of dozens of highly toxic pesticides that are used every day in Latin America. In Guatemala almost a quarter of the pesticides used for non-traditional export crops were rated as extremely toxic, or highly toxic, by the World Health Organization. Carbofuran and methamidophos, along with four other pesticides that are classified in the United States as restricted use, are in the top ten list of imported pesticides in many of the Central American countries surveyed (table 6.1). The restricted-use classification of the U.S. Environmental Protection Agency is used for hazardous pesticides that can be purchased by and used by only trained and licensed applicators because they contaminate groundwater, are highly toxic to humans or wildlife, or are known carcinogens.

These shocking tales of pesticide misuse can be found throughout Latin America. The local communities are trapped on a chemical treadmill, and time and time again we see the deadly combination of heavy use of highly toxic pesticides and poor safety measures. The extensive use of highly toxic pesticides in Latin America has created an epidemic

Pesticide	Toxicity to Birds	Percentage of Countries	Status in U.S.
Terbufos	Extremely high	71	Class I toxin; restricted use
Methamidophos	Very high	57	Class I toxin; restricted use
Carbofuran	Very high	43	Class I and II toxin; restricted use. Granular forms banned in 1994
Methyl parathion	Very high	28	Class I toxin; restricted use
Aldicarb	Very high	14	Class I toxin; restricted use
Paraquat	Moderate	100	Class I toxin; restricted use

Table 6.1. *"Restricted use" pesticides that are among the top ten pesticides imported by seven Central American countries (Belize, Costa Rica, El Salvador, Honduras, Nicaragua, Panama, Guatemala) in 1998–2000. (After Wesseling, 2001)*

of human poisonings and caused terrible health consequences for farmers and their families. Few farmers have even basic knowledge about the pesticides they are using, and few have access to gloves, respirators, or even a place to wash their hands before eating. Many farmers accept the dangerous working conditions because this is their only source of income. Awareness of the social and economic costs of pesticide use is increasing, though, and many countries are slowly moving toward banning the most dangerous pesticides and improving safe handling and disposal of all pesticides.

These problems are not restricted to Central America. The fertile Carachi highlands of northern Ecuador might well be called the potato garden of South America. This region produces 40 percent of the national potato crop in Ecuador, and this remarkable productivity is maintained through the now-familiar pesticide dependency. This agricultural region has been intensively studied by an international group of experts, led by Dr. Charles Crissman, a researcher at the International Potato Center in Peru. Their goal is to teach farmers how to handle pesticides safely and reduce their use of pesticides. In Carachi, each potato field receives more than seven applications of cocktails of insecticides and fungicides, often with several different chemicals in each mixture. Pesticides are bought in powder form and are mixed in a large barrel without using gloves, and then loaded into backpack sprayers that often leak and drip pesticides down the farmer's back and legs. Pesticides are a big investment for farmers, so are stored near or inside a farmer's house to prevent thievery. Farmers favour carbofuran and methamidophos to control the Andean weevil and leaf-eating insects that attack their crops, and these two highly toxic pesticides make up 90 percent of all the insecticides used in the region.

The past few decades have seen a torrential rain of pesticides in Latin America, which has dire consequences for the birds and other wildlife, not to mention the people who live there. We can expect that the horrible example of Swainson's hawks may also apply to many migratory songbirds that spend their winters in agricultural fields.

Surprisingly, few people have looked for pesticide poisoning in songbirds. Nevertheless, there are two clear cases, so far, of migratory songbirds being seriously poisoned by pesticides on their wintering grounds.

The dickcissel, a handsome sparrow with black streaks on the back and yellow highlights on the face and breast, spends the winter in the grasslands of Venezuela. The funny name is a reminder of its breeding habits: males defend territories by singing *dick, dickcissel, cissel*. Stan Temple, a professor of wildlife ecology at the University of Wisconsin, and his Ph.D. student Gianfranco Basili studied dickcissels in Venezuela during the early 1990s and describe a scene reminiscent of passenger pigeons.

Across the hot, dusty llanos, a huge dense cloud of what appeared to be smoke approached us. The llanos, or plains, of central Venezuela are rapidly being converted to agriculture, and fires are common during the dry season. But this great plume was not of smoke but of birds, millions of them, flying together in a tight, undulating, serpentine flock that darkened the sky. As they reached us and flew low overhead, we were engulfed by the noise and draft created by their wing beats. The flock, seemingly endless in length and more than a hundred yards wide, took half an hour to pass.

Dickcissels form enormous nighttime megaroosts that can contain several millions birds, a third of the entire North American population. In Venezuela, the dickcissel is known as *el pájaro arrocero,* the rice bird, and is public enemy number one because of its sheer numbers and appetite for rice and sorghum. By day, dickcissels spread out over the countryside to feed on seeds. A hundred years ago dickcissels fed on the seeds of abundant native grasses, but since the 1950s vast areas of grassland in Venezuela have been converted to agriculture. The bird's winter diet is now almost entirely rice and sorghum, much to the farmers' dismay. A survey of farmers found that more than 90 percent reported crop damage by dickcissels, and one in eight farmers admitted to illegally killing birds with pesticides. Farmers use organophosphates like parathion and monocrotophos as their weapon because these chemicals are so toxic to birds. Farmers poison watering holes used by birds and spray feeding areas early in the morning just before the birds arrive. Farmers have also been known to kill hundreds of thousands of dickcissels in one night by using a crop duster to spray the birds as they sleep in their megaroost. Farmers describe wading knee-deep in dead birds at the roost. Not surprisingly, the Breeding Bird Survey shows a dramatic 35 percent decline in dickcissel numbers in North America during the 1960s and 1970s. The population has stabilized recently, but not recovered, probably because pesticide poisoning is still a common practice today among farmers.

The bobolink has also plummeted in numbers on the breeding grounds (see figure 2.4 in Chapter 2) and until recently very little was known about its wintering habits. Bobolinks descend in huge flocks on the rice fields that have taken over their wintering grounds in South America. Their Latin name, *oryzivorus,* means "rice devourer." Rosalind Renfrew, a researcher at the Vermont Institute of Natural Science, wondered if bobolinks were suffering a similar fate as the dickcissels. She went searching for wintering bobolinks and found small numbers in Paraguay and large flocks in eastern Bolivia. Two nearby night roosts held more than 130,000 bobolinks.

Farmers with well-established rice farms thought that bobolinks were pests and most used guns or firecrackers to scare the flocks away. Although there was no evidence that farmers were deliberately poisoning birds, almost all the farmers interviewed by Renfrew said they used monocrotophos on their fields, the same chemical that killed the Swainson's hawks. Rosalind Renfrew found haphazard dumps of old pesticide containers by the edges of fields, and the labels confirmed that monocrotophos is widely used in Bolivia, even while it is banned next door in Argentina. The pesticides used by the rice farmers also included methamidophos and carbofuran. These pesticides are applied in very large amounts, and there is little doubt they must be killing bobolinks who feed in the fields soon after spraying. Blood samples from live bobolinks showed that the birds had low cholinesterase activity, many reduced by 75 to 90 percent, a clear sign that they had been recently exposed to neurotoxins. Some birds were so poisoned that there was little hope that they could survive in the wild for much longer. Unlike the Swainson's hawks, piles of dead bobolinks were not found, because it is almost impossible to search the enormous waterlogged rice fields and roosts for the bodies of little songbirds.

Grassland birds across North America are a group experiencing the most severe and consistent decline in numbers, and it is reasonable to wonder if they too are victims of pesticides. In the cases of both the dickcissel and bobolink, the discovery of pesticide poisoning was a result of a handful of North American researchers being curious enough to travel to South America to find out what was happening to their birds. Michael Hooper, a professor at Texas Tech University, thinks there are likely similar situations of pesticide poisoning awaiting discovery, not only in the Americas but throughout the world wherever wildlife habitat and intensive agricultural practices overlap. It is simply a matter of looking.

For instance, researchers in Australia sampled birds from 2002 to 2004 in areas that had been sprayed with fenitrothion, a pesticide used to control locust outbreaks. About half the songbirds caught within five days of spraying showed evidence of exposure. Their plasma cholinesterase activity was 60 to 75 percent lower than before spraying. As alarming as this finding is, the actual number of birds affected must have been even higher since extremely sick birds would not have been able to fly into the nets to be sampled. In Latin America, there is good reason to think that migrants are also being exposed, and killed, in large numbers because equally toxic pesticides are used heavily.

The massive increase in crop exports from Latin America over the past few decades has caused large-scale deforestation and loss of natural grasslands, forcing more and more birds to live near people. Over a period of forty years in Costa Rica, the area of cultivated land devoted to bananas, coffee, and sugar cane doubled to 203,000 hectares. By the mid-1990s, new major crops had been developed in Costa Rica, amounting to an additional 122,000 hectares devoted to agriculture, all heavily dependent on pesticides. Loss of forest has not just taken away the best wintering habitat for forest birds; it has pushed birds into areas where they are more likely to encounter people and their agro-chemicals. Worm-eating warblers, Kentucky warblers, and wood thrush seek shelter inside the forest, so are probably not running into pesticides in their daily lives. The birds at risk include the grassland birds and dozens of forest species, among them the American redstart, hooded warbler, black-and-white warbler, and summer tanager, which are routinely found near agricultural fields.

～

Pesticide poisoning is hard to prove because you have to be there soon after it happens, before the evidence disappears. Modern pesticides are considered relatively safe precisely because they are not stored inside the body and break down within several days. A tissue or blood sample from a bird will not tell you if it was seriously exposed to organophosphate pesticides a few weeks earlier because the pesticide itself is rapidly cleared from these tissues. You can test for the pesticide indirectly by seeing if birds, whether dead or alive, have reduced levels of cholinesterase in their brain after the pesticide has wreaked havoc on the chemical messengers in the nervous system. Swainson's hawks and bobolinks, for instance, had cholinesterase levels at least 40 to 50 percent below normal. It is even harder to find the actual pesticide responsible. Freshly killed birds may still have the poison inside their mouth or stomach, though this evidence disappears within hours or a few days. In a crime investigation, if detectives find the victim's body and the murder weapon in someone's closet, then the case is easily solved. The investigation of whether modern pesticides are causing declines in migratory songbirds is not so easy because the murder weapon is rarely found, and neither is the body of the victim.

To get a good estimate of how many wild birds are killed by pesticides, we have to turn to studies in North America, but even there the numbers are sketchy. The National Wildlife Health Center of the U.S. Geological Survey has tracked incidents of large-scale bird kills in the United States since 1980. In twenty years, they documented only 335 "events" that were caused by organophosphate and carbamate pesticides. Ducks and hawks were the most common victims, but slightly over 1,800 songbirds were found dead during this survey. Not surprisingly, it is the songbirds that live in open areas near agricultural fields that are found most often: red-winged blackbirds, common grackles, and European starlings. These numbers are unrealistically low, if taken at face value. The number of songbirds known to be killed by pesticides would amount to only one hundred deaths per year across the entire United States. The few bodies that are found and reported are just the tip of the iceberg, and given the devastation that has been witnessed in Latin America, for every dead bird we find there are likely hundreds or thousands more who suffered the same fate.

Most bird mortality goes unnoticed. The small bodies of songbirds may lie in the middle of a farmer's field to slowly rot in the sun or be carried away by scavengers who have found an easy meal. It is the day-today mortality that happens sight unseen that could add up to huge losses for a species. One way to estimate the total amount of bird mortality, the size of the iceberg if you will, is to carefully look for casualties in a field before and after treatment with a pesticide, though even the most thorough workers will miss some birds and scavengers will eat up much of the evidence before workers get there. Pierre Mineau, a research scientist with Environment Canada, reviewed field studies on carbofuran done in the 1980s to estimate bird mortality after U.S. corn fields were treated. Carbofuran is applied to fields as granules that stay on the surface of the soil, and birds eat them. At that time about six million hectares of corn fields in the United States were treated with carbofuran. Carbofuran ranks among the top four pesticides known to have caused large-scale bird kills, and a single carbofuran granule is enough to kill a small bird.

Mineau's study shows that while carbofuran was in wide use during the 1960s and 1970s it must have killed hundreds of millions of songbirds. The body count after a single carbofuran treatment was astounding, and ranged from 22 birds per 100 hectares in Iowa to a shocking 850 birds per 100 hectares in Utah. The horned lark, a grassland songbird that frequents corn fields, was the most common victim. To estimate the total number of birds actually killed, we have to take into account the number overlooked by the search teams and the carcasses taken away by scavengers. To find out how good the searchers were at spotting victims, dead birds were scattered in a field, then the search teams were sent in to do a count. The search team found only six out of every ten "planted" dead birds. In corn fields in Maryland, researchers placed a known number of songbird carcasses in a field and returned the next day to see how many were missing. Three quarters had been removed by scavengers, so would never have been found by search teams. When Mineau corrected for both the birds missed by search teams and the ones eaten by scavengers, he found the actual death rate was estimated at 305 birds per 100 hectares in Iowa and over 1,000 birds per 100 hectares for Illinois and Utah. With this best estimate of the true rate of bird mortality, the total number of birds killed in corn fields in the late 1970s would exceed eight million birds each year. Today, granular carbofuran is not registered for most uses in the United States and is banned in Canada. In Latin America, though, carbofuran is still used heavily and often makes it onto a country's top ten list of imported pesticides. Birds that live near agricultural areas must be dropping like stones, even if no one is there to keep a tally of the body count.

These bleak statistics on death rates do not take into account the birds that die away from the scene of the crime. Low levels of organophosphate, or OP, pesticides interfere with normal behaviour and seriously handicap the bird's survival. Neurotoxins cause dizziness, confusion, and nausea, and it often takes several days or even weeks for a bird's brain cholinesterase activity to return to normal after exposure. Humans who have been poisoned often complain of blurred vision, and the same is likely true for birds. Birds that initially survive an encounter with a neurotoxic pesticide may die anyway because they cannot survive in the wild. Songbirds are tasty prey for hawks and other predators, so must be constantly vigilant for surprise attacks. Several studies have shown that birds suffering from a pesticide poisoning are easy pickings for predators. Poisoned birds can also die from collisions with buildings, fences, and other objects, and if they live near roadsides could be hit by passing cars. A poisoned bird may also be unable to catch food and suffer dramatic weight loss, which can prove fatal. Imagine trying to fly, catch insects, and avoid predators when you are feeling dizzy, confused, and nauseated.

One of the most detailed studies to look at the behavioural effects of pesticides took place in New Brunswick. The province sprayed large areas of its spruce-fir forest with pesticides beginning in the early 1950s in an attempt to control massive outbreaks of the spruce budworm. At the peak of spruce budworm outbreak in 1976, almost four million hectares of forest were sprayed. The pesticide used most widely was fenitrothion, an OP whose use today is restricted to roach and ant traps. Spraying took place during the breeding season of birds, when the insects were also at their most abundant. To find out how fenitrothion affected the breeding behaviour of white-throated sparrows, researchers with the

Canadian Wildlife Service compared unsprayed and sprayed forests. All birds were caught and banded, and their behaviour, survival, and nesting success were monitored closely. In areas that had been sprayed, 20 percent of the birds died or disappeared (and were presumed dead) within a few days of spraying. The birds that survived showed a wide range of behavioural side effects. Several pairs abandoned their nests or territory, and some females neglected their eggs. Pairs nesting in sprayed sites produced on average only 0.6 young, compared with 2.4 young in the unsprayed forest. Even with intensive searching, only one sparrow was actually found dead. Yet, the overall impact of spraying was 20 percent adult mortality and 84 percent of nesting attempts were disrupted. These Canadian Wildlife Service researchers were able to document the true extent of the damage because they knew when the forest would be sprayed, and they looked carefully at the fate of individual birds immediately after spraying. Physiological tests showed that sparrows living in the sprayed forest suffered a 20 to 50 percent reduction in brain cholinesterase activity compared with birds living in the unsprayed forest. No wonder they could not defend territories and take care of their eggs and young!

Migrants who are preparing to fly thousands of miles also risk getting lost because OP contamination may throw off their navigation system. A bird navigates using its brain and, for older birds, its memory. Much navigation ability is innate, and even young birds can tell the compass directions by using the stars and sun to orient themselves. In the early 1990s, Nimish Vyas, a Ph.D. student at the University of Maryland, discovered that when he fed adult white-throated sparrows a diet tainted with the OP pesticide acephate, they had trouble telling north from south. Acephate is a common insecticide that sparrows encounter in similar concentrations during migration. He used the time-tested trick of putting each bird in a small cage outdoors, where it could see the night sky. The cage was funnel shaped, with walls sloping outward and an ink pad as a floor. When the bird tried to hop in the direction it wanted to go, it left its footprints on that side of the funnel. He did his tests in the early fall, and birds with no exposure to pesticides headed south in their cages. Adults who had eaten acephate-tainted seeds headed in all directions and presumably would have got lost had they been in the wild. Acephate, unlike fenitothion, is still commonly used in North America and Latin America on a wide variety of food crops, including tomatoes, beans, Brussels sprouts, cauliflower, cranberries, head lettuce, and sweet peppers. It is popular in North America for residential use on lawns and gardens. Over four million pounds of active ingredient is used annually in the United States. Acephate is only moderately toxic to birds, but its sublethal effects could be substantial during migration.

Many modern OP and carbamate pesticides are hormone disruptors, and there are great fears that they may cause subtle changes in the animal's hormone levels that can have huge effects on health. Theo Colborn and her co-authors raised the alarm for humans in their bestselling book *Our Stolen Future,* in which they make a good case that hormone-disrupting pesticides take their toll on wildlife and can affect human fetal development with consequences that range from lowered sperm counts in men to increased incidence of breast and prostate cancer.

The ghosts of pesticides past also haunt our songbird populations today. Migratory birds are widely contaminated with an old enemy, the DDT and related chemicals that almost drove eagles, hawks, and other raptors to extinction in the 1960s. Although DDT was banned in the United States long ago, it and other persistent pesticides take a very long time to degrade and are still around us, in our air, water, and food, and inside our bodies. DDT was used widely and legally for agriculture in Latin America for a decade or more after it had been banned in North America. DDT is still used in some countries to combat mosquitoes that are the vectors of malaria, a disease that kills millions of people worldwide each year. There is also evidence that DDT and other persistent pesticides are used illegally in Latin America for farming because they are cheap and easy to buy. One study in a heavily agricultural part of Mexico found that resident house sparrows had extremely high levels of DDT residues in their bodies, and researchers suspected that farmers in the area were using the chemical illegally.

Low concentrations of DDT have been found deep in rainforests in Venezuela, Costa Rica, Ecuador, and Belize, carried there by the wind and rain. One study that tested air samples in the mid-1990s found that concentrations of DDT and its associated breakdown products were vastly higher (992 picograms per cubic metre) in an agricultural centre in Belize than at three other sites sampled in the northern United States (less than 10 pg/m³). Another study found that butter made in Mexico and Brazil had DDT concentrations that were up to twenty times higher than butter made in Canada and the United States. This is precisely why DDT and other organochlorine pesticides were banned for agricultural use in the first place; it is impossible to keep them from tainting the food chain.

Most studies of pesticide contamination of songbirds in the tropics have focused on the older organochlorine pesticides, even though they are not the most toxic to birds and are not used in large amounts today. OC pesticides are popular to study mostly because they are stored in the body for months or years after the bird eats tainted food, so you can tell if a bird has been exposed by simply testing the blood or tissue. For OC pesticides you don't have to be at the scene of the crime, but instead can piece together evidence of pesticide poisoning long after the fact.

Dr. Given Harper, a professor of biology at Illinois Wesleyan University, has led the way in testing migratory songbirds for OC pesticide contamination. He and his colleagues salvaged birds that had collided with communication towers in Illinois during migration, and tested their bodies for a host of pesticides. Harper's tests showed that that 84 percent of migratory songbirds tested contained DDE, 60 percent contained dieldrin, and 46 percent contained heptachlor epoxide. Next, Harper wanted to find out where migratory songbirds were picking up the poisons. A bird flying through Illinois in May could have OCs hitch-hiking in its body that first hopped on board many months earlier in the tropics. If the wintering grounds are the main source of OC contamination, as many suspected, then a migratory bird should arrive in the spring with relatively high levels. By contrast, a songbird that has spent the winter within the United States should have relatively low pesticide loads. Harper tested dozens of songbirds that live year round in North America and found that 91 percent contained OC pesticides, even though these pesticides were banned long ago. DDT and other OC pesticides are common everywhere migrants travel, partly because these chemicals are transported in the atmosphere and move around the globe easily.

The concentrations of DDE, and even dieldrin and heptachlor, found in migratory songbirds are in the order of 1 to 5 milligrams per kilogram and are too low to cause outright death, but with these chemicals it is the hidden sub-lethal effects we should be worrying about. Although pesticides are designed to kill by attacking the nervous system, they often have other devastating effects on the body, such as disrupting the hormones that control everything from sexual development in the embryo to egg production by females. Early lab studies on the toxicity of DDT missed the serious non-lethal effects of this pesticide because at that time the focus was on detecting deaths and carcinogens. DDE, a hormone disruptor, lowers the level of a reproductive hormone called prostaglandin, resulting in thin egg shells in many birds, particularly raptors. Some hormone-disrupting toxins that are passed into the egg affect brain development of the chick and even at low levels can shrink the part of the brain that controls birdsong. The low pesticide burdens that migrants carry in their bodies could be having subtle but serious effects, but it is extremely difficult in practice to carry out systematic tests to find out what they might be and which species are most affected.

Eating food is the most intimate relationship we have with the natural world. A plant or animal that was once alive and thriving is put inside our mouth and swallowed, and the vitamins, proteins, carbohydrates, and other essential elements that made up the apple or tomato now become part of our own body. When you eat that food you become part of the environment and food chain of where it was grown. Most people buy their food in a grocery store, and on a given day can purchase milk and butter made locally, green beans from across the country, and strawberries from another continent. Most of us are members of dozens of different food chains because we buy and eat food that was grown in fields far away, in other provinces, states, and countries. In this way, we share much in common with migratory birds.

Many of the crops grown in Latin America are sent to our grocery stores and end up on our dinner table, so we should care deeply about the chemicals that are unleashed on that food and the surrounding environment. The United States Food and Drug Administration randomly samples a wide range of food types for pesticide residues and reports what percentage of the food items tested had residues and, worse, what percentage violated EPA standards for safe food. The foods tested are not what is actually sitting on the shelf in your grocery store; instead they are samples of raw, unwashed, and unpeeled foods that arrive in U.S. ports or the domestic foods that are on their way to the packaging plant. (Pesticide residues in foods that are ready to eat are typically much lower than raw products and are tested separately.) If illegal residues are found on raw foods, the FDA can seize domestic products or stop shipments from entering the country. The FDA blocks thousands of shipments each year from dozens of countries.

The results of the pesticide-residue testing show the wide extent of pesticide use, particularly in Latin America. In the United States, 37 percent of the foods tested contain some pesticide residue, though the EPA considers the levels low enough to not harm human health. About half the samples tested from Latin America had some residues, significantly more than the domestic produce. "Violative" foods are a more serious matter because they either exceed the levels allowed by the EPA or contain pesticides not approved for use on those foods. Imported foods from Latin America are almost three times more likely to violate EPA pesticide-residue standards than are foods grown domestically in

Food Type	Domestic	Latin American
Grapes/raisins	0%	3%
Strawberries	4%	9%
Apples	2%	3%
Peaches	2%	2%
String beans	3%	29%
Cucumbers	7%	1%
Sweet peppers	0%	2%
Squash	1%	2%
Tomatoes	0%	0%
Broccoli	0%	0%
Potatoes	0%	0%
Sweet potatoes	0%	17%
Average:	**1.6%**	**5.0%**

Table 6.2. *Percentage of food samples where pesticide residues violated EPA standards (2003 FDA Pesticide Residue Monitoring Program). Only goods with greater than twenty-five samples for both imported and domestic categories were included. Violations could be due to an excess of an approved pesticide or detection of a pesticide not approved for use on that food.*

the United States (table 6.2). Almost a third of the string beans imported from Latin America violate EPA standards, along with about 20 percent of sweet potatoes. Almost one out of every ten strawberries fails the test. The high pesticide loads from Latin American foods reflects the heavy use of restricted pesticides that are a threat not only to those environments but to anyone who becomes part of that food chain.

Even though we are not involved with growing the food, we have choices as consumers. We can remember the lessons we have learned from shade coffee and choose to buy crops that use fewer and safer pesticides, or buy organically grown foods. Making wise choices about the food we consume promotes a safer environment for the birds and other wildlife—as well as for the people—who live where the food was grown. Buying "bird-friendly" produce helps to create a market for crops grown with safer and fewer pesticides, which in turn provides a financial incentive to farmers to reduce their dependency on pesticides.

To find out which crops are most bird friendly in terms of pesticide use, Pierre Mineau, head of the Pesticide Division at the National Wildlife Research Centre in Ottawa, and Mélanie Whiteside looked at the acreage of crops grown in the United States and the types and amounts of pesticides used on those crops. Since the 1980s, many new pesticides that have been introduced to the market have a negligible toxic effect on birds. From 1990 to 2003, the general trend in the United States was an overall reduction in the percentage of a given crop that is potentially lethal to birds. For instance, the percentage of corn grown that presents a death threat to birds has dropped from 20 percent to only 5 percent. Cotton, notorious for its heavy and frequent pesticide use, has dropped from 80 percent to 40 percent, and vegetable crops from an already low 5 percent to 1 percent. This steady improvement in the chemical environment for birds has come not because we are using fewer pesticides but because in the United States a new generation of pesticides is replacing the deadly organophosphate and carbamate pesticides.

This bird-friendly approach to crops can be used to identify which foods present the greatest risk to birds, at least in North America. At the level of a farmer's field, Brussels sprouts are grown with repeated insecticide applications and were ranked the highest risk to birds living near these fields (table 6.3). Other crops that are not bird friendly on a per hectare level include celery, cranberries, cabbage, potatoes, sweet potatoes, sweet peppers, and hot peppers. Blueberries should be on the list too because they are one of the few crops that pose an increasing danger to birds over the past fifteen years. The use of low-risk pesticides for blueberries has decreased by 50 percent while pesticides like diazinon that are a high risk to birds have been used more extensively. This is especially worrying because many birds eat the tasty blueberries so are very likely to come into contact with the pesticides.

The number of birds that are at risk nationwide depends on how much acreage is used to grow particular crops. Brussels sprouts are the worst crop at the local level, but since they are a minor crop in the

Local Level	Continental Level
Brussels sprouts	Corn
Celery	Cotton
Cranberry	Alfalfa
Cabbage	Wheat
Potato	Potato

Table 6.3. *The top five crops in the United States that pose the greatest risk of pesticide poisoning to birds. The local level is based on pesticide use per hectare and the continental level is based on total acreage that presents a risk to birds. (From Mineau and Whiteside, 2006)*

United States they do not account for high bird mortality compared with more widespread crops. Corn ranks as the number-one enemy for birds because it occupies such a large amount of land (table 6.3). Safer pesticides are used on corn today than in the past, but even if only one bird were killed per hectare of corn this would still add up to more than five million dead birds each year. Cotton comes in second place because it is a common crop and each individual field receives frequent doses of pesticides. The five crops with the greatest potential for nationwide bird mortality are corn, cotton, alfalfa, wheat, and potatoes.

We can also help our migratory birds by using our consumer power to encourage bird-friendly agriculture in Latin America. Here it is less clear which crops to target, since from what we have seen few of the exported crops are grown with modest use of pesticides that are relatively safe for birds. Detailed statistics on pesticide use are not available for Latin America, though given the heavy use of dangerous pesticides we can expect that a high proportion of crops grown in Latin America, probably in excess of 80 percent, are capable of killing birds. Bird-friendly crops may simply be those that are grown organically.

Consumers can encourage a lower use of pesticides in the environment, and in their own bodies, by buying organic produce and choosing crops that are bird friendly. (I can hear some children cheering at the news that their parents have decided not to serve Brussels sprouts at dinner!) Now when I am in the fresh produce section of my neighbourhood grocery store I look carefully at where the food was grown. I buy organic for domestic crops that are harmful to birds, like celery, potatoes, and blueberries. It is not hard to find breakfast cereal and whole wheat flour that is organic. If the small organic produce section at my store does not have organic celery, I go without and pick a different vegetable for the salad. I buy only organic bananas because bananas receive among the highest pesticide loads of any tropical fruit, so they are responsible for a large fraction of the pesticides that are unleashed on tropical environments. This consumer-driven strategy is a broader version of bird-friendly coffee: it is good for consumers, good for farming families and communities, and of course good for birds and other wildlife.

7 BRIGHT LIGHTS, BIG DANGER
Small-Town and Big-City Hazards to Migrating Songbirds

After many months of living in a scrubby forest on a Caribbean island, the black-throated blue warbler's body begins to change. It is mid-March, and the hours of daylight are a little bit longer and the nights shorter. Although the change in photoperiod is subtle, it nevertheless registers in the bird's brain, triggering the release of hormones that in turn set off a chain reaction. The warbler begins to eat more than usual, its body efficiently converting the food into layers of fat that it stores underneath the skin near its breast bone. The warbler gets chubbier and chubbier, and begins to get restless at night. Soon, it will leave its winter territory and not return for five months. The hormones awake his reproductive organs; by the time the warbler arrives on his breeding territory in early May his testes will have grown a hundredfold. Birds are very economical when it comes to unnecessary baggage during flight; the large internal testes of males shrink to tiny specks over the fall and winter.

Far away, in a tropical forest fragment on the east coast of Mexico, a wood thrush is undergoing similar changes as it hops on the forest floor, flipping over leaves and looking for insects to eat. An indigo bunting male on the Yucatán Peninsula, who took on a drab, unassuming appearance while living in flocks during the winter, turns a crazy jumble of brown and cobalt as he begins to moult back into his brilliant breeding colours. All across Central and South America, the change in day length is perceived by billions of wintering migrants and automatically turns on their "get ready" switch.

Far to the north, in the temperate zone, the daffodils are still in their cold underground shelters and the lawns are covered with a beaten-down mat of dead grass. I measure the progress of spring with my ears, not by the appearance of the yellow flowers dotting the forsythia in our front yard or by the soft, curled leaves that slowly unfold from the Virginia creeper vines on the back fence. While walking our golden retriever in the small park near our house in Toronto, bent over against the strong winds of a March morning, my head snaps to attention when I hear the screaming *kill-deer, kill-deer* overhead. A small shorebird is zig-zagging across the sky at breakneck speed, flying in large looping circles over the entire park. A pair usually nests on the roof of the elementary school, where their eggs, laid directly on the ground, are safe from cats, raccoons, and rats. When I get back to the house I walk in the front door yelling, "Hey, the killdeer is back!" After months of snow and ice, the killdeer is a sure sign that spring is on its way and that other migrants are soon to follow.

Although my neighbours do not notice the killdeer, or the song sparrow that arrives a week later and begins singing in a backyard at the edge of the park, they do notice the robins. In our neighbourhood the robins sing from the rooftops because there are no trees taller than the second-story windows. Fifteen years ago this entire neighbourhood was a farmer's field. The human footprint could hardly be heavier now, with hundreds of homes packed close together, manicured lawns, and a token patch of forest that was saved from the bulldozer. A weathered sign proclaims the forest is a "Neighbourhood Park Woodlot," yet a chain-link fence surrounds the site to keep people out.

In the wee hours of the morning, just before dawn, I lie in bed listening to the male robin singing from the house next door, belting out his rollicking song to another male at the other end of the street. Natives who lived in this area hundreds of years ago must have heard almost identical songs near their summer homes, as did the pioneer families who cleared the forest so they could plow the land. Male robins have used their energetic song to intimidate rivals and woo females whoever their human neighbours have happened to be. These birds are resilient, and despite the massive changes to this piece of land the robins return every spring and give us a chance to eavesdrop on their public displays.

Most forest birds are not so forgiving, and I know the sad-looking woodlot in this suburban bliss cannot possibly attract nesting birds like the wood thrush, scarlet tanager, or rose-breasted grosbeak. Only a couple of miles away, my office at York University looks out over a forest patch only a little larger than the one near my home. I keep a pair of binoculars handy in my desk drawer, in case I see something interesting across the road. A Cooper's hawk is a regular visitor, gliding by like a guided missile on its way to pick off one of the house sparrows that hang around the buildings on campus. During summer even this forest is quiet, home to only the resident chickadees, a couple of pairs of robins, and a cardinal and a red-eyed vireo. Several other small woodlots are scattered around the campus and a few blocks away a narrow strip of trees stretches along Black Creek. Other than this, there is precious little natural habitat for miles around. For most migrants, these tiny woodlots are pretty much a write-off as a breeding site.

During spring migration, it is a different story altogether. I enjoy walking to the parking lot along the well-worn dirt path at the edge of the woodlot instead of using the busy sidewalk along the road. I take my time, keeping my eye out for visitors. Some are birds that breed far to the north in the almost endless boreal forest of Canada but use the woodlot as one of many stepping stones on their journey. I am humbled to see white-throated sparrows barking in alarm as I pass by and a hermit thrush hopping along the ground oblivious to my presence until the last moment. Juncos scratch the ground looking for seeds, flashing their white outer tail feathers, and high in a tree a rusty blackbird squawks loudly like a creaky old door hinge. Although not much use for raising families, this woodlot is a life saver for these migrants whose journey is not over by a long shot; it is a patch of food and shelter amid endless city streets and buildings that offers them a chance to refuel and launch off on their connecting flight.

At our rural home in Pennsylvania the migrants who visit our large woods have it easy, if they can avoid running into the pair of Cooper's hawks who patrol the woods by the old cemetery on the hill. We compare notes with our like-minded friends: "Our phoebe came back yesterday" versus "We haven't seen one yet, but we have a towhee." By mid-April the backyard list is growing steadily: tree swallow, bluebird, song sparrow, field sparrow, red-winged blackbird, common grackle. This is the first wave, birds that spend the winter close by in the southern United States.

The forest in mid-April is still very quiet, though in a month it will be teeming with neotropical migrants. The chickadees are no longer living in their winter flocks but have split up into pairs to start excavating tree cavities for their nests. The male and female take turns working at a small snag, ripping at the rotting wood with their tiny beaks and sending bits flying like shrapnel. An enormous pileated woodpecker explodes overhead with its wild laughter, and farther away a cardinal sings methodically *cheer, cheer, birdy-birdy-birdy*. These are all residents who spent the winter here and are already in full gear building nests.

There are only a handful of migrants in the woods, just a tiny taste of what is about to come. Two male blue-headed vireos argue over an invisible boundary in the darkness of the hemlock trees, singing back and forth as they flit among the treetops searching for the first insects of the season. A hike through the hemlocks is punctuated with an occasional *zee-zee-zee zoo zeeeee,* revealing the black-throated green warblers who are almost invisible among the hemlocks. Deep in the stream valley, a single junco sings a long, breathless trill; his mate will build a nest among the tangled roots of a fallen tree.

In early May, neotropical migrants appear as though a dozen jumbo jets have arrived at the same time at a small airport and unloaded a seemingly endless stream of passengers. The first are almost all males, rushing to their breeding territories a week or so before the females arrive to shop around for good homes and mates. Many males will return to the exact same place in the forest as the year before, a navigational bull's eye after a journey of thousands of miles, and sing from familiar perches, glean insects from the top of the red oak that was a such a good spot for food last spring, and will quickly agree to observe the same old territory boundary with the returning male next door. The fields, marshes, and woods go from almost empty in March to overflowing with birds that live in almost every nook and cranny. The forest is filled shoulder-to-shoulder with wood thrush, Acadian flycatchers, scarlet tanagers, hooded warblers, red-eyed vireos, American redstarts, and many other species of migrants. The field edges near our house become homes for yellow warblers, chestnut-sided warblers, blue-winged warblers, indigo buntings, and mourning warblers. The big rush is over quickly; by mid-May virtually all the species that will breed in the area have come back and have gotten down to serious business. Females waste no time starting their nests, and the next two months becomes a race against time to reproduce.

~

The Gulf coast from Texas to Florida is the first stop in North America for many migrants. It is also their most important stop, because they have just finished the longest and most dangerous leg of their journey. Warblers, thrush, flycatchers, and tanagers, just to name a few, fly across the Gulf of Mexico after departing from the northern shores of the Yucatán Peninsula at sunset the night before. They fly for fifteen to twenty hours non-stop and are pushed to their physical limits. Weather radars along the U.S. coast start picking up clouds of migrants around noon, and they come in wave after wave for the rest of the day. Radar images have shown up to 50 million birds arriving along the coast every few hours during the peak period of migration. As the flocks descend to the ground somewhere inland from the coast, they drop below the radar beam and disappear from the image. As soon as they make landfall they start looking for food. Most have just burned off close to half of their body weight, fat that was laid down in Mexico just a week beforehand.

In a remarkable study, Martin Wikelski of Princeton University measured how much energy a migrating bird actually used up during a typical nighttime flight. This had been done before in wind tunnels, but never in the wild with free-flying birds. Wikelski caught Swainson's and hermit thrushes that were passing through Illinois on their way north to breed, and fitted them with a radiotransmitter. Before letting them go, he injected them with a harmless dose of special water that contained marked hydrogen and oxygen isotopes that would be used up during exercise. The more calories a bird burned, the fewer marked oxygen isotopes would be left in the bloodstream when the bird was tested the next day. Wikelski and his crew drove like madmen through the Illinois countryside at night in a car equipped with a large antenna on the roof, trying to keep up with the birds and follow their flight path from the ground. Birds flew non-stop for four or five hours in a single night, going an average of thirty-seven miles an hour. The crews were able to recapture several of their birds, including one bird that flew for eight hours in a single night, covering 370 miles. When birds were captured early the next morning, they had lost 6 percent of their body mass in a one night. Thrush that stay on the ground for the night instead of flying need about 360 calories of energy per day to maintain their weight and stay alive. The long migration flights require a huge boost in energy input; the birds that will fly for six to eight hours need to pack on an extra 300 to 400 calories of energy to power their wings. This is double what they would need if they stayed on the ground, and these estimates are for an "easy" flight compared with the Gulf crossing.

The successful crossing of the Gulf of Mexico and even the shorter legs of the trip that follow are possible only if birds can find habitat along the way that provides a rich food supply for the tens of thousands of birds that will stop there during migration. Birds cannot afford to eat only as much food as they need to stay alive but must overeat to lay down fat stores that will fuel their long flights. In poor stopover habitat it may take them days to build up enough fuel to continue their journey. Birds do not fly every single night but rather time their movements according to their own energy reserves and favourable weather conditions. Wikelski's study helps us to piece together the number of stopovers a bird normally makes in its long trip north. In the 1970s, banders had the good fortune to catch a thrush in Canada that had been banded only forty-two days earlier in Panama, but this doesn't mean the bird flew for forty-two nights in a row. Wikelski's radiotagged birds flew an average of 155 miles each night, so could make the 3,000-mile trip in just eighteen separate flights; the other two dozen nights would have been spent on the ground at stopover sites. Birds that find themselves in poor stopover habitat can be grounded even in good flying weather because they don't have enough fuel, or at best can limp along for an hour before having to land again. Many of the Swainson's thrushes that Wikelski studied in Illinois did not fly the same night that he had radiotagged them; those with low fat reserves flew for only one hour. At that slow pace, it would take a thrush more than three months to reach the breeding grounds, and the poor bird would arrive at the tail end of the breeding season, just in time to turn around and head back south!

Stopover habitats are crucial for migration. Imagine a highway with exits every sixty miles; if you are low on fuel and the nearest exit has no gas station, you have to keep driving and hope there is a gas station at the next exit. For migrants, the gas stations have become fewer and farther between over the past hundred years as humans have taken over millions of hectares of prime land. Not so long ago the deciduous forests of the eastern United States stretched from the Mississippi Valley all the way to the eastern seaboard and from the Gulf coast up into southern Canada. Today the landscape has been consumed by humans: plowed lands have replaced rich meadows of native grasses and the forests have been replaced by large fields of crops and by housing developments and cities. It becomes critical to find out where birds do stop during migration, and to make sure there is enough food in those places to keep them flying.

Radar has been used to map out the critical stopover habitats that migrants visit when they first set foot in North America. By analyzing images just after sunset, at the very beginning of the night migration, Sid Gauthreaux and others have been able to pinpoint where the first waves of migrants spring up into the air from their stopover sites. The radar image suddenly lights up in blotches of red as the birds leaving their stopover sites first hit the radar beam. In southern Louisiana, most birds arriving after their Gulf crossing stopped anywhere from six to thirty-seven miles inland rather than along the coast proper. The highest concentrations of birds were found in floodplains, the lowland forested wetlands that are highly productive. The drier pine flatlands, though more extensive in area, were rarely used by migrants. Satellite images of the Mississipi coastline give us a bird's-eye view of the landscape that greets the migrants. The rich bottomland deciduous forest that is optimum habitat for migrants makes up only 7.5 percent of the landscape in most regions and is scattered widely in small clumps. Their next favourite habitat, shrubby wet habitat or the drier upland shrub and forest, is more extensive but still covers less than a third of the landscape.

Along the Gulf coast the offshore barrier islands are life rings for spring migrants that have run out of steam crossing the Gulf because they hit a headwind and have burned up their fat faster than expected; they can land on the islands, far short of the mainland. No one knows how many birds do not even make it to the islands and die when they hit the water. Mist-netting stations have been set up on some of the barrier islands to find out which species of migrants are using these stopover sites and what kind of habitat allows them to recover and continue on their journey the fastest. On East Ship Island, about twelve miles off the coast of Mississippi, dozens of species of migrants are caught in the nets each spring, including more than thirty species of warbler. Each spring, about two thousand individuals continue their journey after being closely inspected and measured, then released wearing a numbered bird band. A bander can score the amount of fat on a bird by rudely blowing on its breast feathers to see the skin underneath—the equivalent of lifting up your neighbour's shirt to inspect his belly for pudginess. You can actually see the whitish-yellow fat under a bird's thin skin, and if there is a good amount it will literally bulge out. (The birds don't take it personally, though—being fat is a good thing!) On typical days the nets on East Ship Island are busy but manageable, and most birds who arrive during the day have little or no fat on their bodies, a sign that they landed on the island because they had used up all their reserves. These birds spend several days on the island searching for food in the pine forest and scrub, then continue on their way. The food on the island is not great compared with the lowland wet forests of the mainland, but reaching East Ship is certainly better than landing in the drink.

A couple of times each spring all hell breaks loose because a strong cold front sweeps south overnight and the birds slam into it as if they've hit a Jersey barrier on the turnpike. The trip across the Gulf takes so long that birds that launch off the Yucatán Peninsula at sunset have no idea what the weather will be like the next day when they get close to mainland. When they hit bad weather, a cold front or a thunderstorm, the birds head for the nearest landing pad and pile up by the thousands in a spectacular "fall out." During a fall out, the banding station may have to pull eight hiundred birds from the nets in a single day. Most of these birds did not run out of gas, but had to pull over to wait out the storm; they have plenty of fat on their bodies. They usually leave that night, and are not recaptured in the nets, because they are already gassed up and ready to continue their trip.

Birds have been making these trips for thousands of years, and are well equipped to survive when the chips are down and they find themselves in an unfamiliar place. On nearby Horn Island, biologists radiotracked summer tanagers that had just landed on the island after crossing the Gulf. The behaviour of the birds, and the habitat they use, depended on their own personal energy stores. Fat birds stayed in a small area, often perched quietly for an hour or more, and were most often seen in the scrubby or shrubby habitat that is second rate when it comes to food. Lean birds roamed more than half a mile, were very active and spent most of their time in the pine forest where there is more food up for grabs. A fat bird who arrives early in the afternoon does not urgently need food, and may simply rest in a safe place hiding from predators until nightfall to continue its journey. A bird that is starving has different needs; finding food is its top priority, even if that means being where predators can spot it more easily. Both scrub and forest are important stopover habitat because they each offer vital but different resources to a travelling bird.

This diversity in a bird's basic needs makes the conservation of stopover habitat a complex and daunting job. Some stopover sites, like the Chenier Plain scrubby forest that stretches in a narrow strip along the coast of Texas and Louisiana, is overshot by most migrants who, if in good condition, prefer to land inland. This does not mean that the chenier habitat is low quality or unimportant from a conservation perspective. This coastal habitat becomes absolutely critical during bad weather, when birds are struggling to find any land at all. A visit on a typical day in April might turn up only a few migrants, but these remnants of natural habitat may be teeming with starving migrants during one or two days of the season. For desperate migrants, the coastlines are used in emergencies when their energy demands and their risk of death are at their highest. But these same coastal areas have a burgeoning human population that continues to gobble up and degrade stopover sites, creating a potential disaster for migrants. A good conservation strategy would be one that protects both the large bottomland forests farther inland where stopovers occur regularly, and the emergency stopover habitat along the coast.

The Nature Conservancy has proposed several categories of stop-over sites worthy of protection to ensure that there are no weak links in the chain from Central America up to Canada. Large bottomland forests qualify as "full-service hotels," high-quality sites where birds can quickly accumulate body fat and find shelter from predators. The "Convenience Store" stopover sites are regularly used smaller forest patches surrounded by agricultural fields, houses, or industrial sites. Birds can find enough food to continue on their journey after a few days, or explore for higher-quality sites. Finally, the "fire escape" stop-over sites are used only once or twice a year but are utterly vital to the survival of large numbers of birds. Habitat conservation for birds in North America has traditionally focused on the breeding success of birds, where small forest patches are considered extremely poor places for migrants. This emphasis on breeding ignores the importance of these small woodlots as convenience stores during migration. Many of these small forest patches see their greatest bird diversity in spring and early fall, not during summer. Birds are no dummies and would rather stay in a hotel, *if* they can find one. Birds are frequently forced to the ground by low energy reserves or bad weather, only to find themselves surrounded by agricultural fields or in the midst of a suburban land-scape. Small woodlots and strips of forest along creeks and rivers are their fire escape.

Migrating birds can be seen just about anywhere there is semi-natu-ral habitat, including backyards, parks, and tiny clusters of trees near busy parking lots and streets. I once saw a brown creeper, a tiny song-bird that acts more like a woodpecker, on the side of our brick house in the suburbs inching its way up the wall as though it was on a tree trunk deep in a forest, searching for insects among the crevices. The nearest good-sized tree is two blocks away. Occasionally a dark-eyed junco lands in our postage-stamp backyard and somehow finds the sun-flower seeds that fell from the plate-sized flower heads last fall. In early May, I saw a white-crowned sparrow perched boldly on top of one of a few tiny spruce trees planted near the baseball diamond in the park, the sun lighting up the striking white stripes on his crown as he raised his beak to belt out his song. He was still far from his breeding territory on the tundra in northern Canada, but he was pumped and ready. I wondered if he, or the brown creeper and junco, ever made it to his breeding site. No one really knows the fate of birds who stop over in urban and suburban settings where safety and food are both hard to find.

～

For thousands of years, migratory birds have passed over the Gulf of Mexico, then over the forests, marshes, and fields below them as they made their way north through the United States and Canada. Their DNA carries instructions passed down from the survivors of migration; what works is tried again and again by successive generations, without thought. The instructions that did not work slowly shrivel up and blow away along with the victim of a mistake. Birds automatically take crosswinds into account as they fly, correcting for being blown off course. Young birds don't need a high-school physics class to work this out, any more than my son needs to make mathematical calculations before throwing a baseball. Birds "know" to stay on the ground when the headwinds are strong, biding their time and slowly putting on weight. When the winds shift, they take to the air, riding the warm fronts that push them north. They are not thinking and planning the way you and I might do; they operate largely on instinct and react to the physiological cues that come from their own bodies and the external cues that come from the environment around them.

Young birds do not need to be taught north from south; the basic navigation system is built in, pre-programmed in their brains from birth. A bird only a few months old can easily fly by itself, independent from its parents, thousands of miles and find a winter home in Central or South America. It is born knowing the direction to travel and the rough distance to its species' wintering grounds. Come spring, it can just as easily fly a different route thousands of miles to find a breeding territory even though it has never made the trip before.

As we know, humans are not born with this ability; most of us would be hopelessly lost if blindfolded and dropped somewhere unfamiliar. When I was a six-year-old, lying on the dock at the cottage, my parents taught me how to pick out the Big Dipper and North Star from the millions of stars that make up the Milky Way. My daughter was taught a memory trick for remembering the compass directions in her Grade 2 class: "Never Eat Shredded Wheat," or, even better, "Never Enter Stinking Washrooms." Humans are stuck on the ground and have never needed a built-in long-distance navigation system, so our brains, as big as they are, need to be taught how to navigate.

The built-in navigation system of birds uses a suite of different compasses that work in concert to allow a songbird to zip along at speeds of twenty-five to thirty-five miles an hour through the night without getting lost. To figure out where they are going, birds use familiar landmarks, the sunrise and sunset, the polarized light from the sun that filters through the clouds, the magnetic fields of the earth, and the night stars. Birds use their internal clock to tell time, and then use the position of the sun in the sky to tell east from west. Long ago, experiments with homing pigeons during the daytime proved that birds have a magnetic compass in their brains that can detect the earth's magnetic fields. Birds were fitted with little head caps that sent out a magnetic field, disrupting the natural cues. The birds were released somewhere unfamiliar and far away from their home coop. Most of them got lost if it was a cloudy day and they could not "cheat" and use the sun to tell directions. On sunny days, the birds did a pretty good job of getting home even though their magnetic compass was effectively going in circles.

Some songbirds migrate during the daytime, including birds like the multitasking swallows who catch insects in-flight. Most songbirds, however, make their long flights exclusively at night because the natural air conditioning cools their bodies as their hearts beat some five hundred times per minute, generating heat. The air is also less turbulent during the night, so the birds expend less of their precious energy. Birds that migrate at night use the stars and moon to fine-tune their navigation.

Fascinating experiments were done in the 1970s that, during the migration season, took advantage of the fact that birds get hyped up with jitters that drive them to be on the move. At night, the bird jumps around in its cage trying to interpret the cues available so that it can go in the right direction. If the bird is placed outdoors on a clear night, it can correctly surmise where north is by looking at the stars, and begins jumping on that side of the cage. Researchers put birds in a planetarium where they could turn stars on and off, and even move stars around in the sky. Even though the migrants had a magnetic compass to help them find north, if the stars in the sky were flipped 180 degrees and put in the wrong place, then the birds also flipped the direction they moved in the cage and followed the stars instead of magnetic north.

Recent research on free-flying thrushes has shown that the magnetic compass can sometimes trump the star compass. Bill Cochran, a pioneer in migration research, radiotracked migrating thrushes to test how they navigate. During sunset he shifted the magnetic field around caged thrushes by 90 degrees and found that when the birds were released after sunset they flew west instead of north. These birds were flying under a clear sky and so could easily see the stars, and were experiencing normal magnetic fields from the earth, but apparently could not tell they were going the wrong way. The effect lasted only one night; when exposed to the natural magnetic field of the earth at sunset the next night, the birds corrected their flight path and flew north once again. This study suggests that birds "set" their magnetic compass at sunset before they take off, then use other cues like stars to maintain that direction during the night.

These kinds of clever experiments have shown that birds have a very sophisticated navigation system that allows them to fly for hours at a time in the darkness and to return to exactly the same breeding territory year after year. Nevertheless, the simple nature of the cues that birds use for navigation may be their downfall in today's modern world. The stars that help to guide nighttime migration can be a fatal attraction that brings songbirds face to face with manmade structures like buildings and television towers.

Amid the towering skyscrapers of Toronto's financial district, a man carrying a butterfly net walks intently along the sidewalk scanning the base of the buildings. Around him are businessmen in suits marching down the sidewalk with a newspaper tucked under one arm and a coffee cup in the other. It is only 6:30 on this cool spring morning and the streets are already busy. No one pays attention to the man with the butterfly net; unusual sights are commonplace on downtown streets, and people have learned to tune out the throng of people around them. The man with the net pauses, then walks toward a tall glass-fronted entrance to a building with a brightly lit lobby. A body lies at the base of the glass wall; it is a small ovenbird. He picks up the bird and holds its lifeless form in his hand. The subtle earth tones of its back contrast with the bold streaks on the white breast, and an elegant stripe of rusty brown decorates on top of its head. This is the second ovenbird he has found this morning (figure 7.1).

Nearby a bird is perched on the sidewalk, motionless, with its feathers puffed up in shock. Pedestrians bustle by as the man quietly sneaks up behind the bird, bends over and in slow motion gently picks it up. The white-throated sparrow's eyes are both open, a good sign, and it looks alert, though it is lethargic in his hand. This bird might live, and later this morning it will be released in High Park, a large park that stretches several blocks northward from the shores of Lake Ontario into the city and is an oasis for people and birds alike. The man carefully puts the sparrow in a paper bag and continues on his search. The next stop is another brightly lit glass lobby entrance a few doors down; here a black-throated blue warbler is flying at the window toward the lights, fluttering against the glass over and over. Inside the building are two small potted trees, probably fake but they must seem like a safe haven to the bird, who is confused and exhausted. After a few quick moves with the butterfly net, the warbler is caught and tucked away safely in another paper bag.

The wonderfully fine-tuned system that migrants use to find their

Figure 7.1. *Across eastern North America, ovenbirds, thrush, sparrows, and warblers, attracted to city lights during spring and fall migration, die by the hundreds. (Photo by Bridget Stutchbury)*

way in the darkness is a handicap in this modern world of sprawling cities. Birds are programmed to use the subtle lights of the stars and moon to guide their long flights during the night. It is only in the past hundred years or so that the darkness under their wings has been replaced by enormous cities that light up the sky from miles away. Celestial signposts become masked in cities where bright lights shine from skyscrapers and rooftops, literally blinding birds and confusing their navigation system. Especially on foggy nights and nights with low cloud cover, when they cannot see the real stars, birds stream toward the city lights and circle among the buildings and streets, disoriented and exhausted. Before long, the birds fall like rain. Many hit windows in a frantic but confused effort to escape the strange and hostile environment that is totally lacking in food. Survivors may perch in small shrubs around buildings, only to hit windows as they fly toward the lights inside. The birds that stream north each spring encounter dozens of major cities in a deadly obstacle course (figure 7.2). It is hard to imagine how a bird could make

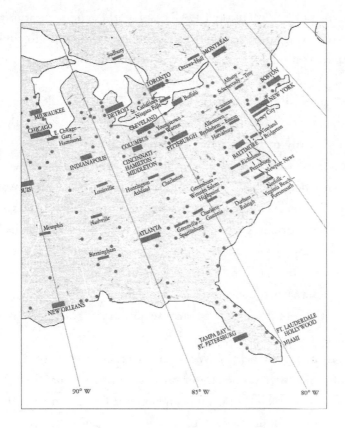

Figure 7.2. *The urban obstacle course that migrants travel through twice a year. Major cities, over 15 miles wide and with populations in excess of one million people, are shown with large rectangles. (Map courtesy of Evans Ogden, WWF, 1996)*

the trip from the Gulf coast to Canada without flying near a major city.

Toronto lies on a bird super-highway, and tens of thousands of birds pass overhead in a single hour during the peak of spring migration. Volunteers in Toronto have been combing the streets each spring and fall since 1993 and find more than two thousand trapped or dead birds each year. The Fatal Light Awareness Program, or FLAP, in Toronto has been a leader in migratory bird conservation, even challenging other cities, like Chicago, to a contest to see who can save the most birds. FLAP has worked closely with the City of Toronto to bring the plight of migratory birds into the awareness of ordinary people.

To get the public's attention, FLAP displays the otherwise anonymous victims of one migration season. In stocking feet and with gloved hands, two volunteers are bent over, intently working in the grand rotunda of the Royal Ontario Museum. Around them are neat rows of dead birds, arranged artistically by size, shape, and colour. Twelve woodcock alternate in two short rows followed by several northern flickers. Below them are twenty-eight brown creepers; the whip-poor-wills are clustered together a few rows away, and beside them are the hermit thrush, Swainson's thrush, and wood thrush. There are a few dozen rows of small warblers and two rows of even smaller ruby-throated hummingbirds. One section is reserved for chickadees; these are not neotropical migrants but in this year they underwent a large short-distance migration as they moved south from the boreal forest. These birds dropped like flies when they came through the city, unaccustomed to the buildings and glass they ran into. In all, the colourful though macabre tapestry of bodies was built out of two thousand birds of eighty-nine different species.

The body count is shocking. Worse, no one really knows the full extent of the toll either within one city or on a continental scale. Snapshots of parts of Chicago, New York, and other major cities paint an ominous picture. A single building in Chicago used to cause fifteen hundred migratory bird deaths each year. Chicago is on a major migration route because it is at the south end of Lake Michigan, a crossroads for birds. About five million birds, representing roughly 250 species, fly through the city on their way north. Chicago now has a "Lights Out" campaign that was inspired by FLAP. Almost all the major skyscrapers in Chicago, including the Sears Tower, turn off their floodlights during the main migration season.

The Audubon Society in New York City has a program called "Project Safe Flight," which has been monitoring bird casualties since 1997. Before the 9/11 disaster, the World Trade Center was a major obstacle for migratory birds, and the Audubon Society had successfully campaigned for netting over some windows so birds would harmlessly bounce off. The ghost of the WTC, the Tribute in Light memorial, was a giant magnet to migrating birds with its eighty-eight massive spotlights that lit up the night sky one night in 2004. That year, the two towers of light began to sparkle as the brilliant spotlights reflected off moving objects that had entered the beams. Thousands of migratory birds had been drawn to the lights and circled around confused and blinded.

The birds that are found by volunteers are but a tiny fraction of the total number that die when they are lured into our urban areas by the bright lights. Cities are so big that it is nearly impossible to survey enough streets thoroughly, or every morning, to arrive at an accurate estimate of mortality, let alone to rescue all the birds that still have a slim chance of escaping the maze of glass, concrete, and congested streets. With energy reserves burned and no food to be found, birds do not last long. In Toronto, ring-billed gulls have learned where easy meals can be had and attack the weak, puffed up birds who are sitting miserably on the sidewalk. FLAP's main goal is not to salvage dead birds, but to rescue, rehabilitate, and release the birds that they find dazed but still alive. In a typical year they find a depressing eight hundred-odd birds that have died, but are able to rescue almost twice as many and relocate them to High Park, where they can at least find food and shelter.

Toronto is turning off its lights. Most people have no idea that birds pour through the city every night and are appalled to learn how many birds are killed; turning off the lights is a win-win solution because both birds and energy are saved. In the mid-1990s, FLAP persuaded managers of more than a dozen tall towers and skyscrapers in Toronto to dim their lights during migration. A publicity campaign, "Lights Out Toronto," was launched in 2006 by the city and its partners to encourage all business owners and residents to turn off their lights between 11 p.m. and 5 a.m. during the spring and fall migration seasons. By persuading residents and workers who share their city with millions of fragile visitors to turn off the lights late at night, FLAP has made it possible for thousands of birds to pass through the city unharmed.

Toronto is the first city in the world to implement a migratory bird protection policy for building design and lighting. All new buildings are to consider a bird-friendly design and minimize lighting at night, including unnecessary floodlighting that serves only for showing off the building. Ground lighting that is pointed skyward is deadly for migrants. Highly reflective windows, particularly when trees are part of the landscaping, can cause hundreds of fatalities every migration season.

The lighting systems inside the buildings need to be designed so that they *can* be turned off at night when not needed. Many office towers have advanced lighting systems where five or so floors are controlled by the same switch; if one lawyer needs to work in her office late at night, then five entire floors stay lit up. The director of a Toronto wildlife rehabilitation centre tells the story of a great blue heron that was trapped in a Home Depot store. The bird was cornered and sitting quietly, and rescuers had their nets ready; they asked the store manager to turn the lights off so that they could sneak up on the bird. He couldn't, because the lights were controlled via computer at a control centre somewhere in Georgia. Rescuers had to phone Georgia and negotiate with the powers that be to turn off the lights in a building in Toronto. We homeowners take it for granted that we can easily flick a switch and save a bird, but for some commercial buildings this will require an overhaul of the electrical system. Even then, what is good for birds is good for business; some buildings can save hundreds of thousands of dollars a year in electrical bills by dimming the lights during migration.

Skyscrapers are not the only buildings that kill birds; even two-story office buildings or homes can be lethal. The impressive diversity of migrants that pass through my university campus can be most easily seen by looking in the chest freezer in my lab. I have dozens of little birds stored in plastic body bags, victims of collisions with the almost invisible glass of the windows on campus. Tired and desperate to find food, the migrants fly toward what they think is an opening, then hit the glass hard, breaking their skulls or suffering fatal brain injuries. My undergraduate students patrol the buildings on campus during migration and collect the victims. Birds that do not breed here are nevertheless well represented in the avian morgue: ovenbirds,

Chestnut-sided Warbler *(singing male)*
Chestnut-sided warblers sing their songs "Pleased-pleased-pleased to meet-cha!" along forest edges and in the dense, thorny tangles of sunlit gaps within the forest. (Photo by Lang Elliott)

Hooded Warbler *(pair feeding young)*
Male hooded warblers, like most songbirds, deliver many beak-loads of wriggling caterpillars to help feed their hungry nestlings. This pair of adults has been banded with coloured and numbered leg bands. (Photo by Joan Howlett)

Scarlet Tanager (*male singing in forest*)
Scarlet tanagers are best seen early in the spring before the trees in the forest have leafed out; males sing infrequently once paired and seem to disappear into the canopy. (Photo by Marie Read)

Indigo Bunting (*male on redbud*)
Male indigo buntings lose their showy colours late in summer; they become a drab buff brown and form wintering flocks that move through weedy tropical fields in search of seeds. (Photo by Marie Read)

Bobolink *(male singing)*
Male bobolinks have a comical breeding display, easily seen in open fields where they breed.
(Photo by Marie Read)

Yellow Warbler
(male singing)
The yellow warbler is familiar to many people because its breeding range covers most of North America and its nests are often found in backyards and parks. (Photo by Marie Read)

Rose-breasted Grosbeak
*(male singing in apple tree)
The powerful bill of the rose-
breasted grosbeak is used for
crushing seeds and catching
insects, but this bird is also an
ardent fruit-eater in late summer
and on its tropical wintering
grounds. (Photo by Marie Read)*

Painted Bunting *(male perched)
The painted bunting looks as if
it came from a child's colouring
book; males are often found in
cages at busy markets in Mexico,
where it is a popular choice as a
pet bird. (Photo by Marie Read)*

black-throated blue warblers, hermit thrush, and even scarlet tanagers, yellow-bellied sapsuckers and ruby-throated hummingbirds. I salvage their bodies so I can make taxidermic mounts, beautiful feathered imitations of the real thing that are nearly life-like even though they are stuffed with cotton.

As I carefully dissect a black-throated blue warbler, I find it hard to believe that something so small and fragile could have been living on a Caribbean island only a month before. Its insides are dominated by the large breast muscle, as in a miniature version of a Thanksgiving turkey. The large mass of muscle is the V-16 engine that powers the wings during non-stop migration flights that can last more than ten hours. The leg bones are as slender as toothpicks and snap easily, and the brain is smaller than the fingernail on my pinkie. If this male had not hit the window on campus, within a week's time he would have been giving his buzzy *I'm so la-zyyyyy* song in the northern woods and be nothing of the sort as he courted mates and sparred with neighbouring males.

Although these migrants met a violent end, their bodies will be used for years to come to help their comrades. There is no better way to show children, parents, and students the wonderful diversity of migrants that few of them will ever see in the wild. Children, particularly, are enthralled by the bright colours and patterns, and the silky feel of the feathers.

I took my bird collection to my daughter's Grade 2 class and had the kids sit in a circle on the carpet. One by one I passed the colourful treasures around the room, telling stories about the birds' lives: where they live, what they eat, what they sound like. The favourite, by far, was the hummingbird, because it is so tiny yet has such a long beak; the metallic red shield on the male's throat flashes on and off like a neon light as you turn the bird ever so slightly in your hand. The ruby-throated hummingbird males, though not much bigger than large bumblebees, fly for more than fifteen hours non-stop across the Gulf of Mexico on their trip to Canada. To get ready for the long flight north from their tropical island homes, the black-throated blue warblers eat our equivalent of twenty hamburgers a day and almost double their weight in a few weeks' time. Small hands cradle the birds and gently stroke their smooth feathers as though tender loving care can reverse the birds' fate.

~◡

Birds fly into almost any tall structure that knifes up into the sky. Most songbirds fly at altitudes of two thousand feet or less, a strategy that has worked perfectly well for thousands of years. Once above the treetops, birds enjoy wide open spaces and can barrel along as fast as a car even though their night vision is actually quite poor. Birds can make out the rough outline of the landscape below them as well as the horizon that lies ahead, but rely mostly on their magnetic compass and the stars to guide them. You could do this too, on the ground. Imagine yourself on a football field in the middle of the night, with the lights turned off. If I stood at the far end with a small flashlight pointing skyward, you could easily sprint safely toward me so long as you could roughly make out the ground lit by the dim stars and moon. If we tried this again, after I secretly drove a few dozen metal posts into the ground, it wouldn't be long before you crashed into a post at full speed. It would be even worse if one of the posts had a light on it since you very likely would mistakenly veer toward the post thinking it was my beacon.

Radio and television towers are notorious killers, as are the tall emission stacks of coal-burning plants and factories. All these structures are lit at night so that planes do not crash into them, but this has the opposite effect on birds, which are drawn to the lights, especially during bad weather. In the fall of 1977, one television tower in Elmira, New York, killed at least four thousand migrants, including more than a thousand bay-breasted and magnolia warblers and hundreds of ovenbirds and Swainson's thrush. A couple of years earlier, a tower in Youngstown, Ohio, killed three hundred ovenbirds during one fall migration. Two towers in Nashville, Tennessee, killed more than six hundred ovenbirds and eight hundred Tennessee warblers *in one night*. On clear nights, birds tend to fly at a higher altitude, above many of the towers and structures, and may be able to veer around the towers at the last minute. On foggy or stormy nights, birds fly closer to the ground and are attracted to the tower lights; they may never see what hit them.

We cannot live without our televisions, radios, cellphones, and pagers, and take them for granted without much thought as to how they affect the world around us. Communication towers, some more than two thousand feet high, blanket the migration paths of birds in the United States. Any tower taller than 200 feet must be lit at night, according to Federal Communications Commission regulations, as well as towers that are near airports or highways. A disturbing website, *www.towerkill. com*, shows the location of the towers state by state, and breaks them down by the tower's height; they are practically everywhere. In all, there are more than fifty thousand lit towers in the United States, and another five thousand new towers, if not more, are being added every year. The U.S. Telecommunications Act of 1996 requires television stations to provide high-definition broadcasts, which will mean the construction of hundreds of "mega-towers," each stretching to one thousand feet tall, and each equipped with multiple lights and dozens of guy wires. At this rate, the total number of towers in the United States is likely to double in the next ten years. This is a different kind of obstacle course, made of thousands of sharp needles instead of long blocks of unforgiving concrete.

The U.S. Fish and Wildlife Service conservatively estimates that between four and five million birds are probably killed at communication towers each year, though admits the actual number may be ten times greater. Just as with building collisions, it is difficult to systematically count the victims at towers and arrive at an accurate estimate of total mortality on a continental scale. We do know that almost all neotropical migrant songbirds are at risk from tower collisions; over the years, close to 230 species have been found dead under towers. Several species that are being killed in large numbers are listed as "Extremely High Priority" on the Partners in Flight Watch List, including the Swainson's warbler, cerulean warbler, Bachman's sparrow, and Henslow's sparrow. Their populations are declining fast already, so losing huge numbers at towers certainly adds to the downhill slide. Other species experiencing more modest declines are also found in staggering numbers at towers, and two are on the top ten list for victims of tower kills: Tennessee warbler and blackpoll warbler.

Research done on tower kills has mainly documented the number and types of victims, so naturally the work is done at towers that are already known to be a problem. The dozens of known deadly towers are widespread in the eastern United States, where most of the searches have been done, and include relatively short two-hundred-foot towers all the way up to the massive two-thousand-foot towers. Surprisingly little is known about what features of towers present the most risk to birds flying at night. Careful, large-scale, and systematic comparisons between different kinds of towers are needed. There is some evidence that taller towers are more deadly because they have more lights and are held up by dozens of guy wires that are just as lethal to a bird as the tower itself. Towers that use white strobe lights that flash every two to three seconds seem to be less lethal than towers that use blinking red lights or constant red lights. Sid Gauthreaux used mobile radar to look at bird flight behaviour and found that more birds circled or hovered near red-lighted towers, which ultimately could lead to a greater risk of collision with the tower or guy lines. Studies using radar and nocturnal flight calls are the most promising way of testing how different tower lighting and placement can keep the number of bird kills to a minimum.

Wind turbines are exploding in number too, and look like something out of a bad horror movie, towering three-hundred-foot windmills with giant blades whipping around that we imagine could chop just about anything into tiny pieces. They look intimidating and dangerous and have sparked an outcry from the public and conservation groups because birds are being killed. Since the early 1980s, wind farms have sprung up across the United States, beginning in California, with hundreds and sometimes thousands of turbines at one facility. The United States is currently home to more than fifteen thousand commercial turbines, with thousands more planned or under construction. This green energy produces no greenhouse gases and is a home-grown, renewable energy source. Is this too good to be true?

Early wind farms in California, such as the 73-square-mile Altamount Pass farm that has some seven thousand turbines, sparked the debate when dozens of raptors were found dead under the turbines. Although the collision rate amounted to less than one bird per turbine per year, the huge number of turbines meant that the body count in a single year came to a disturbing 30 golden eagles, 181 red-tailed hawks, and 49 American kestrels. As it turns out, this site was one of the worst places they could have chosen for a turbine farm. Raptors live at unusually high density in this region because of the large small-mammal population. The first-generation turbines had open lattice-like towers that allowed birds to perch and nest on the towers, bringing them close to the deadly spinning blades. The Altamount Pass facility still operates many of these outdated turbines, so high numbers of raptors are still killed each year. Many changes have been made to wind farms to reduce bird collisions. Newer turbines are tubular in design with no perches or nesting sites that might attract raptors, and are spaced farther apart than at the older farms. The turbines' long blades rotate more slowly, less than thirty times per minute, though still fast enough to kill unwary birds.

Millions of songbirds migrate through California twice a year, yet wind farms have documented very low mortality in this group. The Altamount Pass study found 114 dead songbirds; almost all of these were grassland residents breeding in the area. The San Gorgornio Pass farm, with 360 turbines, was searched for over a year but turned up only a handful of songbirds who also were breeding residents. The nighttime flyers apparently made it through pretty much unscathed. Although California wind farms are more dangerous for raptors and apparently have little impact on migrating songbirds, wind farms in other parts of the country appear to be a threat mainly to songbirds. Wind farms in Minnesota, Wyoming, Colorado, Oregon, and Wisconsin find that almost 80 percent of the fatalities are migrating songbirds who hit the turbines at night. This geographic difference reflects the scale of songbird migration, heavier in the Midwest and East, and the lower abundance of raptors at these sites.

Many conservation organizations support wind farms because of the obvious need for clean renewable energy resources to replace fossil fuels as a source of energy. At the same time, conservation groups and naturalists find themselves in bitter fights and lawsuits with the wind-energy industry because they believe not enough care is being taken to assess sites for wind farms, or to manage wind farms to minimize bird deaths. Large wildlife kills can happen at wind farms if they are placed in critical migratory paths. A case in point is the discovery in 2004 of more than two thousand dead bats in just six weeks at two facilities in the mountains of Pennsylvania and West Virginia.

Migration routes can be mapped with radar and topographical features of the landscape. Migrating hawks rely heavily on ridge tops and congregate in predictable places, and migrating songbirds often follow lakeshores and coastlines. Unfortunately, these are also the places where strong, consistent winds are found. Wind farms are being planned for the Great Lakes and offshore on the east coast and Gulf coast. The incredibly high migratory bird traffic, hundreds of thousands of migrants flying near the turbines every day, could result in much higher fatalities than wind farms located inland. A "fall out" day on the Gulf, when migrants head for the nearest terra firma, could lead to spectacular kills of the same magnitude we see at towers and buildings.

Scientific and independent evaluation of sites for wind farms is essential to ensure that the thousands of new turbines that will be erected over the coming decade do not kill millions of birds and other wildlife. If wind farms are monitored closely during operation, then turbines can be turned off at critical locations, or times of year, to minimize their impacts on wildlife. Just as some major cities in the east turn their lights off at night during migration, the turbines could be turned off for a few hours every night to allow safer passage for birds. Even after massive development of new wind turbines, this wind energy is expected to meet only 5 percent of energy needs in the United States over the next few decades. We could achieve a similar boost to our collective energy budget, and reduce fossil-fuel emissions, by using less energy in the first place.

Migration has always been a dangerous affair and migrants have always died by the thousands, falling exhausted into the Gulf of Mexico or being eaten by a Cooper's hawk at a stopover site. Death during migration has increased in recent decades as stopover habitat has been lost and the night sky filled with obstacles. Recent studies on warblers have estimated that about 85 percent of the deaths that happen all year take place during migration or somewhere on the wintering grounds. When more birds die en route, the only way populations can sustain themselves is if breeding success improves dramatically to make up for the shortfall. As we will see in the chapters that follow, migrants are losing out on their breeding grounds too. They are under siege at both ends of their journey.

8 STALKING THE SONGBIRDS
Cowbirds, Cats, and Other Predators

The freshly built spiderwebs light up like jewels in the morning sun, the dew gathered along the long strands that are drooping under the weight of the silvery droplets. I feel a bit guilty when the carefully woven webs collapse by the dozens as I walk toward the woods. I know that I am the first one down the well-worn path this morning; not even a deer or raccoon has beaten me to it. My boots are already soaked from the heavy dew; I might as well be wading in water. Tree swallows in the field are busy arguing over the nest boxes as they circle around noisily scolding each other with harsh chatter, and a lone bluebird whistles his song from the power line overhead. The bright sun is still low in the sky, and the remnants of the morning fog obscure the forest ahead as though I am in a dream. The field ends, and the path dives into the forest like a tunnel through the thick raspberry plants, wild rose, and witch hazel along the edge. In moments I am standing in the forest, and a calm blanket settles over me.

The air is cool and refreshing, and the ground underneath is dry. Streams of sunlight cut through the dark hemlock trees and dance on the forest floor, spotlighting clumps of ferns. Walking into our forest is like an embrace with a close friend; comforting, familiar, and relaxing. The Blackburnian warbler sings his barely audible high-pitched *see-see-seeee,* and his neighbour the black-throated green warbler belts out his bold *zee-zee-zee, zoo-zeee.* The wild grape vines draped from the high branches of the hemlocks are so thick at the base that I cannot close my hand around them; they must be a hundred years old. Nearby, ghosts stand guard as a reminder of past forests. A few giant skeletons of American chestnut trees are still standing in a small cluster, huge stumps that were killed by the Chinese blight decades ago.

Our humble patch of forest in Pennsylvania measures about one mile long and half a mile wide, and I can walk from one end to the other in under an hour. A bird's-eye view of our forest reveals it is actually an island surrounded by fields (figure 8.1). The landscape is made up of forest patches scattered among the distinctive scars of long, rectangular blocks of land stripped clear of trees for raising dairy cows or planting corn, potatoes, cabbage, and other crops. I like to imagine that I am immersed in nature, even though I can still hear dogs barking, cars going by on the road below, and the occasional train whistle. A couple of years ago we started seeing black bears in these woods, a small symbol of wilderness for these parts. Even common sights bring a special peace of mind and a smile to the face: a long-legged and gawky fawn flushed out of its hiding place or a nearby barred owl haunting the forest with its loud, rumbling question, *WHO cooks for YOU, WHO cooks for YOU-all?* The spell is broken when my two-way radio crackles, or if I see one of my students noisily crunching through the woods. I often turn my radio off, much to the chagrin of my husband, who likes to call me when he sees something notable during his own morning travels.

Most of those neighbours whose woods join ours have been seduced

Figure 8.1. *Aerial photo of the landscape surrounding my 150-hectare study site (outlined in white) in Crawford County, Pennsylvania. Forest cover is about 40 percent in this area, and forest patches are bisected by roads and strips of agricultural fields.*

into the quick cash that comes from local logging companies. We get several offers a year; they will even write you a tempting cheque the same day they drop by with a sales pitch, an advance on the value of the lumber way back in the forest where most owners rarely venture. The recently logged areas are a jumble of fallen branches, amputated stumps, and thick, impenetrable tangles that are a stark contrast to the open understory of a mature forest. Although some birds, like indigo buntings, mourning warblers, veeries, catbirds, and rufous-sided towhees, thrive in these hot, sunny tangles, the deep forest birds like Acadian flycatchers have lost their homes.

The great onslaught on the temperate forests of eastern North America happened long ago, from 1750 to 1920, a period when some hundreds of millions of hectares of forest were cut to make way for farms and towns. In the late 1800s, about 170 million hectares of forest were converted into cropland. Michael Williams, professor of geography at Oxford University, writes, "To the American pioneer the beauty of the forest and its destruction was of little consequence. The aesthetics of the scene were subordinate to practical problems of clear-ing—simply, trees and stumps meant toil." Isaac Weld, who travelled among the American pioneers of the late 1700s, thought they had an unconquerable aversion to trees because they cleared the land quickly, wherever they settled. By the early 1900s the "virgin" forest of eastern North America had all but disappeared.

The forests came back with a vengeance during the 1900s as the coun-try matured into a developed and industrial nation. Farmers gave up their marginal lands in the East in favour of the richer lands out west or stopped farming altogether to take jobs in the quickly growing cit-ies. Forested lands had become a scarce resource, so logging companies began a long-term strategy of replanting vast areas that were scheduled for rotating harvest decades later. Fire control became widespread to reduce the loss of valuable timber to fires and also increased the area of regenerated forest. Demand for wood dropped dramatically as fossil fuels became the primary source of energy for transportation, heating, and industry. From 1910 to 1960, about 27 million hectares of cropland were abandoned in the eastern states and allowed to grow back into for-est. This is three times the area of forest that was cut during the same period, so there was a net gain in forest cover for the first time in a few centuries. Since 1960, the rate of conversion of cropland back to forest has accelerated to almost half a million hectares per year.

Although the eastern forests are coming back, most of the hardest-hit regions are still missing more than 60 percent of their original forest. The forest that is standing today is larger in collective area than fifty years ago, but is made up of thousands of small fragments. In central Missouri only 25 percent of the original forest cover stands as forest today; the rest is agricultural lands. In southern Ontario, where the deciduous for-est once stretched from Toronto to Windsor, the forest cover in even the most forested areas covers only about 15 percent of the land. My research site in northern Pennsylvania, just on the other side of Lake Erie from Ontario, has about 40 percent forest cover, which makes it a great place to study birds. Not only is forest cover still low in most places but the forest lives as scattered and wildly shaped jigsaw puzzle pieces set into a background of private and heavily used land. The migrants who pour into these regions to breed often have no choice but to live in these small forest patches.

The questions of whether small forest islands are good enough habitat to sustain forest songbird populations, and just exactly how big a patch should be, have obsessed conservation biologists and wildlife managers for several decades. Migrants get only a few short months to breed, and the population numbers hinge on the number of young birds that hatch out of their eggs and leave their nests to successfully fly south in the fall. The job, then, is to measure nesting success and failure in different types of forest patches.

~~⌒~~

To know whether birds are successfully breeding, you first have to find their nests so you can count their eggs and see how many young live long enough to leave their parents' territory and start lives of their own. It is easy enough to find a songbird's territory because the male's song advertises his ownership. Finding the nest on the territory can be like finding a needle in a haystack. A typical territory is roughly the size of a football field and somewhere hidden among all the shrubs and trees is a small nest built by the female. There are literally thousands of possible places it could be, so you have to think like a bird to guess which one caught the eye of the female.

There is a certain art to searching for a nest. Your eyes become trained to pick out suspicious-looking dark clumps in the vegetation. Most of these clumps will be false alarms, just leaves or twigs that got tangled up in branches as they fell. Visitors are delighted when I point out a wood thrush or red-eyed vireo nest, though at first they cannot see it at all. "See the big maple tree in front of us? Follow the trunk up to the first main branch on the right, follow that branch until it forks, then follow the top fork." After a long pause punctuated by frowns, someone says, "I see it." To me it was plain as day, but to the rookies it is hard to pick out from the seemingly monotonous green leaves and brown tree trunks.

Our brains and senses can be easily trained to develop a search image for objects that are important in our lives. I can't do my research without finding lots of bird nests, but my ten-year-old son is more interested in cars. Douglas has a search image for Porsches and knows all the models; with barely a glance he can casually pick one out from the dozens of cars ahead of us in the traffic and announce "Turbo 911." Even if you have never heard of a search image you have one. We are predisposed to notice the faces and movements of our loved ones and friends, and even in a crowd or grocery store we can effortlessly take in the details that we catch from the corner of our eye; it might be the hair, the glasses, the coat, the walk, or more likely, a subtle combination of all these cues. Familiarity is the key to being an ace nest finder; you have to get to know the small feathered creatures who build and live in these carefully crafted homes.

It is much easier to find a nest by having the bird show you where it is. You have struck gold if you find a female gathering nest material. If you can keep her in sight for several minutes she will fly straight to her nest, which hopefully is not too far away. "Keep your eyes glued on her, and don't use your binoculars," I teach my new field assistants. Binoculars have such a narrow field of view you'll easily lose the female when she makes her move. It takes several days for a bird to build a nest from a thousand different pieces of sticks, strips of grapevine bark, spiderweb-bing, leaves, and fine deer hair to line the inside of the nest. The female is usually in charge of home construction and she makes hundreds of trips to the nest carrying bits of building material. When she is fran-tically at work she does not hide her activities as she hops along tree branches pulling at sticks and bark to get supplies, picking up leaves off the ground, or hovering at spiderwebs collecting the natural glue that helps to hold the nest together.

The nest architecture and building materials vary from species to species so the search methods and personal acrobatics depend very much on whom you are looking for. For scarlet tanagers I spend most of my time looking way up into the high branches of trees and after an hour feel like someone has given me a karate chop to the back of the neck. Tanagers build a large, sticky nest that sits halfway along a sturdy branch far up in the treetops. To find a hooded warbler nest, I look down at the shrubs and spend most of my time bent over at the waist peering into low bushes or squatting on my heels trying to peek up into a low shrub. A hooded warbler builds a loosely woven nest with lots of dead leaves hanging off the bottom and nestles it in the crotch of a shrub or sapling at about knee height. These "needles" come in different shapes and sizes, and can be reliably found in certain parts of the haystack, which makes the job a touch easier.

Another way to find nests is to listen. There is usually a trick to finding the nest of a particular species, a special sound to listen for that can help you zero in on birds who by necessity visit their nest. Blue-headed vireos hang their small basket nest from the V near the tip of small branches and camouflage the outside of their nest by sticking on white spiderweb egg cases and small grey sheets from old bald-faced hornets' nests. Male blue-headed vireos are unusual among our migratory songbirds because they help their mate build the nest and incubate the eggs. The male and female take turns sitting on the four speckled white eggs, and together keep the eggs covered more than 95 percent of the time. The gleaming clutch of eggs stands out sharply from the dark basket of the nest and, if not covered, would attract the attention of a hungry blue jay or crow. The parents stay on hand to hide the eggs and chase away predators that discover the nest. The nest exchange is done quickly but with fine-tuned coordination. As the male approaches the nest he switches from his usual repertoire of songs to his nest song, in which he repeats the same two or three phrases over and over: *chow-dee, chow-dee, chow-dee.* This signals the female that he is approaching, and she will answer with her soft nasal *yank, yank* calls. In a flash the male darts to the nest and the female hops off just before he lands. To find a blue-headed vireo nest, I sit quietly and listen to the male; when he switches to his nest song I move in close to stalk him and listen for the female's quiet *yank.*

There are different nest-finding tricks for different species. A female hooded warbler gives loud metallic *chip* calls while she is nest building, and to find a scarlet tanager nest I listen for the soft, raspy nest song of the male just before he delivers food to his incubating female. A good nest searcher is someone who is happy spending hours becoming part of their surroundings, quietly and patiently looking and listening. The mental radar scans for slight movements of females who are gathering nest material, or parents carrying food for their young, and the ears are wide open to listen for subtle sounds amid a chorus of loud birdsong.

It is easy to forget the nuts and bolts of field studies when digging through the results of forest-fragmentation studies. Somewhere buried in the paper is the subtle mention of the number of nests that form the groundwork for these important statistics; 123 ovenbird nests, 52 red-eyed vireo nests, 230 wood thrush nests. These numbers are the result of many, many long days in the field by teams of field assistants and graduate students, and end up boiled down to a few graphs and tables in a journal article. There is no other way to chronicle the loss of eggs and young and the failed nesting attempts that are part of everyday life for breeding songbirds.

The late-May morning is cold, and a light, silvery frost coats the leaves at the edge of the forest. A female hooded warbler has slept alone in a dense grape vine tangle safely above the ground, but she wakes as soon as the weak light of dawn creeps into the forest. She starts looking for insects even though she can barely see because she is so very hungry. Over the past day and night, deep inside her body, she has made an egg that weighs about 10 percent of her own body weight. She has used her own body's store of energy and nutrients to build her precious cargo, which is loaded with high-protein yolk and a calcium-rich shell. When the sun peeks over the horizon and lights up the tops of the trees, she flies to her empty nest and wriggles into it, settles down and rhythmically pumps her tail. Her mate is far away on the edge of the territory, feeding and

singing. After a long thirty minutes she flies off the nest without looking back, and has left behind a small white egg lightly speckled with
brown. She will begin making her second egg very soon; her ovary is
about to release an ovule that will be fertilized before it drops into her
long, winding oviduct, the egg maker. The egg is built layer by layer
with yolk, egg white, and then the outer shell; it takes a full day. Her
second egg will be ready to add to the nest the next morning, but in the
meantime she will spend all day eating, eating, and eating.

The next morning, while it is still dark, the female hooded warbler
is asleep in her shelter unaware of the danger near her nest on the other
side of the territory. A dark shape flies toward the nest and perches in
a nearby shrub, then sits motionless for several minutes. It flies down
and squats in the nest for about thirty seconds, then just as suddenly
flies off into the dim forest carrying something small in its beak. When
the hooded warbler arrives at her nest half an hour later, she does not
notice that the egg in her nest is much bigger than it was the day before.
The larger egg belongs to the female cowbird who has just stolen the
little warbler's egg to make room for her own. The warbler settles down
to lay her second egg, not knowing that her first now lies broken under
a tree just a short distance away. A couple of days later, after she lays her
fourth and final egg, she sits patiently on the nest to keep the eggs warm
day and night for almost two weeks.

One day the larger egg has a tiny hole in the middle, and the female
warbler can hear tiny knocking sounds from inside. The nestling finally
breaks out of the shell, a whole day before the other eggs hatch. The
female eats the egg shell (nothing goes to waste) and then flies off to find
her newborn some food. An hour later the empty-handed male arrives
at the nest for the first time since it was built. He has noticed his female
taking food to the nest, and quickly confirms there is a mouth to feed, so
he starts making regular deliveries to the nest. The first-hatched chick
is the cowbird, and over the next few days it grows much faster than the
other, smaller chicks in the nest. The warbler parents come and go at a
frantic pace, but the large chick seems insatiable and keeps begging with

its loud, ungainly call for more food. The female warbler and mate are programmed to feed the hungry mouths in the nest, and do not even notice that the cowbird nestling looks totally unlike the other nestlings. The lion's share of the food goes to the large, gawky cowbird nestling, and by the fifth day two of the little warbler nestlings lie dead in the nest from starvation. The parents remove the dead nestlings without a thought and go back to finding caterpillars. The hard-working parents end up with two offspring for all their efforts, one a cowbird and one their own.

Cowbirds are viewed by songbird lovers as public enemy number one and are often blamed for the songbird decline because they have such a huge impact on the nesting success of their unwitting hosts. Cowbirds are also vilified because we do not admire the sneaky tactics of the female. She never builds a nest or takes care of her own eggs and young. Instead she sneaks up to a songbird nest then dumps her egg and steals one of the victim's eggs in the equivalent of an avian drive-by shooting. Hosts are victims of a carefully planned attack; a female cowbird finds the nest while it is being built, visits the nest regularly so she knows when to add her own eggs, and may even come back to the nest during the daytime to remove a host egg. Over the next month, the victims use up vast amounts of time and energy caring for the foreign youngster and lose many of their own offspring in the bargain. Cowbirds are serial killers who attack dozens of host species; a single female can lay more than twenty eggs in one breeding season. Many hosts produce only one batch of kids per summer, meaning they have no second chance to make up for the lost reproduction that comes with caring for a cowbird chick. Clearly this is a bad deal for songbirds, and more cowbirds will mean many more victims and lower nesting success.

Cowbirds are unwelcome visitors to eastern North America and to the far southwest. They were once restricted to the open grasslands of the Great Plains in the centre of the continent, where they followed bison herds, hence the name "cow" bird. When the eastern forests were cut down, the cowbirds moved east into the newly opened landscape that had once been a vast, inhospitable forest. For more than a hundred years, cowbirds have been attacking species like hooded warblers, scarlet tanagers, and Acadian flycatchers that had rarely, if ever, seen cowbirds before. Cowbirds have invaded all but the largest of forest tracts and parasitize more than a hundred species of hosts. In the late 1800s, cowbirds also expanded their range into the southwestern states and are also moving into the northern forests of Canada and Alaska. Conversion of the forest into agricultural landscapes not only gave cowbirds access to new hosts, it also increased the amount of food available for cowbirds, which love seeds and commute out of the forest each day to gorge on plentiful supplies of grain in the fields.

The combination of abundant naive victims, open lands, and a ready food supply allowed cowbirds to thrive in areas far outside their historical range. They have become so plentiful in fragmented landscapes that a single host nest often contains not just one but sometimes three or four cowbird eggs. These hosts are especially vulnerable to cowbirds because there has been no long history of evolutionary attack and defence that would endow the hosts with built-in defences to recognize the foreign eggs and dodge the bullet by abandoning their nest or tossing out the foreign egg.

Cowbird nestlings are well adapted for their lives as con artists. They hatch earlier than their nest mates, grow faster, and are loudmouths. The parents robotically feed the hungriest nestlings first, a system that worked perfectly well before the cowbird invasion. The cowbird is big and reaches up high out of the nest with incessant loud begging calls that dupe the parents into giving it most of the food. Not surprisingly, the nesting success of hosts is much lower when a cowbird has attacked. Not only do they lose an egg or two to the female cowbird but their own small young have to compete with the bully on the block. Ovenbirds who have been tricked into raising a cowbird produce half the number of their own young, while red-eyed vireos and wood thrush lose close to a quarter of their young. When two more cowbirds eggs hatch in the nest, even the most energetic parents may not be able to raise any of their own offspring. Some hosts, like blue-headed vireos, rarely manage to raise any of their own young if there is even a single cowbird chick in the nest.

To get a feel for how forest clearing has changed the lives of songbirds, we can compare the success of birds that breed in expansive forests, a taste of what life was like several hundred years ago, with that of those who are living in forest fragments. A mammoth study by Scott Robinson, a biologist with the Illinois Natural History Survey, Therese Donovan, a biologist with the U.S. Geological Survey and the University of Vermont, and many colleagues looked at the nesting success of forest birds in the midwestern states. More than five thousand nests in Illinois, Missouri, Wisconsin, and Indiana were found over several years of field work. Songbirds nesting in large continuous forests were rarely parasitized, but the same species were five to thirty times more likely to have a cowbird egg in their nest if they lived in a forest fragment. You would have to look in almost a hundred wood thrush nests in these continuous forests to see even a single cowbird egg, but if you were in forest fragments a remarkable seven out of every ten nests would contain one or more cowbird eggs. Red-eyed vireos, wood thrush, and ovenbird nests held two or three cowbird eggs *each*. This study may show us the worst-case scenario for songbirds because forest loss in the Midwest has been so severe and the extensive agricultural landscape is heaven for cowbirds. But even in forests farther to the east, cowbirds are common and often parasitize close to a quarter of songbird nests.

Cowbirds are such a scourge in forests and their tactics so underhanded that most wildlife lovers root for the songbirds and would be happy to be rid of cowbirds altogether. Many groups energetically advocate widespread culling of these birds in an effort to give songbirds a chance against this sneaky enemy. Cowbird control certainly has been critical for saving a number of endangered songbird species who live in specialized habitat and have small breeding ranges. Here, the songbird populations have been driven down first and foremost by habitat loss, and the cowbirds are delivering the knockout punch.

The least Bell's vireo is a dull-looking grey bird that specializes on riverside habitat of willow, cottonwood, and alder and historically ranged throughout south and central California. Even the song is not much to write home about, described as loud and unmusical, with an overall jerky, sputtering quality. Urbanization, agricultural development, heavy grazing by cattle, and mining have eliminated these vireos from the Central Valley, and they are now hanging on by a thread in the southwestern corner of California. With 95 percent of their original habitat destroyed, it is no wonder they are an endangered species. Cowbirds invaded this region in the early 1900s, and with the forested habitat so fragmented could easily find and parasitize the vireo nests. Vireos are among the hardest hit of any cowbird host because they can rarely raise their own young if there is a cowbird in the nest. In the early 1980s a large-scale cowbird control program began as a last-ditch effort to save the least Bell's vireo from sure extinction. A few birds nested each year at Camp Pendleton, a large military reserve south of Los Angeles. Cowbirds were trapped in the spring using dozens of large drop-in traps, cages with a V-shaped roof. The cowbirds' natural flocking tendency is their downfall; birds flying nearby hear and see live decoy birds in the cage and drop down into the trap to join the flock. About two thousand female cowbirds are killed annually in thirty to forty traps throughout Camp Pendleton, which has reduced cowbird parasitism from 50 percent of nests to less than 1 percent of nests (figure 8.2). This control measure allowed a spectacular recovery of the vireo population, which quickly climbed to more than five hundred breeding pairs.

This amazing recovery of an endangered species might lure us into thinking that cowbirds are solely to blame for songbird declines. The example of the Kirtland's warbler is a good lesson that cowbird control by itself does not necessarily lead to a species' recovery. The Kirtland's warbler has a small breeding range that has always been restricted to a narrow strip across the lower peninsula of northern Michigan; this little bird is named for Jared Kirtland, a physician in Cleveland who found one dead after it flew into a building. It took decades before anyone

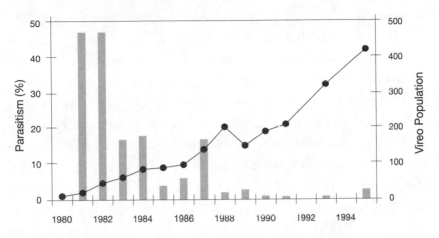

Figure 8.2. *The recovery of the least Bell's vireo (see line) in southwestern California due to control measures that virtually eliminated cowbird parasitism (dark bars). (Based on Griffith and Griffith, 2000)*

knew where it bred, and several more decades to discover its wintering grounds on the Bahama islands. This warbler is highly specialized on a particular breeding habitat; it breeds only in Jack pine forest that is in the early stages of regeneration after a forest fire, where the trees are shorter than sixteen feet. The warblers nest on the ground under the branches of the small trees, so once the trees grow tall the birds lose the natural cover that conceals their nests. They also prefer pine forests that are on dry sandy soil because this allows heavy rains to quickly drain away so nests are not flooded. Jack pine is adapted to grow in regions with fires, and its cones open and release their seeds only after being scorched by fire. Increasing human populations and suppression of forest fires have put a stop to the natural cycle that provided a steady supply of the recently burned forest that is habitat for the warbler. By the early 1970s the entire species had shrunk to a paltry two hundred singing males; desperate action was needed.

At first the cowbird was blamed for the small numbers of warblers. About 70 percent of the Kirtland's nests were being parasitized by cowbirds when the very first large-scale cowbird control began in the 1970s. Soon, traps were spread over three counties to trap female cowbirds, and almost two thousand females were killed each year. The control efforts initially seemed like a great success, because parasitism dropped to only 6 percent of nests, and reproductive success jumped from one to more than three young per pair each summer. Clearly, cowbirds were suppressing the reproductive efforts of this endangered species. Problem solved? Not quite. Unlike the least Bell's vireos, the Kirtland's warbler population did not rebound, because its specialized habitat was still in short supply. The young had no place to breed. After ten years of intensive cowbird control with no increase in the warbler population, focus shifted to habitat management. Fires were set deliberately to create stands of Jack pine that in ten years would be perfect for Kirtland's warblers. Bingo! The population increased sharply in the 1990s with the combination of habitat creation and cowbird control. By 2005 more than thirteen hundred Kirtland's warbler males were defending territories, an increase of over 600 percent since the early 1970s. Today, huge areas are actively managed by careful logging, burning, seeding, and replanting to ensure that at any one time some fifteen thousand hectares of nesting habitat are available to the bird. Humans are working hard and spending large amounts of money to do what nature once did by itself with no help at all.

Most songbirds are likely more threatened by habitat loss than by cowbirds. The Breeding Bird Survey has shown that even though cowbird numbers have gone down in the East since the 1960s, the songbird host populations have continued to decline. Cowbirds depend on open fields and agriculture, and this cowbird-friendly habitat has declined as the amount of forest has increased steadily as farms are abandoned. It is true that cowbird parasitism can be very high in forest fragments, but songbirds face an even bigger problem: predators who wipe out their entire nests.

~~

During early spring, our forests are full of delicious eggs. A given hectare of forest contains, at any one time, dozens of nests of various songbird species all filled with eggs. These eggs, and any birds lucky enough to hatch from them, are highly sought-after food for a whole suite of predators, including snakes, small mammals, deer, and even other birds. A female who has just finished laying her valuable eggs has only a fifty-fifty chance that her nest will not be noticed by a predator before her young are ready to leave the nest. Songbirds are accustomed to losing their nests, and the victims simply try again, and again, until they run out of time and have to start packing on weight for their migration journey.

Songbirds have a number of tricks up their sleeve for deceiving predators or, the more direct approach, driving them away altogether. The female hooded warbler sits tight on her nest even when you get within a couple of paces from the nest; she freezes and looks right at you, pretending she is invisible. If the predator has not yet spotted the nest, it might very well walk on by. If you get very close, within inches, she will leap off the nest and run along the ground away from the nest, dragging her wing pathetically along the ground. She is trying to distract the predator's attention away from her nest with her broken-wing act—injured prey are easy targets. When she gets safely away from the nest she flies up into a tree and switches to her aggressive *chip* calls, the equivalent of barking at the predator to go away.

Blue-headed vireos are small but feisty and do not hesitate to attack predators much larger than themselves. To find out if males help to defend the eggs in the nest, I set up blue jay decoys near blue-headed vireo nests. Although males and females are usually preoccupied with their domestic duties of incubating, they turn into kamikaze attack pilots when a predator is near the nest. The male and female coordinate their attack by perching in the branches above and on each side of the blue jay. At the same instant they dive down and in a one-two punch each hit the blue jay model as they pass by each other in opposite directions screaming their low, raspy growl of *cher, cher, cher.* They perch, turn around, pause, and do another simultaneous attack. Pairs can keep this up for twenty minutes or more, a relentless attack that in real life must succeed in discouraging some predators from finding the nest.

The predators that eat birds' eggs do not necessarily find nests the same way that we do. Humans, for instance, do not sniff out nests with their noses as a squirrel might. We rely on our eyes and sometimes our ears to locate nests. I would fire any field assistant who was silly enough to go out at night to look for warbler or vireo nests, yet many important nest predators, like skunks, opossums, and raccoons hunt at night. Some predators, like chipmunks, seem to randomly search for nests by climbing stems and running along branches. I've seen them walk right under a warbler nest and not even notice it. Songbirds are faced with so many different kinds of predators who find nests in so many different ways that it is no wonder that only half the nests ever produce young.

Although normal background levels of nest predation seem high to us, forest fragmentation increases nest predation. In his classic study, Dave Wilcove, a Ph.D. student at Princeton University, used fake nests to measure predation. He put out quail eggs in straw-coloured wicker basket nests in the continuous forest of the Great Smoky Mountains National Park, which straddles the border of Tennessee and North Carolina, and compared nest predation with small forest patches in Maryland. Only two out of every hundred fake nests in the Great Smokies were disturbed by predators, compared with a stunning 70 percent for suburban woodlots and 50 percent for rural woodlots. Predators identified by the tracks left behind on coated cardboard squares near the nest included dogs, cats, raccoons, opossums, skunks, and blue jays. Artificial nest experiments do not give the entire picture because the wicker baskets do not look like real bird's nests and there are no parents coming and going to tip off predators. Still, these studies were the first to suggest that nest predation is higher in fragments. Later studies in the midwestern United States did use real nests, thousands of them, and found that nest predation was high (60 percent) in large continuous forest but even higher (70 to 80 percent) in small forest fragments.

The combination of high cowbird parasitism and high nest predation means that overall nesting success is often terrible in forest fragments.

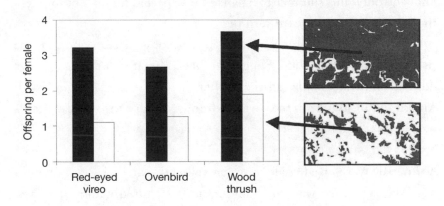

Figure 8.3. *Reproductive success of females nesting in continuous forest (dark bars) and fragments (open bars) in the midwestern United States. Landscapes to the right show the extent of forest cover (shaded area) for a 6-mile-wide snapshot of the intact versus the fragmented forest landscapes. (Based on Donovan et al., 2005)*

The large study in the Midwest found that females produce many fewer nestlings each summer if they are unlucky enough to be living in a forest fragment (figure 8.3). One yardstick for measuring whether a habitat is good enough to sustain a population is to consider whether a breeding female will be able to replace herself in her lifetime. The size of a population is a balance between the new birds that are added by breeding and the adults that are lost from the population when they die. If a fully grown daughter is added to the population to offset each death of a breeding female, then the population will remain steady. For birds breeding in the forest fragments of Illinois, breeding females do not produce nearly enough young to replace themselves. In the worst fragments, females would have to make more than ten nesting attempts per summer to produce a single daughter to replace her if she dies. In reality, females are lucky to make even four nesting attempts before they run out of time to breed and have to pack their bags and head south. In eastern Ontario, near Ottawa, forest cover is only 13 percent in some areas, and the remaining forest is highly fragmented. Ovenbird, rose-breasted grosbeak, wood thrush, veery, and red-eyed vireo females cannot produce enough young in a summer to balance the expected number of mothers that will die before the next summer.

Adults living in fragments have poor nesting success, and may be risking their own lives too. Songbirds face a threat that their ancestors did not: an abundant and efficient killer that has stalked prey in North American forests only in the past few hundred years: the domestic cat.

~~~

A tiny, pale warbler, a female common yellowthroat, had been caught in mid-May while she was nest building and was fitted with a tiny back-pack that held a radiotransmitter. Over the next week researchers fol-lowed her movements for a few hours every day as she finished her nest, laid eggs, and began incubating her clutch of four eggs. One day, she was gone and her eggs were stone cold.

Scott Tarof, a postdoctoral researcher at the University of Wisconsin, went out that afternoon to help a graduate student find out what had happened to their female. The bird's radio signal was coming from the pasture across the road from the study site. The two walked into the pasture thinking they would find the radio tag lying on the ground, but were puzzled when the signal suddenly started coming from the far edge of the pasture. As they walked in that direction, the signal moved again; this time it was several hundred yards away in the opposite direc-tion. There was no common yellowthroat to be seen or heard, so they thought they were going crazy or maybe the equipment was not work-ing properly.

After a few hours of frustrating false leads looking for the radio tag in the hot sun, they finally got a steady signal from a clump of grass in the corner of the pasture. They zeroed in on the signal only to find a chewed-up transmitter in a pile of cat poop. The female warbler had been eaten by someone's cat, and Tarof had unknowingly been following the cat that still had the bird, and its radio tag, inside it.

Cats that are allowed outdoors are a huge problem for birds nest-ing in suburban and rural agricultural areas. Surveys of homeowners in southeastern Michigan found that each home had about two to four cats that went outside for at least part of the day. Cats eat adult birds that nest near the ground, like common yellowthroats, and also birds that land on the ground to gather nesting material or look for food. Nestling and juvenile songbirds that cannot fly well are easy prey for roaming cats and often show up on people's doorsteps.

To estimate the numbers of birds killed, homeowners in Michigan were asked to count up the dead animals their cats brought home. On average, each cat killed about one bird a week, and though this may not sound like much, the damage adds up because there are so many free-ranging cats hunting near homes and farms. The six hundred cats in this study would have killed more than six thousand birds during a typical ten-week breeding season alone. A similar study in Wichita, Kansas, asked homeowners to bag the contents of the litter box so researchers could later search through the feces looking for feathers. They found bird remains in about 10 percent of the samples, even though the homeowners had not reported seeing their cat bring back a bird in recent days. This suggests that kitty is not as innocent as owners think and that surveys of cat predation underestimate the true scale of the problem. When the Wichita study ended, the homeowners were asked if, given the results of the study, they would now keep their cats indoors; 73 percent said no.

Cats are only doing what comes naturally, but their predation on birds is not a natural part of the ecosystem. Domestic cats were introduced to North America when the Europeans arrived and only became popular in the late 1800s. The number of cats living in the Unites States alone has doubled since the 1960s, and now stands at well over 75 million. Unlike natural predator populations, which decline when their own numbers get too high or their prey declines, pet cats are housed, fed, and given vaccinations against disease. Even well-fed cats kill birds, and declawing cats or putting bells on the collar does not stop them from catching birds. Also, for every loved and cared-for pet cat, there is at least one homeless feral cat that also roams our meadows and woods.

The spotlight on bird predation by cats was sparked by a study in Wisconsin during the early 1990s that estimated that free-ranging cats in rural areas killed anywhere from 8 million to 217 million birds a year in that state alone. In some parts of the state, there are close to one hundred free-ranging cats per square mile, a density that far exceeds any native mammalian predator.

Owners want their cats to have a good life, and for many owners this means giving their cat plenty of outdoor time. Ironically, pet cats that are kept indoors may be better off because they are less likely to contract deadly diseases from free-roaming and feral cats, and of course will not get lost or hit by cars. Outdoor cats live an average of only three years compared with fifteen years or more for indoor cats. The American Bird Conservancy, a non-profit advocacy group for bird conservation, began a "Cats Indoors!" campaign in 1997 to promote a win-win solution for cat owners and birds. The Humane Society of the United States has a similar "Safe Cats" program and gives tips on how to help cats (and the owner) adjust to life on the inside. Cats are not to blame for the songbird decline, but keeping cats indoors will mean that birds nesting in wood-lots near farms and homes will have a better chance of staying alive and producing a healthy number of offspring.

Fragments are called population sinks because they drain the population size of migratory birds. Imagine a sink half full of water. From the faucet comes the new water that is added each summer via breeding, and the drain is where the water disappears forever as a result of adult mortality that can happen any time of year. The amount of water in the sink depends on the balance between the amount of water coming in through the faucet and the amount going down the drain (figure 8.4). If you turn the faucet on full blast and there is a very small drain hole, the water level will quickly rise. If there is a big drain hole and you turn the faucet down to a trickle, before long the sink will be empty. Fragments are sinks because the trickle of water that is left after cow-

"Sink" Population   "Source" Population

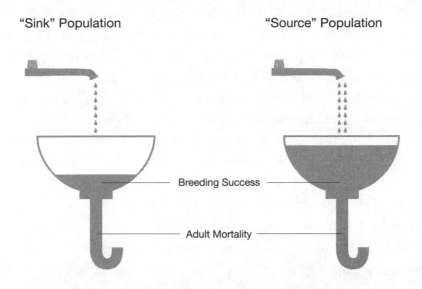

Breeding Success

Adult Mortality

Figure 8.4. *Population size can be envisioned as the water level in a basin, with births as the water coming in from the faucet and deaths as water going down the drain. Migratory bird populations are more like a bathtub with many faucets and many drains, which represent the different habitat patches where birds breed.*

bird parasitism and high nest predation does not keep pace with the death of adults.

Large continuous forests are usually "source" populations because nesting success is quite high, so more birds are being added to the population through births than are going out through deaths. An example of a source population is the Great Smoky Mountains National Park, which is the largest national park in the eastern United States. It is heaven from a wood thrush's point of view—more than 200,000 hectares of continuous forest. An estimated ten thousand nesting pairs of wood thrush live in this forest, and each pair produces almost three nestlings during the summer. Nest success is high because cowbirds are rare; nest predation was higher than expected though still an improvement over small fragments. This national park produces a surplus of almost three thousand females each year, over and above the number of daughters required to replace the local breeding females who have died.

If birds were stuck on their small forest fragment, eventually the local population would go extinct for lack of new birds being added to the population. Bird populations do not disappear from fragments entirely, because the sink is refilled each spring with new recruits that come from outside the fragment, from the sources. This is like dumping a bucket of water into a sink just before all the water goes down the drain. The recruits are the surplus young that were born the summer before in large forests. Fragments are refilled even in regions like Illinois, where there is little forest cover, because young songbirds returning from their wintering grounds usually end up far from their birthplace.

It is hard to know exactly how far away from home a young bird moves, because the odds of finding a banded bird hundreds of miles away are so slim. Once in a while someone will catch a breeding bird that is already banded and find out that it was banded as a nestling somewhere far away. For instance, the Beaverhill Bird Observatory in central Alberta banded a juvenile tree swallow that ended up breeding the next summer nine hundred miles away, in Long Lake, Minnesota. Such reports are scarce but they tell us that fragments can be refilled from very distant source populations. Although we rarely know where juveniles end up, we do know that few come back to breed in the same place they were born. At my study site in Pennsylvania, I banded more than a hundred hooded warbler nestlings each year, but the next summer only one or two came back to breed there. Most of the empty territories are filled with birds that have no bands on their legs, meaning they must have come from somewhere off my study site.

The extensive mixing of young birds that were born in different places means that a migratory bird population is more like a giant bathtub with many thousands of different faucets and drains. When large forests are converted into tiny forest patches, the many faucets that once flowed strongly are reduced to mere trickles. As forests are cut altogether and lost as breeding habitat, many of the faucets are turned off. With less water coming into the tub, the water level will drop. When populations are viewed as the sum of their parts, it becomes more obvious that source populations are crucial for sustaining a healthy population size. At the same time, protecting only a handful of large forests, like the Great Smoky Mountains, may not be enough to stop the birds from slowly going down the drain.

～

Most studies of habitat fragmentation in North America have focused on the eastern forests of southern Canada and the United States. The European immigration wave, and their axes, started in the east and swept across the continent. Early colonists did not have a choice between the hard work of clearing towering trees for a small homestead in Massachussetts and the much easier job of plowing up rich prairie grasses. The eastern forests were cut first, and more extensively than anywhere else up to that point. This focus on the east leaves out dozens of species of migratory birds that breed in the western forests of the United States and the gigantic boreal forest of Canada. These types of forest are very different from the eastern forest in how they are used by people, the types of predators that live there, and the extent to which forests end up as isolated islands.

Western forests are distinctly different from the moist, extensive forests of the east. The climate is drier and the birds and trees have co-evolved in a system of widespread and frequent forest fires that have long made the forest patchy and uneven in age. The impressive topography adds another layer of diversity, and birds are presumably well accustomed to coping with patchy environments compared with their counterparts in the east. The western forests of the United States also have a very different pattern of fragmentation and land use. The amount of forest cover is high in many parts of the west, where logging, rather than agriculture, is the main pressure on the forest. Cleared areas are embedded within extensive forest, the opposite of eastern forests, where forest islands are embedded in open landscapes. After logging, the cleared areas regenerate into young forest, so the matrix surrounding older mature forests is not open land with intense human activity, like we see in the east.

In western forests, small fragments are not necessarily sinks. Tom Martin, a biologist with the U.S.G.S. Montana Cooperative Wildlife Research Unit in Missoula, found that birds in western forest fragments were not more likely to find cowbird eggs in their nests. The threat from cowbirds depends on the amount of agricultural land nearby, which cowbirds depend on for food. Forest patches surrounded by regenerating clear-cuts may not be enticing to cowbirds, and thus birds in those fragments are relatively unaffected by parasitism.

The results for nest predation were even more surprising. In the western forests, birds in large forest patches suffered *higher* nest predation than birds in fragments, the reverse of what is usually found in eastern forests. The nest predators in the West are made up of a different set of animals, who respond differently to fragmentation and land use changes than predators in the east. Studies in Montana and Alberta also found more nest predation in larger forests, and suggested that small mammals, like red squirrels, were to blame. Red squirrels avoid small forests, so birds nesting in small fragments enjoy a relatively safe summer. The opposite is true in the eastern forests where many of the key nest predators, such as crows, blue jays, skunks, and raccoons, are more abundant in agricultural settings and small forest patches.

Even less is known about the effects of forest loss in the biggest migratory bird nursery in the world, the boreal forest of North America. This forest stretches across the entire northern half of the continent, from Newfoundland all the way to Alaska, and is one of the world's biggest ecosystems that is still intact. It covers almost a third of the entire continent and is home to one quarter of the world's remaining forest. This enormous area is home to billions of neotropical migrants, including such species as palm warblers, Tennessee warblers, Cape May warblers, bay-breasted warblers, blackpoll warblers, yellow-bellied flycatchers, and Philadelphia vireos.

The boreal forest is a patchwork of different forest types and ages that are interspersed with peatlands and lakes; this unique habitat has been shaped for thousands of years by the cold, dry climate and by frequent fires and insect outbreaks. Commercial logging removes the forest, of course, and causes widespread and long-term changes to the forest structure and age. Old stands of Jack pine and spruce are replaced with huge areas of regenerating scrubby forest. An experiment that deliberately created forest islands in northern Alberta found that the numbers of neotropical migrants declined in small forest patches, but the effect was not as strong as one would find in an eastern deciduous forest because boreal birds are predisposed to cope with habitat change. Logging may result in huge population sinks for forest birds not through the creation of forest islands but rather by large-scale removal of older stands, which forces birds to move elsewhere or attempt to breed in younger successional forests. Birds that prefer open scrubby habitat, like common yellowthroats and alder flycatchers, colonize recently logged sites. The losers are the forest specialists, who decrease dramatically in numbers after logging, among them the bay-breasted warbler, Canada warbler, Cape May warbler, and black-throated green warbler.

The boreal forest, as vast as it is, is under siege from commercial logging, mineral extraction, and oil and gas development. It has earned its unfortunate claim to being the biggest toilet paper, facial tissue, and magazine factory in the world, as it is being logged at a rate of several hectares a minute to fuel the demand for paper products in the U.S. markets to the south. The United States buys about 80 percent of Canada's timber exports, and almost 50 percent of U.S. newsprint comes from the boreal forest. Oil and gas exploration and hydroelectric projects threaten areas bigger than most states. The fast-paced and unsustainable resource extraction is gobbling up the forest. Scott Weidensaul, acclaimed naturalist and author, thinks there is hope. "Because this region is so huge, though, we have a chance to get it right this time—to upend the typical approach to conservation. Instead of protecting a few patches of natural habitat, we have the opportunity to save immense, functioning ecosystems as the matrix, with islands of carefully managed development in between."

Many groups are working to make this vision a reality. The Boreal Forest Conservation Framework has brought major conservation groups like the World Wildlife Fund, the Nature Conservancy, and Nature Canada together with key industrial paper and energy companies, along with a variety of nature and birding organizations, coffee companies, and outdoors stores. Their common goal is to protect 50 percent of Canada's boreal forest region—in other words, to forever save one million square miles of this forest. The remainder of the forest would be harvested using ecologically sensitive and sustainable forestry practices. The international standard for sustainable logging is set by the independent Forest Stewardship Council. The FSC, founded in 1996, certifies both the logging practices and the sourcing of wood and paper products that consumers buy off the shelf. The area of boreal forest being logged to FSC standards in Canada has risen dramatically in recent years to 17 million hectares by 2006, in part because major consumers like Home Depot and Ikea now buy FSC wood products. In turn, forest industry giants like Tembec plan to bring their enormous commercial logging operations, which cover some 16 million hectares, under FSC standards.

Forest Ethics, an environmental advocacy group, took Victoria's Secret to task in 2004 for mailing out more than a million glossy catalogues every day. Much of the paper comes from trees cut in the boreal forest, enough to make 100 million catalogues each year. Full page ads in the *New York Times* and hundreds of protests were used to pressure the lingerie company to stop using paper from the boreal forest, to use FSC-certified products, and to increase the amount of recycled paper in its catalogues. The aggressive public campaign ended successfully in December 2006 when Limited Brands, parent company of Victoria's Secret, unveiled a new forest-protection policy. Other catalogue distributors will be expected to live up to these new standards. (In 2004, some 18 billion catalogues were mailed to U.S. consumers by such companies as Sears, J. Crew, and L.L. Bean.)

Another group, the Boreal Forest Network, is made up of major U.S. conservation organizations working to raise the awareness of the boreal forest among U.S. consumers who are ultimately fuelling its destruction. We have already encountered bird-friendly coffee and bird-friendly vegetables, so why not bird-friendly toilet paper? The Natural Resources Defense Council, one of the members of the network, provides consumers with a simple shopper's guide to bird-friendly disposable paper products like toilet paper, paper towels, facial tissues, and napkins (*www. nrdc.org/paper*). Many of the most popular brands, like Kleenex, Puffs, Charmin, Cottonelle, Bounty, and Scott, use no recycled paper in their products and also bleach their paper with chlorine, which can contribute to water pollution.

Consumers can help the northern forests and their birds by becoming environmental shoppers. The boreal forest is too valuable to our world's environment to cut it down for catalogues and toilet paper.

~~~

Forest nesting birds have received the most attention by researchers and others trying to figure out what is driving songbird populations down. The decline of grassland birds has been just as precipitous, if not more so, yet this group has been overlooked until recently. Birds in trouble include the Baird's sparrow, a species restricted to the Midwest, as well as species that breed in grasslands across the United States and southern Canada, such as the eastern meadowlark, bobolink, and horned lark. Grasslands are one of the most endangered ecosystems in North America because they can be converted so easily into productive farmland; more than 90 percent of tallgrass prairie has been lost. Native grasslands were maintained by grazing mammals like bison and frequent fires, and so grassland songbirds are adapted to a mosaic of habitat types, with some species preferring short, sparse vegetation while others zero in on taller, denser vegetation. Now that the native grasslands are largely gone, our birds are making do on agricultural lands, where the habitat is severely altered through heavy grazing by cattle and mowing. Hayfields that are mowed in May or June, before young birds are independent, wipe out the nests of grassland birds.

Fragmentation of grasslands is a serious threat to many songbirds. A large-scale study of native grassland fragments, in the 1990s, focused on four species of common grassland birds: grasshopper sparrow, Henslow's sparrow, eastern meadowlark, and dickcissel. More than three thousand nests were monitored in thirty-nine grassland fragments ranging in size from a measly 24 hectares to huge preserves larger than 40,000 hectares. Nest predation was much higher in the small fragments, where four out of every five nests were destroyed. Cowbird parasitism was not higher in small grassland patches, probably because cowbirds are abundant everywhere in this open landscape. Small grassland fragments appear to be population sinks much like the small forest patches of the East, and in both cases cut short the reproductive efforts of songbirds.

Loss of bird habitat on the breeding grounds does not kill birds outright, like pesticides, cats, buildings, and towers, but is just as dangerous for the future of birds. Individual warblers, thrushes, and bobolinks may survive perfectly well during the summer months when life is easy, even in a small patch of habitat, but many will not produce enough offspring to balance the deaths that will come that fall, winter, and spring. The high mortality on the wintering grounds and during migration outstrips the birds' breeding efforts, so the population as a whole slowly loses ground. The loss of millions of songbirds each year from North America will have a strong and accelerating ripple effect on the ecosystem. The ecological roles that neotropical migrants play are familiar by now: they eat insects and move seeds. The details differ from how these same species affect tropical environments because insects and trees in the north are peculiarly adapted to the harsh change in seasons that comes with winter.

Most northern plants wait until late summer and early fall before they produce their fruit. This timing is no accident; the seeds are dispersed by birds and trees have to wait until their customers are ready to order fruit from the menu. Early in the spring, when the migrants arrive, there are so many protein-rich insects available that few birds would look twice at a fruiting tree. Plants cannot compete with insects when it comes to providing a healthy meal; even the most nutritious fruits pale in comparison to a juicy caterpillar. Later in the summer, fruit becomes an important food for migrants because insect larvae diminish in numbers and the birds have hungry young to feed and have to overeat to get ready for migration. Many migrants opt for fast food, and from the plant's point of view this is the best time to make fruit. There are twice as many mouths to feed in late summer, after the birds have bred, and the many migrants who are on the move make an abundant and efficient dispersal system for plants.

Red elderberry is among the earliest-fruiting woody plants in the northeastern United States, and its hundreds of tiny red fruits are eaten by forest birds in late June and early July. In our forest in Pennsylvania, the fruit is eaten almost entirely by neotropical migrants, particularly scarlet tanagers, rose-breasted grosbeaks, and veery. Other customers include thrush, cardinals, catbirds, vireos, towhees, and woodpeckers. Later in July, the deep red berries of the chokecherry beside our house are devoured by eastern kingbirds, and cedar waxwings are frequent visitors to the branches of the black cherry tree at the edge of the forest that droops under the weight of tens of thousands of fruits. Even on crisp mornings in early fall, I see flocks of migrating robins moving through the forest by the hundreds, swarming around the native grape vines that hang high in the hemlock trees. Fruit fuels the migration of many birds, and plants in turn have clever adaptations for attracting birds. Most bird-dispersed fruits are bright red, but the sassafras, devil's walking stick, alternate-leaved dogwood, and pokeberry all have black fruits and instead attract birds with bright red stalks that hold up the fruit. This colourful flag, the "open" sign, keeps flashing long after the bulk of the fruit has been eaten, keeping the customers coming through the door to eat the remaining fruits. Virginia creeper goes one step further; the leaves of this vine turn bright red long before the leaves of the tree that hold up the vine, so that birds can find its fruit, which would otherwise be hidden from view.

The importance of birds in moving seeds is clearly seen where open land has been abandoned. George Robinson and Steven Handel, of the Department of Biological Sciences at Rutgers University in New Jersey, worked to reclaim an old landfill on Staten Island, New York, by planting native tree species. Although the saplings survived, they did not grow well and did not produce their own seeds. Instead, the real gains in plant growth and biodiversity came for free, with the rain of seeds from birds and other animals. Although workers had planted eighteen species of saplings from a nursery, birds brought in about twenty new species through natural seed dispersal. The nursery saplings, though not so useful in terms of their own growth, provided perch sites for birds, where, obligingly, they would defecate. The rapid and extensive regrowth of the eastern forests in the past decades has been financed by migratory songbirds.

Deciduous trees in the north cannot afford the energetic and chemical price of loading their leaves with toxins, as many tropical plants do, because the expensive leaves are going to fall to the ground anyway in the fall. It is cheaper to have harmless leaves and suffer the insect damage, then start fresh each spring. Insects have a heyday on the new growth and are well adapted to take advantage of the super-abundance of tasty plant food. On the wintering grounds, birds eat mainly large adult insects, but when it comes time to breed, their main food supply is the small insect larvae and caterpillars that consume the forest. One pair of breeding migrants can easily eat thousands of these insects on their territory, and with dozens of different bird species sharing the same space in the forest they do a very good job of suppressing insect numbers. There is nothing better to feed baby birds than a nice soft, juicy caterpillar. Birds have been hunting caterpillars for themselves and their nestlings for tens of millions of years. Caterpillars have been eating leaves for even longer and are very good at turning leaves into caterpillar flesh. As vegetarians, caterpillars have no equal. Trees have not stood by idly; they evolved spines, or made their leaves smoother and tougher, all to discourage the caterpillar hordes. It is war between the trees and the caterpillars, a war of attrition that can easily get out of balance.

It is war, too, between caterpillars and their arch-enemy, birds. Caterpillars don't want to be eaten and, obviously, they go to great lengths to avoid becoming carte du jour. Some have spines, often poisonous ones. In a fit of evolutionary one-upmanship, some caterpillars take the very poisons that plants first used to discourage them and store them in their own bodies to make themselves poisonous to birds. Witness the monarch butterfly, whose caterpillars incorporate heart-stopping poisons, cardiac glycosides, from their milkweed fare. Perhaps the caterpillar's most cunning achievement is to look exactly like bird poop, something no bird would dream of eating!

Far and wide, most caterpillars avoid birds the easy way—they hide. Many hide in the day and eat leaves only at night, when the birds are asleep. Since they cannot eat when they are hiding they can't turn leaves into caterpillar flesh nearly as fast as they are capable of doing. Birds quickly learn that a damaged leaf means a hiding caterpillar nearby and peer more closely at the leaves. As a counter-strategy, some caterpillars have evolved a body shape that "fills in" the section of the leaf they just munched, hiding the leaf damage from hungry birds. The long history of evolutionary strike and counterstrike between birds and insects ties them together ecologically, so when birds are suddenly taken out of the equation, insects quickly increase in numbers.

Experiments in New Hampshire that used netting to keep birds from eating caterpillars found that warblers and thrush reduced the number of caterpillars on leaves by 50 percent. The reduction was strongest in late June and early July, when parents had extra mouths to feed. A similar experiment in Missouri showed a big impact of birds on insect numbers, but also showed how the trees benefited from their feathered bodyguards. White oak trees that had no birds to protect them from leaf-eating insects lost twice the area of leaves to insect damage, and the tree grew more slowly because it could not generate as much energy. On a larger scale, we can expect that the decline of forest migrants will slow the growth of our valuable forests.

From time to time our forests have to cope with insect explosions that can denude the forest, which cuts deep into the forestry industry, which should thank birds that these outbreaks do not happen more often. The spruce budworm is a native pest of the spruce and fir forests of eastern North America and regularly undergoes epidemic outbreaks. These periodic and natural outbreaks have been happening for thousands of years, and many migrant bird species take advantage of the bumper crop of food. Entire communities of warblers, thrush, kinglets, sparrows, vireos, nuthatches, and juncos gorge on the spruce budworm, allowing them to raise many more young than usual. Blackburnian warblers and Cape May warblers are particularly tuned in to spruce budworm and eat more of them than other birds; their populations quickly increase in the years after an outbreak because they produce so many well-fed offspring. Many species crowd into infested areas, packing more birds into the same amount of space because there is so much food to go around. One study in New Hampshire "collected" (shot) songbirds to find out exactly how many budworms they were eating. Based on what was found in the stomachs, and the numbers of birds living the forest, the researchers estimated that the bird community eats in excess of 120,000 budworm larvae in each one-hectare patch of forest. When spruce budworm populations are low, these birds eat about 80 percent of the larvae, keeping numbers at low levels and lengthening the time between major outbreaks. It is only in rare years when the pest explodes in numbers that even the birds cannot eat enough to slow the budworm down. As the numbers of migrants dwindle, the frequency and severity of budworm outbreaks will increase.

In the 1950s the forestry industry tried to take over the job of budworm controller by using pesticides. Pesticides are a poor substitute for forest birds. Fenitrothion, a popular chemical used in the 1970s, not only killed insects but also killed birds and severely hampered the ability of survivors to breed. We saw earlier the effect on white-throated sparrows; with nests abandoned and failed, there were fewer mouths to feed and fewer parents alive. The pesticide was knocking out the birds that would provide long-term insect control after the outbreak had subsided. Putting this into dollars and cents, one study suggested that bird predation on the western spruce budworm is worth almost $5,000 per square mile in tree growth that results from natural insect control. Healthy bird populations add up to tens of millions of dollars in real economic value to the forestry industry each year; birds are worth saving! In the boreal forest, birds make up nearly three quarters of all the vertebrates in the forest and are a potent force in that ecosystem. The forest grows better with a healthy bird population, and in turn, a healthy bird population depends on a large and healthy forest.

9 LIVING ON THE EDGE
Birds Need Not Just Homes But Neighbourhoods

Cross-dressing, illegitimate children, males strutting around show-ing off in front of the ladies, females who crowd around the best-looking males, raised voices and fights, spouses cheating on each other; this isn't a raunchy Maury Povich show but a day in the life of a song-bird. Birds also experience the more mundane aspects of married life, of course: choosing a first home, bringing home the bacon, and taking care of the kids. Most songbirds live together in pairs for at least part of the year, combining their efforts to defend scarce resources and raise offspring. I admire the industriousness and teamwork when I see a male and female American redstart busily searching for food among the maples and grape vines, taking turns commuting to the nest every few minutes with a delivery.

Songbirds live in neighbourhoods and know each other as individuals by the sound of their voices and by the subtle markings of their feathers. I can stand in one place in my forested backyard and can hear four male hooded warblers, three male scarlet tanagers, five red-eyed vireos, and others. They can hear each other too. Individual pairs are surrounded by males and females of the same species who are friends and foes, potential mates and competitors. Social interactions happen every minute of the day, whether they are between a male and his mate, two rival males singing on their respective territories, or even a female having a brief affair with the male next door.

The source-and-sink model of forest fragmentation treats birds as little black boxes that produce eggs. It is a bean-counting approach that does not concern itself with the amazing lives of birds and their fascinating behaviour. For birds, choices are at the root of everything. They choose where to nest, whom to mate with, how hard to defend their nests from predators, how many eggs to lay in one nest, and how much care to devote to their offspring. Population size is a balance of the births and deaths in the population, but what happens at the anonymous population level is the sum of an infinite number of choices made by individual birds who are struggling to produce kids and stay alive. I want to go beyond measuring just the nesting success of the population and focus on the behaviour of breeding birds when they are faced with forest fragments.

Last summer a pair of chickadees nested in a small cavity that they had excavated in the base of the pear tree in our backyard. One day while I was reading at the picnic table I heard the male singing his crisp and ringing *fee-bay, fee-bay.* I looked up to see him perched in the pear tree, and then he darted to the entrance hole carrying something in his beak. The female popped her head out of the hole, and he quickly fed her. Over the next hour he returned three more times with food for her, singing each time as he approached. Behavioural ecologists are obsessed with "why." Why did he sing near the nest hole? His song was so very loud and easily would be heard 150 feet away. If he simply wanted to signal to his mate that he was on his way home with the takeout, he could use quiet call notes. Surely his singing would attract the attention of smart blue jays and crows, just as it had attracted my attention. Why did he bother to feed her in the first place? There is plenty of food around in these woods, and females of most species don't get handouts from their mates. Incubation feeding is common in chickadees, so I knew I was watching not an oddball male but rather a characteristic behaviour of a species that had been around for many generations.

The guiding principle for answering the why question is to think in evolutionary terms, rather than to try to read the minds of birds or think of them as human-like in their minute-to-minute decision making. Birds themselves do not understand why they make certain choices; the simple instinctual rules that govern their lives were inherited from their parents. The parent bird uses the time-tested rule "feed the hungry chick" and so is easily tricked by the cowbird nestling. Young females do not need to learn where to build a nest or how to construct it; even a first-time breeder knows whether to pick up sticks as opposed to grass and whether to place the nest in a shrub or high on a tree branch. This is not to say that birds do not learn a great deal through their own experience, but they are born with a broad suite of genetic instructions that are the result of hundreds of generations of trial and error that their ancestors went through. Genetic instructions that predispose a bird to make poor decisions will be weeded out over the generations, because such birds have low survival rates and do not produce many young who will carry those faulty instructions. Behavioural ecologists study wild birds to discover the consequences of different behaviours for a bird's ability to stay alive and healthy, get mates, defend territories, intimidate rivals, and produce healthy young.

Red-winged blackbirds are among the first migrants to return in spring, and are a common sight along roadsides. The males look tough; their long, pointy bill is typical of blackbirds, and they have a sleek all-black body that is punctuated by the in-your-face red epaulets that decorate their shoulders. To stake out a territory a male perches on a wire, leafless tree, or weathered bullrush where he is in plain sight, hunches and fluffs up his back to look big, lets out an ugly-sounding and raspy *crick-keer-reee* and at the same time spreads out his red epaulets in a magnificent display of machismo. Why do male red-winged blackbirds have such large and conspicuous red badges?

The rush to be back first is driven by intense competition for high-quality territories in marshes or the tall vegetation in roadside ditches. Early studies on redwings showed just how important the red badges were in defending territory. Some of the top males in the marsh were captured and their brilliant red feathers were dyed black. When released, the males quickly went back to singing and displaying on their territories, but without the macho signal. The neighbours repeatedly snuck onto the territory, ignoring the blackened males' otherwise impressive displays and attempts to chase them away, and eventually stole parts of the territory. Without the red badge, the threats carried little weight. The reproductive costs of losing space are high because males who get the biggest and best territories attract a harem; three to five females may decide to nest on one male's territory. Male redwings can get away with this impressive mating feat because they do not help to feed the nestlings; the male can focus his efforts on defending his territory from rivals and attracting females. The dyed males ended up with both smaller territories and fewer mates, demonstrating the clear disadvantage for males that are unfortunate enough to inherit small red epaulets from their parents.

Birds must choose between one important activity and another. Males cannot sing and eat at the same time; a male who spends a large amount of time singing to impress females or scare rivals will quickly get very hungry. One the other hand, the male who eats his fill at the expense of singing may lose his territory or find himself living alone and without any young to show for his efforts. Male blue-headed vireos face the dilemma that they cannot be in two places at once; they have to choose between incubating the eggs or leaving the nest to confront incoming males. Males help their mates incubate the eggs, and when off the nest the male typically patrols his territory's boundaries and sings frequently to remind his neighbours that he is alive and ready to chase them away.

What is a male to do if an intruder shows up while he is quietly sitting on the eggs? Jump off the nest and attack or take care of the eggs and let the intruder get a toehold in the territory? My student Ioana Chiver did song playback experiments to simulate a territorial intrusion. If the male was off his nest at the time of the playback, he would come tearing over to the playback site within two minutes to try to find the fake male intruder. If the male was on his nest incubating, he just sat there while the "intruder" kept singing a short distance away. Males waited for their mate to come back to the nest to take her turn at incubating; when they finally got the green light to leave the nest, they flew straight to where they had heard the intruder, even though the recording had stopped as much as ten minutes earlier. Males remembered exactly where they had heard the intruder, and though they were late on the scene they were clearly following up on the security threat. Our big surprise was that when an intruder began singing on the territory, the female came back to the nest much earlier to relieve her mate; she was cooperating with him. Females weren't being altruistic, but rather they lose out too if part of the territory is annexed by an intruder and those food resources are suddenly out of bounds when it is time to find food for the kids.

One of the most important choices that birds face is where to breed in the first place. A poor breeding territory can doom a pair to endless nesting attempts after repeated cowbird and predator attacks, and they may go home to the tropics empty handed when it comes to what really counts, adding to the next generation. Our migrants who arrive in the spring face a very different landscape than their ancestors did a few hundred generations ago. Although the native peoples certainly managed these forests extensively with fire and agriculture, they did not mow down the forests and leave as much as 95 percent of the landscape deforested. The behaviour of forest birds has been shaped by ancestors that lived in large extensive forests that stretched for dozens or hundreds of miles. Today, migrants have to choose between living in one of the many small fragments or competing for a territory in one of the larger patches of prime real estate. The choice seems pretty clear for most species; small forest fragments often sit empty and unused even though they are big enough to support one or more pairs of a given species. In Maryland, for instance, ovenbirds occupy only one out of ten of the tiny forest patches that scatter the landscape. Even reasonably good-sized ten-hectare patches are unpopular. Other forest species such as red-eyed vireos, wood thrush, and scarlet tanagers are also much less likely to occupy a small forest patch. To one degree or another, this choice to avoid small forest patches is seen in dozens of forest songbird species and holds true in many different parts of their breeding range.

The classic explanation for why breeding forest birds avoid small fragments is based on the idea that forest birds do not like the edge of a forest. The logic makes perfect sense. Forest birds nest inside the forest, of course, so that must mean that they do not like the forest edge, where light-loving shrubs and bushes grow up in a dense wall. Inside the forest the light is heavily filtered by the forest canopy and there is relatively little understory, so it is easy to walk through the forest even if there are no trails. The edge is a very different environment for birds, as it is warmer and windier than the interior. Even in ancient forests, the edge may have been an unsafe or undesirable place for forest birds because it was poor habitat and perhaps also held more nest predators, so birds who stayed away from edge habitat could have produced more off-spring. The simple decision rules that evolved over hundreds of years in response to natural edges may have inadvertently equipped songbirds with a rule that works well in today's world; avoiding edges also means that they will avoid small forest fragments.

Small fragments contain mostly edge habitat and offer few places for birds to hide from the edge effects (figure 9.1). Cutting things to pieces automatically creates more edge. Imagine a Friday-night family-size pizza that comes in a large rectangle with two dozen square pieces. My kids always pick out the pieces from the centre, the pizza interior, because there is no crust. On our large pizza there are eight delicious centre pieces, and four corner pieces that have two crust edges each (for Mom and Dad to eat). The rest of the pizza has just one edge of crust.

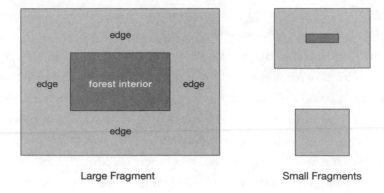

Large Fragment   Small Fragments

Figure 9.1. *Small fragments contain mostly edge habitat and have little or no forest interior.*

Now imagine that instead we had ordered a family-size "fragmented" pizza—the same amount of pizza but cooked in four separate smaller rectangles instead of one large pizza. This pizza would not have any crustless interior; every single piece would have some crust. A large forest patch offers more interior forest and less scrubby "crust" than the same area divided into several smaller pieces. If forest birds avoid edge habitat, then this could quickly explain why they also avoid small fragments.

The idea that edges are hostile places for forest birds has been around for a long time, so long that many people take it as a given. The birds that were known to prefer large forest patches, like ovenbirds, scarlet tanagers, and red-eyed vireos, were called forest-interior birds, a name that equated a preference for large forest with an aversion to edge. Hooded warblers are often depicted as the poster bird for forest-interior species in part because of the male's handsome black cowl. One chapter in a recent book on declining birds is called "The Hostile Edge" and shows a male hooded warbler feeding a cowbird chick in his nest. Hooded warblers are certainly area-sensitive throughout their breeding range. In Pennsylvania, for instance, only one out of every five small fragments in our area is actually occupied by hooded warblers. Hooded warblers, however, do not avoid edge habitat. Radiotracking studies by my students found that males who live in fragments spend a third of their time singing right along the forest edge, and females sometimes build their nests in the dense shrubs at the forest edge. Edges are used late in the season too, when parents move their newly mobile family toward the scrubbier edge of the forest and spend several weeks there feeding the young as they slowly become independent. One of the first papers I published on hooded warblers was called "Response of a Forest-Interior Songbird to the Threat of Cowbird Parasitism," though I realize now that hooded warblers are not really forest-interior birds.

Hooded warblers are not alone in their extensive use of edge habitat. Scarlet tanager males routinely sing along edges, and I often see parents feeding fledglings along the edge, perhaps because plenty of fruit is available in these sunnier spots. Red-eyed vireos, scarlet tanagers, and wood thrush are common in our forest, and their territories go right down to the edge of the forest. Ovenbirds, a species that is often labelled as forest-interior, act very differently in our forest. My husband, Gene, mapped the ovenbird territories in our forest for many years and found that they always set up shop along the northern edge of the forest or in a smaller cluster of territories along the southern edge. These edges offer safety from chipmunks, the ovenbird's main enemy, who are less abundant along the edges of this forest. Gene even tried enticing ovenbirds to breed in the forest interior by playing ovenbird song over speakers for several weeks at a time to make it seem as if birds were happily settled there. No real ovenbird ever set up a territory inside the forest, even with that much encouragement. It's not as if our ovenbirds are just dummies who forgot they are supposed to be forest-interior birds. Studies in other parts of the breeding range have found that ovenbird breeding success is not always lower for the pairs who live on the edge. The idea that the forest edge is universally bad habitat for ovenbirds, and other forest birds, needs a second look, maybe even a third.

It turns out that most species that avoid small fragments are not actually avoiding the edge. In a review of all the studies done, only the Acadian flycatcher clearly avoided edges. In our forest, Acadian flycatchers are usually found along the dark stream valleys, where towering hemlock trees block out direct sunlight with their thickly blanketed evergreen branches. Given the incredible popularity of the idea of the hostile edge, it is pretty surprising that even the most hardcore area-sensitive species—ovenbirds, red-eyed vireos, and scarlet tanagers—showed no overall pattern of edge avoidance. Why not? Could it be that the edge is actually not a hostile place after all? The high levels of cowbird parasitism and predation in small fragments may have duped us into thinking that edges are the source of the problem.

Even the big forest-fragmentation study in Illinois that found such incredibly high levels of cowbird parasitism did not find that nests near edges were harder hit. Cowbirds were so superabundant that songbirds could find no refuge, even far inside huge forests. Anywhere cowbirds are even moderately common they are seen throughout large forests. In eastern New York, where forest cover is in an impressive 55 percent, nest searchers regularly saw male and female cowbirds in the interior of a 1,200-hectare forest patch. Female cowbirds that were radiotagged spent their egg-laying hours of the morning far inside the forest looking for nest-building hosts.

Songbirds may be able to escape cowbirds only in heavily forested regions where cowbirds are uncommon to begin with. In southern Indiana, where forest cover was high and cowbird parasitism low, researchers did find an edge effect for some species. It was strongest for the red-eyed vireo and worm-eating warbler, where about half the nests along the edge were found by cowbirds. But edge-nesting wood thrush were relatively free of cowbirds whether they nested along the edge or in the interior of the forest.

The other driving force behind the notion of a hostile edge is the danger of nest predators like crows, squirrels, or raccoons. Just like cowbirds, many nest predators are more common in agricultural fields because there is so much easy food up for grabs. If nest predators are more abundant in the fields, the thinking goes, then birds nesting near edges are likely to be at higher risk. The idea gained momentum from a couple of early studies that found high predation near edges. In Michigan, a study of the bird community near the forest edge found that predation dropped suddenly about 160 feet into the forest. The highest density of nests was near the edge, thanks to birds that specialize on edge habitat such as northern cardinals and indigo buntings. This high abundance of eggs may have acted as bait and rewarded predators that stalked the edge for their helpless victims. A later study in Wisconsin found that a shocking 82 percent of nests near the edge were attacked by predators compared with only 30 percent in the forest interior. Researcher David Wilcove, using artificial nests loaded with quail eggs, also found higher predation near edges.

Despite this seemingly impressive evidence, the jury is still out because so many other studies that have thoroughly looked for a predator edge effect, even those using artificial nests, have found none at all. Whether or not birds can escape from predators by moving deeper into the forest depends on who exactly is doing the dirty deed. Crows, snakes and raccoons have dramatically different abilities to move across the landscape, forage at different times of the day and night, use different cues for finding nests; they also have different tendencies to be attracted to agricultural settings. Why *would* all these different predators prefer to hunt on the edge? Some predators like raccoons are more abundant near edges and fields, but chipmunks and snakes probably are not. Crows and blue jays are notorious nest predators and can easily fly deep into the forest to look for tasty treats. If raccoons are eating most of the eggs, then there may be some relief in the forest interior. On the other hand, if chipmunks or crows are the number-one enemy, then edge nests will not experience unusually high nest predation. Forest fragments in Maryland, Michigan, and Illinois likely have a different suite of nest predators, which may explain why some studies find edge effects and others do not.

We started with the question of why forest birds avoid small fragments. The concept of the "hostile" edge is still popular in many circles but has not earned its stripes; it may apply in certain circumstances and places but it certainly is not universal enough to explain why songbirds so consistently prefer large forests. To answer the question, we need to return to the basics of bird behaviour and remember that our migrants are incredibly social animals that live in neighbourhoods and not just individual birds seeking out suitable trees for their nests.

~⌒

Purple martin landlords know all too well that birds crave a busy social life. The purple martin is a large, graceful swallow that nests in colonies of dozens of breeding pairs. Martins readily occupy backyard birdhouses. Centuries ago, native Americans grew and dried gourds, cut an entrance hole in them, then hung them in rows to attract nesting purple martins. The early European colonists were captivated by these entertaining bird cities, and built ornate and colourful wooden houses with dozens of nesting compartments. Today, throughout eastern North America, a subculture of purple martin landlords dotes on their martins and discuss practical advice, problems, and natural history through organizations like the Purple Martin Conservation Association. Many people are landlord wannabes; they have a nice backyard with plenty of room and even a pond, but cannot attract purple martins to actually live in the handsome and expensive housing.

At our farm in Pennsylvania we have tried for some twenty years to attract purple martins, but have yet to have a single pair stay long enough to lay an egg. (Purple martins are scarce in northwestern Pennsylvania because they were virtually wiped out by Hurricane Hazel in 1954, and the population has still not recovered.) At one point our offerings included a large wooden apartment house near the pond as well as two aluminum houses with gourds hanging from each corner, perhaps a total of a hundred nesting compartments in all. There is absolutely nothing wrong with the actual housing or the backyard; it is perfect martin habitat. Gene and I are both martin connoisseurs and have spent years watching and researching martin behaviour, but the birds seem to thumb their noses at us when they come for brief visits to check out the housing. We are stuck in a Catch-22: you cannot easily start a martin colony unless martins are already living there, or near there. Each year Gene announces optimistically, "This year we will get martins." We have some hope, because every spring we try to fool the martins by putting wooden martin decoys on the houses and, most important, playing back martin song and chatter to simulate a thriving colony. The now-popular dawn song recording, sold to purple martin landlords across the country, is one Gene made years ago at a large colony in Maryland. Early in the morning we start the tape player under the houses, and the dawn song and other martin noises are broadcast from speakers for about twelve hours at a time. After a while this becomes noise pollution, the incessant *chee-cher, chee-cher* call interspersed with the pleasing gurgling song of the male.

The martin beacon does work: every day in spring young birds are arriving from the south and need to find a colony and mate for their first breeding attempt. They can hear the enticing sounds from high above our farm, and swoop down to investigate. These birds are not simply looking for a good house; they are looking for a good neighbourhood. The females are especially picky. Many times we have had a young male claim a house, gurgling away proudly on the roof or the porch and enjoying his riches. Yet when a female comes to visit, she circles the house a few times and maybe even dares to perch on the porch for a moment to peek inside the entrance hole to the bachelor's pad. After a few minutes she loses interest and invariably flies away to find a real colony; after a few days the solo male gives up too and he is not seen again.

The dawn song is a vocal magnet that older male martins use to attract newcomers to join the colony. During the predawn hours when it is still dark, older males take to the sky singing their hearts out, and act like a homing beacon advertising the colony to homeless martins passing by. These older males are not being altruistic, though there may be some element of safety in numbers because a predator that comes near the colony will be mobbed by the whole community. Older males advertise their colony for very selfish reasons: they plan to sneak copulations with young females. Although purple martins are revered by many a landlord, their sex lives would make most of us blush. Females who are paired with young males often copulate with the older males in the colony, even out in the open for all to see. DNA testing has shown that the old males are successful; almost half of the young males in a colony will be cuckolded. The young females can have their cake and eat it too. Although they arrived too late to pair with an old male, they can still get his high-quality DNA for their offspring, and meanwhile their young mate helps to raise her young. The older males have been tested by life, and proven their worth genetically speaking, because they have already survived almost two years of exposure to disease and have survived a couple of trips to Brazil and back. The old males have a very good reason to fly around in the predawn hours singing, because this brings in more willing females to the colony and more partners for them to mate with.

Richard Wagner first discovered this kind of behaviour during his Ph.D. at Oxford, where he studied razorbills, small, stocky seabirds that nest in crevices under boulders. He discovered that the razorbills at his study site in Wales had a special rock that they used as a singles bar. Mated females who had breeding territories in the colony would fly over to the mating arena and flirt with other males, most of whom had females back at home among the boulders. Only a handful of the dozens of males who hung out at the arena were chosen by females for extramarital copulations. The razorbill colony was monogamous on the surface, with every male and female paired for the purposes of rearing young, but meanwhile males and females were sneaking off to the mating arena. The similarities between the razorbills and purple martins are striking; in each case females gain an advantage by living in a colony because there is a pool of high-quality males who are all too willing to supply high-quality DNA for their kids.

If colonial birds like razorbills and purple martins like to nest near each other so females can be near older males, maybe the same is true for forest birds. This seems to be the case for the least flycatcher, a bird that clusters its territories within secondary forest. Least flycatchers are small, nondescript birds known for their vocal stamina rather than their musical talents; males sing their monotonous *chi-beck* song about twenty times a minute, in other words, more or less non-stop and for hours at a time. Territories are compact and crammed together, with ten to twenty pairs forming a tight neighbourhood. The first males to arrive form the initial cluster and are joined a few days later by other males, who settle around them. These clusters are widely spaced in the forest, about a half-mile apart, even though there is perfectly good nesting habitat in between. Occasional solitary males are scattered through the forest, far from the clusters, and these males usually cannot attract a female to nest with them. The slate is wiped clean every year because very few birds return to the same area to breed, and the exact place in the forest where clusters spring up is different from year to year. It is almost as if the newly arriving birds throw an imaginary dart at the forest and set up a new neighbourhood wherever it lands.

Scott Tarof, when he was a Ph.D. student at Queen's University, found that the dense "colonies" of least flycatchers are hotbeds of sexual behaviour. Territories are so small and close together that females can easily interact with males living next door and males are often seen copulating with females who are not their mate. Males frequently sneak onto each other's territories, and females do too. Females also seek copulations from neighbours by staying at home and giving quiet *whit* calls and fluttering their wings in a stereotyped invitation; in at least two cases the neighbour male obliged. With all this extra-pair sexual activity, it is not surprising that DNA testing showed that six out of ten females produced some young who were not fathered by their own mate. Colony formation in least flycatchers seems to be driven by mate choice, just as with purple martins and razorbills. Female flycatchers prefer to join colonies because this is where they can have a choice among males and easily obtain extra-pair copulations. A solitary male may have a territory in a beautiful section of forest teeming with bugs and offering lovely nesting sites, but he is shunned because he has no neighbours.

The importance of social attraction in forming new breeding populations has also been shown in the endangered black-capped vireo. This species has a small breeding range in Texas, Oklahoma, and northern Mexico and prefers early successional habitat with dense shrubs and trees for nesting. Open pastures dominate the landscape, and a combination of fire suppression and grazing means that good-quality shrub habitat is in short supply. Fort Hood, Texas, has extensive scrub habitat and one of the largest black-capped vireo populations in the country. The vireos are heavily parasitized by brown-headed cowbirds, and an intensive cowbird control program, like the ones done to protect Kirtland's warblers and least Bell's vireos, has allowed the black-caps to breed successfully. The cowbird removals by themselves did not increase the black-capped vireo populations, though, even though plenty of habitat was available. Instead, the territories were clustered together, and the birds were ignoring good habitat nearby. To jump-start the population of this endangered species, researchers tricked the birds into thinking the other areas were already occupied. During the entire breeding season, they played back vireo song and call notes each morning from a solar-powered stereo-speaker system. In the first year of the experiment, they successfully attracted 73 vireos to settle and breed in sites that had been empty up until then. Once the vireos began using a site, they returned the next year to breed, even though the sound recordings were no longer being played. The returning birds were acting as natural lures and a tradition of using that particular site had been put into motion.

Social attraction probably also explains why forest birds avoid small fragments. Although we like to think that birds are wonderful role models for blissful monogamy, in fact most neotropical migrants are obsessed with extra-pair sex, just like the least flycatcher and purple martin. When I first began studying hooded warblers in the early 1990s, it didn't take me long to realize that hanky-panky is an everyday occurrence in their lives.

I started my study by systematically catching and colour-banding all the territorial males in the area, so I knew which male lived on which territory. In early June a young male, a first-time breeder, arrived and set up a territory in the scrubbier forest near the edge of the study site. This rookie was easily fooled by my stuffed decoy and song playback and was soon wearing bands. Within days he attracted a female, also a young bird, and she made up for lost time by frantically building a nest low in a wild raspberry bush. The nest was easy to find because she gave frequent *chip* calls as she looked for nest material and commuted back and forth to her chosen nest site about ten times in just half an hour. When the nest was almost finished I put a few mist nets on the territory so I could catch her. At first I had no luck because of all the bird traffic; every time I went to check the net there was a different male hanging there. The first morning I caught three of the already-banded neighbouring males, and the next day was no better: I caught four different males in three hours. In all, I had caught seven of the nine males who lived in the neighbourhood. It doesn't take a genius to figure out why all these males were suddenly visiting this new young female. But how did they know she was there and getting ready to lay her eggs?

Standing on the trail a hundred yards away from this hot zone, I could hear my answer: the female's *chip* calls were loud enough to be heard on neighbouring territories and were a dead giveaway that she was nesting. Diane Neudorf, who is now a professor at Sam Houston State University in Texas, was my very first Ph.D. student and studied these female calls. She wanted to find out whether males really were hearing a "come and get me" from neighbouring females. She discovered that by listening, neighbour males tell if a female is likely to be receptive to his copulations. A female who is nest building or getting ready to lay eggs will *chip* very erratically, with many pauses interspersed between her calls: *chip, chip . . . chip . . . chip, chip . . . chip.* A female who is already incubating gives call notes only when she comes off her nest to look for insects to eat, and her calls are given with a rhythmic, rapid cadence: *chip, chip, chip, chip, chip.* Sure enough, neighbour males are much more likely to visit a chipping female when she is fertile and has not yet finished laying eggs. From the male's point of view, once the female has laid all her eggs, there is little point in visiting her because he has no chance of fertilizing eggs.

A typical scene involves a female who is in the bushes happily chipping away looking for food or nesting material while her own mate is singing in a tree twenty or more paces away. Suddenly a second male perches in a sapling near the female, his feathers sleeked down in alarm as he quickly looks one way and another, looking for the female. The territory owner appears just as suddenly and perches in another sapling, and the duel has started. Both males hunch their backs and droop their wings in a posture that exaggerates their body size. A few moments pass as neither statue gives an inch in this staring contest, and then the territory owner loses his patience and flies at the intruder, screaming a wild and long *chippity, chippity, chup, chup* attack call. If the intruder is lucky he will fly home with his tail between his legs, so to speak, and escape untouched. Sometimes, though, the intruder will be knocked to the ground, and the chivalrous mate will violently peck at the victim's head and claw him as the two birds fight on the ground. An intruding male takes his life in his hands when he enters another male's territory and tries to sneak a copulation with the female. I have seen dozens of extra-pair copulation attempts in hooded warblers; sneaky males are caught red-handed about one out of every five times they approach a female. Don't let the tiny size and beautiful manicured looks fool you—these birds can be vicious. And meanwhile, the female is still chipping from a few paces away watching her suitors go at it.

It is one thing for males to swarm around a receptive female, but how many males actually produce offspring as a result of their advances? Here you need genetic testing to find out which males, if any, actually fertilized an egg. Tiny blood samples are collected from the small nestlings a few days after they hatch, and each nestling's DNA is compared to that of the parents who are taking care of the kids. "DNA fingerprinting" is a term familiar to most people because of the way it has completely revolutionized crime investigations. The pieces of DNA that work best for identifying the guilty party are ones that are highly variable in a population, meaning that there may be twenty or more unique sequences for that section of DNA. Every individual has two copies of each section of DNA; one copy was inherited from its father and the other from its mother. There are so many different combinations of variants that very few individuals will carry two copies of the same variant. To imagine this scenario, let's pretend that we have randomly handed out different combination of socks, twenty different colours in all, to a large group of men. Not many guys will end up with two socks of the exact same colour, and there will be dozens of different colour combinations among the men in the room. Still, there is a small chance that two men will have the same-coloured socks, say, one red sock and one blue sock.

A single section of DNA, or marker, does not give an actual genetic "fingerprint" that allows precise identification of an individual, because more than one individual in the population can have the combination. To make our genetic identification test more accurate, we have to use several different DNA markers that each target a different section of DNA. For instance, we can give our test group of men different-coloured gloves and shoes. Now if you randomly pick one guy, he might have a red and a blue sock, a brown and a black shoe, and a white and a green glove. The other guy in the room who had red and blue socks ended up with purple and green gloves and grey and white shoes. We now have our individually unique "fingerprint," because no one in the room has exactly the same combination of colours at all three markers. At the genetic level, DNA left at a crime scene that is tested with eight to ten different markers can in theory match only one single individual in the entire world.

How do you match up a nestling with its genetic parent? Going back to our simple sock analogy, the happy couple consists of the mother who has a yellow sock and a black sock, and the father wearing one red and one blue sock. If the couple was truly monogamous, their nestlings should have inherited either a black or yellow sock from the mom and a red or blue sock from the dad. If actual testing shows a nestling has a yellow sock (from the mom) and a green sock (from whom?), we have good reason to think that the female must have mated with a third party. To find out which male is responsible, we need to search for a male wearing a green sock.

Among hooded warblers, DNA testing showed that about 40 percent of the nestlings were sired by neighbour males rather than the female's hard-working mate. Almost half the females in the population were cheating on their spouses. It's clear how philandering males benefit from extra-pair copulations. A male who sires an illegitimate nestling on a neighbouring territory has no equivalent of child support payments and he is completely off the hook when it comes to taking care of that nestling. Some males sired all the young in their own nest as well as several nestlings on nearby territories, doubling or even tripling their personal reproductive success through their secret rendezvous.

But not everyone is a winner is this promiscuous mating arrangement. Some males that were busy being good dads, delivering beakful after beakful of wriggling green caterpillars to their nest of young, actually were not the genetic father of any of the offspring in their nest. To make matters worse, they did not even have any illegitimate young on neighbouring territories. These males had a territory, and a mate, and had even successfully raised young, but genetically speaking they had failed to reproduce.

Male intrusions and male-male chases are so frequent it's easy to be left with the impression that females are innocent bystanders. After watching and listening to females closely for an entire summer, Diane Neudorf had not seen females wandering around the way that males do. It seemed females were content to stay on their territories chipping and waiting for males to come to them. To find out for sure, Diane put tiny radiotransmitters on nesting females so that she could play private detective and keep tabs on the female's movements. Diane and I were surprised to discover that females are just as unfaithful as their mates and regularly sneak away to visit males on other territories. Females are very secretive when off territory and do not make their trademark *chip* calls, so we would never have known the female had even left her territory without the radiotransmitter signal. Female warblers are more likely to leave their territory in search of extra-pair partners if they are mated to a male who sings infrequently. Song rate is a reliable measure of the male's health and stamina, and females who mate with the good songsters are likely to produce healthier offspring.

To get a feel for what is going on behind the scenes in a hooded warbler community, let's imagine a suburban street with a row of neat brick houses down each side and fences that separate the backyards. A newly married couple lives in each home, and a few have newborn babies. It is a beautiful spring morning and some of the guys are outside their homes washing the car, mowing the lawn and finally taking down the Christmas lights. A couple of the wives are pulling weeds from the flower garden, sweeping the porch or raking the lawn. Suddenly a man runs out his back door, hurdles the fence into his neighbour's yard and quietly slips in the back door of his neighbour's house. The woman who had been weeding stands up suddenly, walks quickly across the road and disappears into her neighbour's house for a few minutes. A fight breaks out a few doors up as a slim, well-dressed man in a black cap and yellow golf shirt sneaks close to a woman on her hands and knees planting petunias, and her husband rushes out of his house, violently pushes the intruder to the ground and then chases him out of the front yard yelling at the top of his voice. This is everyday social life for a hooded warbler, with domestic duties on the territory juxtaposed with promiscuous mating attempts. There is nothing personal or unnatural about the frequent copulations and the scuffles between males; this is just as much a part of daily life as singing, building nests, and feeding nestlings.

If the sex lives of birds make it important for them to live in neighbourhoods, then is this why they avoid small fragments? Birds who live in fragments may be losing out on the chance to get extra-pair copulations. Contrast the suburban street we just visited with life in a rural area, where farmhouses are a mile or two apart on quiet country roads. Instead of seeing quick visits between houses many times an hour along the street, we would see an occasional farmer make the long trip all the way down the road to the neighbour's house. He would leave his own house unattended for almost half an hour at a time, and even an energetic male would have only enough spare time to visit a few different neighbours in an entire day. The wives who are busy with domestic duties may not even bother to take the time and energy to go so far to visit prospective sperm donors. It makes sense that extra-pair copulations will be much harder to get when birds are living far apart.

To find out how forest fragmentation affects the social life of hooded warblers, my graduate student Ryan Norris radiotagged pairs living alone in forest fragments. He was quite worried that his thesis might turn out to be pretty boring if males and females did not leave their forest fragments. The conventional wisdom at the time was that hooded warblers were forest-interior birds and so would not like the forest edge, let alone fly across open fields. We did have some DNA results from a handful of nests that were in isolated forest fragments showing that some of the young did not belong to the male who lived there. Either the female had left the fragment herself, or some other male must have flown in from elsewhere. Ryan needn't have worried about a dull summer; racing across corn fields trying to catch up with a bird is not an easy task when you are loaded down with binoculars, a radio receiver on your belt, and an awkward hand-held antenna. Ryan discovered that most males made trips off their home fragment and travelled an average round-trip distance of half a mile on each trip. A few males travelled much farther, up to 1.5 miles away from their home, and spent almost a third of their time "on the road." Clearly, in a fragmented landscape males were putting much more time and effort into trying to get extra-pair copulations.

Females, though, had the opposite reaction to living in forest fragments. They rarely left their own territory, and if they did it was only if another forest fragment was very close by. Flying long distances across open areas is time consuming, and likely very risky if there are hawks around waiting to snatch up an easy meal. For a female, the small gains from mating with a high-quality neighbour just don't outweigh the difficulties of trying to go and meet him at his place. Females living on a small fragment played it safe and waited for males to come to them. With longer and harder trips off-territory for males, and females staying at home, the amount of promiscuous mating was much lower in forest fragments. DNA testing showed that forest fragments reduced extra-pair matings by 50 percent compared with large forests where territories were packed together like peas in a pod. Forest fragmentation disrupts the natural social behaviour of hooded warblers and other migrants, so it is no wonder they avoid nesting in small, isolated fragments.

There is another important social cost to living in fragments; males often cannot attract a female to nest with them on the fragment. In many songbirds, including ovenbirds, red-eyed vireos, hooded warblers, and scarlet tanagers, as many as half of the males who occupy forest fragments are unmated. The biodiversity of birds in fragments is low to begin with, but is even lower when unmated males are taken into account. Singing males give the appearance of a productive breeding population, but in fact the females are missing, so the fragments have a low productivity even before cowbirds and predators have a chance to attack nests.

⁓

There are few birds like the scarlet tanager that make you hold your breath and say "wow" every time you see one. The name does not do justice to the brilliant red that radiates with such intensity; when the bird is sitting in the sun, you don't want to take your eyes off it because you may never see such an amazing sight again. The jet-black wings of older males provide a stunning contrast, making the red appear even brighter. When a male is courting a female, he perches beneath his mate and droops his black wings down while hunching his back to show off his colours. I wanted to study scarlet tanagers because I wanted to know if mating behaviour would help to explain why they avoid small frag-ments. My new postdoctoral student, Gail Fraser, started the project by radiotagging a male that was defending a territory in a small, isolated forest fragment. Full of enthusiasm, she returned the next day to fol-low him for two hours, but was disappointed that her receiver was not picking up his radio signal. Gail waited for half an hour, but heard no song and got no signal. Fearing the worst, she thought the male might have been killed the night before, perhaps because he was wearing his new backpack. (What a way to begin a field season!) That afternoon she stopped at the same fragment on her way home and out of curiosity turned on her receiver. She was startled to hear a loud, metallic *beep, beep, beep.* The male was only about one hundred feet away inside the forest. A few minutes later she caught a glimpse of him high overhead in the canopy. He looked fine, but where had he been that morning?

At four-thirty the next morning, when it was still dark, Gail returned to the male's fragment to record his dawn song and start following him. She got there well before he was due to wake up so she could quietly sneak into position to record his song. Male tanagers start the day about an hour before sunrise by singing almost non-stop for half an hour or more. Their predawn song is distinct from their regular daytime song; males punctuate their dawn song by adding a *chik-burr* at the end. But Gail could not pick up a signal from her receiver. She drove down the dark country roads listening for his signal, and soon found him in a fragment more than half a mile away. It was still dark, so she still had time to get close to him before he started singing. As she was getting her equipment out of the car, the signal got a bit stronger, then weakened from the opposite direction. The signal was now coming from the same direction as the fragment where she had just been fifteen minutes earlier. Gail drove back to that fragment to find her male happily singing away. The male had slept in one fragment, and then flown off in the dark to dawn-sing in another fragment.

This kind of behaviour had never before been described, or even suspected, in a forest songbird. The males who were fragment-hopping were all unmated young males who had not been able to attract a female to nest with them. Unmated males can use the patient strategy of staying in one place and singing all day long, hoping that eventually a female will come. A different strategy is to wander around trying to impress as many females as possible in the hopes that one day a female will say "I do." Male tanagers have the same problem as hooded warblers: the best habitat is the large forest, which is claimed by the older males. This is also where most of the females are, so young males are pushed out into the fragments and often do not attract a mate for nesting.

Migratory birds see more than just the trees in a forest. When they arrive in spring to select breeding territories, they do not simply size up the forest for its nesting sites and food supply. Of paramount importance is whether or not they will lead a productive social life; males need to be able attract mates, and both sexes benefit from pursuing copulations with neighbours. Forest fragments disrupt all aspects of pair formation and mate choice, and as a result reduce the breeding success of migrants beyond the big losses they already experience from excessive cowbirds and predators. In terms of managing forests and landscapes to increase bird biodiversity, we have to do more than add trees and nest sites to forests. Birds need other birds; as the numbers of migrants continue to fall, this will only disrupt the mating system even more, and in turn the population decline will accelerate.

Epilogue
Answering the Cry of the Songbirds

As I sat at my kitchen table one morning in late May, putting the final touches on this book, I could barely believe that songbirds really were in trouble. As daylight gradually crept in through the windows, the backyard of our farmhouse exploded with voices. The first was the dawn song of the tree swallow, joined soon after by the eastern phoebe, yellow warbler, indigo bunting, wood thrush, hooded warbler, scarlet tanager, cardinal, field sparrow, house wren, American redstart, common yellowthroat, song sparrow, and least flycatcher. There are lots of birds are around, aren't there? The slow, insidious decrease in numbers is hard to notice because it happens over a time span of decades. Stories from oldtimers about their days birding as teenagers could too easily be written off as exaggerations stemming from fond memories. Without the forty years of monitoring by the Breeding Bird Survey and bird-banding stations, we would not know that a crisis is unfolding across two continents.

Although bird watching and bird feeding are among the fastest-growing pastimes in North America, there remain millions of people who have never experienced the joy of seeing a wood thrush, Kentucky warbler, eastern kingbird, or bobolink. What does it mean to them that songbirds are disappearing? It is hard for people to be concerned about the loss of something they have never seen, or have no use for. If I read a newspaper headline announcing that spinach would no longer be sold in grocery stores, I would be slightly curious but not alarmed, because I don't especially care for this vegetable and rarely buy it. Would a ban on guanabana sales spark a public outcry? (Most people in North America have never even heard of this tasty tropical fruit, though in Panama it was my favourite flavour of milkshake.) How many people in Toronto, Pittsburgh, or Chicago know what an eastern loggerhead shrike is, or would care if they knew that in a decade or two it will probably be extinct in the wild?

On April 26, 2005, the world learned that the ivory-billed woodpecker had been sighted in eastern Arkansas, in the wilderness of the White River National Wildlife Refuge. Many thought this bird was extinct because it hadn't been seen in decades. That evening I sat with my eyes glued to the national news to revel in the biggest environmental story in decades. After twenty minutes with no mention I was starting to feel depressed, but then finally, after a story on how cough medicine was being moved behind the counter because people were using it to make methamphetamines, there came a short announcement of the rediscovery of this giant woodpecker. The media's cursory interest was such a disappointment that I felt tempted to run down the street knocking on doors, giving the amazing discovery its due. In 2006, ivory-bills were seen in the Florida panhandle, giving me hope it is not too late for them to make a spectacular comeback.

In the past few decades the environmental crisis has grown from the confined problem of extinctions of individual species to a full-blown global biodiversity crisis. We are losing entire groups of animals and plants, not just one species at a time. The migratory songbird declines are not limited to just a handful of unlucky birds; instead, dozens of species are in a chronic downhill slide. They come from every walk of life: grassland birds as well as forest birds, birds that spend the winter in Mexico and those that go all the way to Argentina, insect eaters and fruit eaters, those that breed in the far north and others that prefer the southern states. Their common decline tells us that our environmental problems are sweeping in scale, large enough to affect birds as they travel across two continents.

If a species goes extinct, or its population drops to very low numbers, the ecological roles that it played in nature are lost. Some species are so specialized that their services cannot be replaced by other animals, so their loss creates a ripple effect. The bellbird that disperses the seeds of the *Ocotea endresiana* tree in Costa Rica is an example. The scale of biodiversity loss is so huge today, and includes such plummeting numbers, that we risk losing the general basic services that sustain ecosystems. Although fewer than 2 percent of bird species have gone extinct in the past five hundred years, by some estimates the total number of birds has dropped by 20 to 30 percent. In the coming century, roughly 30 percent of birds and mammals worldwide will be threatened with extinction or will become so small in number that they are functionally extinct. Their jobs as pollinators, fruit-eaters, insect-eaters, scavengers, and nutrient recyclers will not get done, and this will disrupt ecosystems and affect everyone on the planet.

This is such a serious problem that in 2005 the United Nations issued a Millennium Ecosystem Assessment that lays out the consequences to human society of the collapse of ecosystem services around the globe. The underlying principle of the assessment is that people cause deterioration of ecosystem services, which in turn causes a deterioration of the quality of human life. The health of the world's ecosystems changed more rapidly in the second half of the twentieth century than at any time in human history. Cultivated lands now cover about one quarter of the earth's land surface, and forests have effectively disappeared from twenty-five countries, and another two dozen have lost more than 90 percent of their forest cover. About a third of the world's coastal mangrove forests have been destroyed in the past two decades. This enormous consumption of resources is driven by human population growth; our numbers have doubled in the past forty years and will double again before 2100.

What goes around comes around. Even if we live in cities we cannot escape the fact that we are intimately connected to the natural world. This truth has hit home most deeply with the suspicion, then certainty, that humans are warming up their planet. Mining fossil fuels then burning them in cars, homes, and factories has altered the global atmosphere and triggered a noticeable change in climate. The amount of carbon dioxide in the atmosphere has increased by about 20 percent since 1960. Global temperatures have already increased by almost one degree Celcius, and even the most conservative projections suggest the temperature will climb another two degrees Celcius by the end of this century; some of the bleakest predictions forecast an increase well over six degrees Celcius. Ecologically and economically, it makes a huge difference whether the future unfolds as a best-case or worst-case scenario. To stop this accelerating increase in temperature, not even to bring it back down to normal levels, we need to reduce our carbon dioxide emissions by 70 percent before 2050. At the same time, we need to shore up the ecosystem services that naturally keep carbon dioxide levels in check.

Forests are a storehouse for carbon, so are intricately linked to our global climate. Trees and other plants use carbon dioxide for their growth and store carbon in their tissues; the boreal forests of the northern hemisphere likely store more carbon than is contained in the world's known fossil fuel reserves. The boreal forests of Siberia absorb 10 percent of the human-caused carbon dioxide emissions each year, and North America's boreal forests probably match that amount. It simply doesn't make sense to clear-cut boreal forests even though they may seem like an endless resource that is ripe for the taking. We need those intact forests more than ever before, and we need birds and all the other key players in the ecosystem to maintain healthy forests.

Tropical forests are being cleared at the highest rate in the history of mankind, and the amount of original forest that has been lost is expected to double by 2050. When tropical forests are cleared they are usually burned, releasing their stored carbon into the air in quantities that rival fossil-fuel burning. Deforestation releases carbon into the atmosphere and at the same time cuts short the forest's natural role in using up the carbon dioxide already in the atmosphere. Global warming is expected to affect northern climates most severely, and threatens the boreal forest that the world depends on already for cleaning up our carbon emissions. Global warming is expected to speed up over the next hundred years because climate change will cause widespread shrinking of the boreal forests, which will in turn reduce the ecosystem's ability to buffer carbon dioxide increases in the atmosphere. Tropical deforestation in the Amazon and logging in the remote boreal forest does affect the lives of people living far away in cities.

Birds have noticed the change in climate. Nest records from thousands of tree swallow nest boxes dating back to the early 1950s allow us to look for changes in the timing of their breeding in response to global warming. Female birds are careful to time the laying of their eggs to match good spring weather; females cannot afford the expense of making eggs unless their own bodies are in good condition, and once laid she has to sit on the eggs and keep them warm. If a female tree swallow jumps the gun, it will be hard for her to find flying insects in the cold weather, and she may be forced to abandon the clutch to save her own life. Since the 1950s, tree swallows in North America have advanced their breeding by about nine days, coinciding with an increase in air temperature over the same period.

Climate change affects the nesting success and survival of neotropical migratory songbirds as well. Over the short run, the natural ups and downs of global climate change are generated by cycles driven by changes in the temperatures of the Pacific Ocean near the equator.

During an El Niño year, ocean temperatures are unusually warm, which triggers global changes in air circulation high in the atmosphere and changes in rainfall patterns. This short-term climate change gives us a chance to get a preview of what will happen in the future if such changes were more permanent. A long-term study of black-throated blue warblers found that over ten years, the survival of birds on their winter territories in Jamaica dropped during both El Niño years that happened during the study. Black-throated blue warblers are territorial and eat insects during winter, so face an annual food shortage during the dry season in February and March. Rainfall in Jamaica becomes unusually low during El Niño years, making food even harder to find, and fewer birds survive. On the breeding grounds in New Hampshire, climate patterns affect breeding success. Females laid fewer eggs in El Niño years, and their nestlings left the nest skinnier than in normal years. Global warming is expected to increase the severity of El Niño years, so migratory songbirds will be shaken with higher death rates in winter and in summer will produce fewer young to replace them, driving populations even lower.

We have learned that birds are not just bio-indicators of environmental change; they are nature's blue-collar workers, helping to sustain the environment that we share with them. The planet's ability to cope with increasing carbon dioxide levels depends in large part on the health of our forests; healthy forests will soak up more carbon dioxide and buy us more time to get our carbon emissions under control. Birds are intimately tied to the health of forests, and vice versa. Tropical deforestation is cutting migratory bird populations off at the knees; they are losing their best wintering habitat and suffer lower survival and often longer-term consequences too, like delays in migration and lower breeding success. Tropical deforestation also has a hidden cost: it forces migrants out into agricultural landscapes where they find less food and are likely to encounter deadly pesticides. Migrants connect the ecosystems of the tropics and the northern forests; their own healthy populations depend on both, and so do our human populations.

In many ways we live in a fantasy world, consuming resources on our planet with abandon and ignoring the realities of how ecosystems really function and support life and human society. It is almost as though we are living a Hollywood version of Gretchen Daily's challenge question: what animals and plants would you need to take with you if you wanted to set up a human colony on a distant planet? Will our grandchildren be happy living on a planet that will have at least 12 billion people by the end of this century, doubling our already crowded world? Certainly not, especially if they also have to live with a projected 50 percent decrease in the amount of tropical forest, a boreal forest that has been logged over half of its area, and global climate change. Where will their clean air, fresh water, and rain come from? Without nature's services intact, including the forests, birds, and bees, it will be difficult to support such a large human population.

How can the vicious cycle be broken? The global problems of over-population, overconsumption of natural resources, broken ecosystems, rising temperatures, and increasing world poverty seem inevitable and overwhelming. Even solving one part of the problem, the collapsing bird-migration system, seems insurmountable. Consider all the environmental roadblocks birds face during their journey: tropical deforestation, lethal pesticides, loss of important habitat used for migration, cats, colliding with buildings and towers, and, as if all this was not bad enough, loss and fragmentation of their rich breeding grounds.

Yet there is hope for migratory birds and the state of the planet. There are simple actions we can take every day that will help to promote a healthier world for birds, for ourselves, and for our grandchildren (table 10.1). We can help our migrants find safe winter homes by buying shade coffee as well as bird-friendly produce like organic pineapples and bananas. To help save the boreal forest, North America's bird nursery, we can buy "green" paper products made from recycled paper and wood products from forests that were harvested sustainably. It is so easy! People living in major cities can turn their lights out at night, and everyone can keep their cats indoors and ask their neighbours to do the same.

What to Buy or Do		Why
Buy shade coffee or sustainable coffee that is organic and fairly traded	•	Increases tropical forest habitat for birds and other wildlife; conserves soil; provides fair profits for farmers; fewer pesticides in environment
When buying produce from Latin America, such as bananas and pineapples, choose organic when available	•	Reduces the amount of dangerous pesticide use in the tropics; fewer birds killed; safer for farmers and consumers
Buy organic, or avoid altogether when possible, the North American crops that pose the greatest risk to birds: alfalfa, Brussels sprouts, blueberries, celery, corn, cotton, cranberries, potatoes, and wheat	•	Reduces the amount of dangerous pesticides in the environment; fewer birds killed; safer for farmers and consumers
Buy wood and paper products that are certified by the Forest Stewardship Council	•	Increases amount of forest being logged sustainably and responsibly; better habitat for birds and a healthier forest
Buy disposable paper products (toilet paper, paper towels, tissues) that are made from recycled paper and that are not bleached with chlorine	•	Reduces logging pressure on forests; increases habitat for birds; creates less pollution
Turn off the lights at night in city buildings and homes during peak migration periods	•	Fewer birds killed and injured by hitting buildings; saves electricity
Keep your cat indoors	•	Fewer birds killed; healthier and longer lives for pets

Table 10.1 *How You Can Make a Difference*

Our day-to-day choices add up to an enormous ecosystem boost for birds and other wildlife.

Birds are worth saving, not just for practical reasons but because they are a fascinating window on nature and the history of life on earth. They teach us how the natural world works at its most basic level. Inside their bodies, migrants are fine-tuned flying machines that can navigate precisely over thousands of miles without the benefit of electronic wonders like Global Positioning Systems. Their internal clocks tell them when to breed and when to migrate, and trigger precise hormonal changes that affect their entire bodies from head to toe to match the change in seasons. Over many thousands of years songbirds have shaped the natural world around us; trees make fruit and flowers for them, insects hide from them, and predators hunt them down. Songbirds are beautiful to see and hear, and their fascinating behaviour reminds us of our own lives: moving to a new home, finding food, choosing partners, and the challenges of raising children.

On a cool spring morning in late April, the sun shone brightly through the trees, giving them a ghostly pale green glow as their young leaves peeked out of the buds on the branches. A small group of curious onlookers stood under a tree beside a picnic table; the group included a mother and her two daughters, an older woman in a broad-rimmed white hat with binoculars around her neck, and a young man who had just arrived and was still wearing his bicycle helmet. The young girls had built a small fort out of branches to keep themselves amused while they waited.

The visitors were there to see migrants at a bird-banding station in a large park near downtown Toronto. During the migration seasons, the Toronto Bird Observatory catches migrants that have stopped in the park to rest during their long trip. That morning I was helping with a program we call "Birds in the City," an invitation to the city's residents to come out and see the songbirds that are all around them and that share their crowded space during spring and fall.

Volunteers from the TBO had just done a net run, and came back holding several cotton bags that were wriggling and jumping. The crowd gathered around as Richard Joos, from the TBO, took each bird out its bag, one by one, and in his gentle, calm voice carefully showed them how you tell the magnolia warbler from the American redstart. Richard explained that the redstart was a young male, flying north to breed for the very first time; it had pale yellow and grey colours instead of the bold orange and black of older males. The tiny whiskers at the edge of his mouth like whiskers on a cat, are called rictal bristles; they help the bird scoop flying insects into his mouth. Richard spread the long outer tail feathers and pointed to the large yellow spots; the bird flashes his tail open and shut while feeding, trying to flush insects out of their hiding places. Young and old, the visitors stared intently at the tiny bird in Richard's hand, listening to every word.

Each bird had dozens of stories to tell, but there were others waiting in line so Richard passed the redstart to me. I held it up close to the youngest girl, who was about six years old, and she gently stroked her finger down its smooth back. I asked her to touch his tiny chest and feel the strong flight muscles that had carried him thousands of miles in the past few weeks. He had a long trip ahead of him tonight and would be flying under the stars long after she had gone to bed. At his next stop, though, he would not have any spectators, and instead of finding himself in the middle of a city he would be surrounded by forest far to our north. I showed the older girl how to hold the bird; the redstart looked directly at her as she gently closed her small fingers around his body. She was nose to nose with him, and her eyes lit up as she looked back at the bird, smiling. Time stood still for a moment. Then in slow motion she opened her hand, and in a flash the redstart was gone.

ACKNOWLEDGEMENTS

The catalyst for *Silence of the Songbirds* was my appearance on the front page of the *Toronto Star* one New Year's Day, when I was given the honour of being among ten diverse people chosen as "People to Watch" in the coming year. This sparked two separate phone calls that led to this book. The first was from a member of a private foundation in Toronto, interested to know if I had any plans to use my research for environmental education. Yes, I replied, I was planning on writing a book (but actually had done nothing about it!). She was much more interested in my idea to bring kids and their parents face to face with songbirds that pass through the city during migration. A few days later Jim Gifford, an editor at HarperCollins Canada, called to ask whether I had ever thought of writing a book about my life with songbirds. And there began my journey.

Acknowledgements

Silence of the Songbirds focuses on my own experiences with migratory birds but also describes the work of many excellent scientists who have been tackling this problem for years. I could not possibly include all the important research on this subject and have deliberately glossed over some of the controversies surrounding the measurement of bird declines and the debate over whether winter versus breeding-ground events are more to blame. One can debate at great length exactly which species are declining, by how much, where they are declining the most, and whether banding stations or breeding bird surveys yield the most accurate estimates of population changes. The important point is that many species are in trouble and face serious threats on every part of their trip: on wintering grounds, during migration, and on breeding grounds.

I can think of at least one respected colleague who will cringe in disgust when he reads the term "wintering ground." There is no such thing as winter and summer in the tropics. Instead, there is the dry season and the wet season, so it would be more accurate to describe our migrants' tropical homes as their non-breeding grounds. Professionals may object to my including flycatchers with the songbirds because flycatchers are technically sub-oscines within the order Passeriformes (perching birds, known for their "thumbs" rather than their lovely voices). The birds with elaborate songs are the oscine group of perching birds, which includes the warblers, thrush, orioles, vireos, and their cousins.

My husband, Gene, was always the first to lay eyes on my rough drafts and got used to finding me in the kitchen pounding away on my laptop first thing in the morning, the coffee in the pot already cold. Our children, Douglas and Sarah, were even more relieved to see the book finished; the dedication at the beginning of this book borrows words from our friend Barbara. My students, friends, and family commented on rough drafts of various chapters, sometimes the entire manuscript, including Kim Jones, Lance Woolaver, Rina Nichols, Pam Bezic, Katie Goetz, Joan Howlett, and Marian Morton. Dr. Pierre Mineau, an expert on pesticides and birds, was very helpful in answering my many questions and reading that chapter. Many other colleagues answered specific question about their research. Thanks to my editors, Jim Gifford of HarperCollins Canada and Jackie Jackson of Walker & Company, for their enthusiasm and guidance. Finally, my research studies and graduate students have been supported all these years most notably, but not exclusively, by the Natural Sciences and Engineering Research Council of Canada. Through the York Foundation, I am donating my proceeds from this book to support research on migratory songbirds.

Sources

1: Paradise Not Yet Lost

Ford, H. A., G. W. Barrett, D. A. Saunders, and H. F. Recher. 2001. Why have birds in the woodlands of Southern Australia declined? *Biological Conservation* 97:71–88.

Fuller, R. J., D. G. Noble, K. W. Smith, and D. Vanhinsbergh. 2005. Recent declines of populations of woodland birds in Britain: A review of possible causes. *British Birds* 98:116–43.

Johnston, D. W., and J. M. Hagan III. 1992. Geographic patterns in population trends of neotropical migrants in North America. In *Ecology and conservation of neotropical migrant landbirds,* eds. J. M. Hagan III and D. W. Johnston, 75–84. Washington, D.C.: Smithsonian Institution Press.

Newton, I. 2004. The recent declines of farmland bird populations in Britain: An appraisal of causal factors and conservation actions. *Ibis* 146:579–600.

Pimm, S., P. Raven, A. Peterson, C. Şekercioğlu, and P. R. Erlich. 2006. Human impacts on the rates of recent, present, and future bird extinctions. *Proceedings of the National Academy of Sciences* 103:10941–46.

Şekercioğlu, C. H., G. C. Daily, and P. R. Erlich. 2004. Ecosystem consequences of bird declines. *Proceedings of the National Academy of Sciences* 101:18042–47.

2: Canaries in the Mine

Audubon, J. J. 1871. *The birds of America, from drawings made in the United States and their territories.* Vol. 5. New York: G. R. Lockwood.

Black, J. A busy night on the Buffalo NEXRAD. http://www.physics.brocku.ca/People/Faculty/black

Daily, G. C. 1997. *Nature's services: Societal dependence on natural ecosystems.* Washington, D.C.: Island Press.

Evans, W. R. 2005. Monitoring avian night flight calls—The new century ahead. *Passenger Pigeon* 67:15–24.

Evans, W. R., and D. K. Mellinger. 1999. Monitoring grassland birds in nocturnal migration. *Studies in Avian Biology* 19:219–29.

Gauthreaux, S., Jr., and C. G. Belser. 2005. Radar ornithology and the conservation of migratory birds. In *Bird conservation implementation and integration in the Americas: Proceedings of the 3rd International Partners in Flight Conference 2002,* eds. C. J. Ralph and T. Rich, 871–76. General Technical Report PSW-GTR-191. Albany, Calif.: U.S.D.A. Forest Service.

Hickey, J. J., and D. W. Anderson. 1968. Chlorinated hydrocarbons and eggshell changes in raptorial and fish-eating birds. *Science* 162:271–73.

Kelley, T. 2006. Listening to the faint flutter of birds passing in the night. *New York Times,* May 21.

Oaks, J. L., M. Gilbert, M. Z. Virani, R. T. Watson, C. U. Meteyer, B. A. Rideout, H. L. Shivaprasad, S. Ahmed, M. J. I. Chaudhry, M. Arshad, A. Ali, and A. A. Khan. 2004. Diclofenac residues as the cause of vulture population decline in Pakistan. *Nature* 427:630–33.

Prakash, V., D. J. Pain, A. A. Cunningham, P. F. Donald, N. Prakash, A. Verma, R. Gargi, S. Sivakamar, and A. R. Rahmani. 2003. Catastrophic collapse of Indian white-backed *Gyps bengalensis* and long-billed *Gyps indicus* vulture populations. *Biological Conservation* 109:381–90.

Pretty, J., and R. Hine. 2005. Pesticide use and the environment. In *The pesticide detox: Towards a more sustainable agriculture,* ed. J. N. Pretty, 1–22. London: Earthscan.

Sauer, J. R., J. E. Hines, and J. Fallon. 2005. The North American Breeding Bird Survey, results and analysis 1966–2005. Version 6.2. 2006. Laurel, MD: U.S.G.S. Patuxent Wildlife Research Center.

Terborgh, J. 1989. *Where have all the birds gone?* Princeton, NJ: Princeton University Press.

U.N. Millennium Ecosystem Assessment. 2005. *Ecosystems and human well-being: Synthesis.* Washington, D.C.: Island Press.

3: The Breeding Bird Survey

Blancher, P. 2003. *Importance of Canada's boreal forest to landbirds.* Ottawa: Canadian Boreal Initiative. http://www.borealbirds.org/bsi-bscreport.pdf.

Faaborg, J. 2002. *Saving migrant birds.* Austin: University of Texas Press.

Faaborg, J., and W. J. Arendt. 1992. Long-term declines of winter resident warblers in a Puerto Rico dry forest: Which species are in trouble? In *Ecology and conservation of neotropical migrant landbirds,* eds. J. M. Hagan III and D. W. Johnston, 57–63. Washington, D.C.: Smithsonian Institution Press.

Hussell, D. J. T., M. H. Mather, and P. H. Sinclair. 1992. Trends in numbers of tropical and temperate wintering migrant landbirds in migration at Long

Point, Ontario, 1961–1988. In *Ecology and conservation of neotropical migrant landbirds,* eds. J. M. Hagan III and D. W. Johnston, 101–30. Washington, D.C.: Smithsonian Institution Press.

Lloyd-Evans, T. L., and J. L. Atwood. 2004. 32 years of changes in passerine numbers during spring and fall migration in coastal Massachusetts. *Wilson Bulletin* 116:1–16.

Peterjohn, B. G., J. R. Sauer, and C. R. Robbins. 1995. Population trends from the North American Breeding Bird Survey. In *Ecology and management of neotropical migratory birds,* eds. T. E. Martin and D. M. Finch, 3–39. New York: Oxford University Press.

Robbins, C. S., J. R. Sauer, R. S. Greenberg, and S. Droege. 1989. Population declines in North American birds that migrate to the neotropics. *Proceedings of the National Academy of Sciences* 86:7658–62.

Sauer, J. R., and S. Droege. 1992. Geographic patterns in population trends of neotropical migrants in North America. In *Ecology and conservation of neotropical migrant landbirds,* eds. J. M. Hagan III and D. W. Johnston, 26–42. Washington, D.C.: Smithsonian Institution Press.

4: Birds in the Rainforest

Archard, F., H. D. Eva, H. Stibig, P. Mayaux, J. Gallego, T. Richards, and J. Malingreau. 2002. Determination of deforestation rates of the world's humid tropical forests. *Science* 297:999–1002.

Bearhop, S., G. M. Hilton, S. C. Votier, and S. Waldron. 2004. Stable isotope ratios indicate that body condition in migrating passerines is influenced by winter habitat. *Proceedings of the Royal Society of London B* 271:S215–S218.

Cordeiro, N. J., and H. F. Howe. 2003. Forest fragmentation severs mutualism between seed dispersers and an endemic African tree. *Proceedings of the National Academy of Sciences* 100:14052 56.

Da Silva, J. M. C, and M. Tabarelli. 2000. Tree species impoverishment and the future flora of the Atlantic forest of northeast Brazil. *Nature* 404:72–74.

DeFries, R., A. Hansen, A. C. Newton, and M. C. Hansen. 2005. Increasing isolation of protected areas in tropical forests over the past twenty years. *Ecological Applications* 15:19–26.

Durand, L., and E. Lazos. 2004. Colonization and tropical deforestation in the Sierra Santa Marta, southern Mexico. *Environmental Conservation* 31:11–21.

Estrada, A., and R. Coates-Estrada. 2005. Diversity of neotropical migratory landbird species assemblages in forest fragments and man-made vegetation in Los Tuxtlas, Mexico. *Biodiversity and Conservation* 14:1719–34.

Ferraz, G., G. J. Russell, P. C. Stouffer, R. O. Bierregaard Jr., S. L. Pimm, and T. E. Lovejoy. 2003. Rates of species loss from Amazonian forest fragments. *Proceedings of the National Academy of Sciences* 100:14069–73.

Gascon, C., T. E. Lovejoy, R. O. Bierregaard Jr., J. R. Malcolm, P. C. Stouffer, H. L. Vasconcelos, W. F. Laurance, B. Zimmerman, M. Tocher, and S. Borges. 1999. Matrix habitat and species richness in tropical forest remnants. *Biological Conservation* 91:223–29.

Geist, H. J., and E. F. Lambin. 2002. Proximate causes and underlying driving forces of tropical deforestation. *BioScience* 52:143–50.

Grau, H. R., N. I. Gasparri, and T. M. Aide. 2005. Agricultural expansion and deforestation in seasonally dry forests of north-west Argentina. *Environmental Conservation* 32:140–48.

Greenberg, R., P. Bichier, A. Cruz-Angon, C. MacVean, R. Perez, and E. Cano. 2000. The impact of avian insectivory on arthropods and leaf damage in some Guatemalan coffee plantations. *Ecology* 81:1750–55.

Greenberg, R., M. S. Foster, and L. Marquez-Valelamar. 1995. The role of the white-eyed vireo in the dispersal of *Bursera* fruit on the Yucatán Peninsula. *Journal of Tropical Ecology* 11:619–39.

Hansen, M. C., and R. S. DeFries. 2004. Detecting long-term global forest change using continuous fields of tree-cover maps from 8-km Advanced Very High Resolution Radiometer (AVHRR) data for the years 1982–1999. *Ecosystems* 7:695–716.

Lepers, E., E. F. Lambin, A. C. Janetos, R. DeFries, F. Achard, N. Ramankutty, and R. J. Scholes. 2005. A synthesis of information on rapid land-cover change for the period 1981–2000. *BioScience* 55:115–23.

Mann, C. C. 2005. *1491: New revelations of the Americas before Columbus.* New York: Alfred A. Knopf.

Marra, P. P., K. A. Hobson, and R. T. Holmes. 1998. Linking winter and summer events in a migratory bird by using stable-carbon isotopes. *Science* 282:1884–86.

Marra, P. P., and R. L. Holberton. 1998. Corticosterone levels as indicators of habitat quality: Effects of habitat segregation in a migratory bird during the nonbreeding season. *Oecologia* 116:284–92.

Mayaux, P., P. Holmgren, F. Achard, H. Eva, H. Stibig, and A. Branthomme. 2005. Tropical forest cover change in the 1990s and options for future monitoring. *Philosophical Transactions of the Royal Society B* 360:373–84.

Morton, E. S. 1990. Habitat segregation by sex in the hooded warbler: Experiments on proximate causation and discussion of its evolution. *American Naturalist* 135:319–33.

Norris, D. R., P. P. Marra, T. K. Kyser, T. W. Sherry, and L. M. Ratcliffe. 2003. Tropical winter habitat limits reproductive success on the temperate breeding grounds in a migratory bird. *Proceedings of the Royal Society of London B* 271:59–64.

Philpott, S. M., R. Greenberg, P. Bichier, and I. Perfecto. 2004. Impacts of major predators on tropical agroforest arthropods: Comparisons within and across taxa. *Oecologia* 140:140–49.

Remsen, J. V., Jr. 2001. True winter range of the Veery (*Catharus fuscenscens*): Lessons for determining winter ranges of species that winter in the tropics. *Auk* 118:838–48.

Renjifo, L. M. 1999. Composition changes in subandean avifauna after long-term forest fragmentation. *Conservation Biology* 13:1124–39.

Rappole, J. H. 1995. *The ecology of migrant birds: A neotropical perspective.* Washington, D.C.: Smithsonian Institution Press.

Rappole, J. H., and E. S. Morton. 1985. Effects of habitat alteration on a tropical forest community. In *Neotropical Ornithology*, eds. P. A. Buckley, M. S. Foster, R. S. Ridgely, and F. G. Buckley. Ornithological Monographs 36:1013–21.

Rappole, J. H., E. S. Morton, T. E. Lovejoy III, and J. L. Ruos. 1983. *Nearctic avian migrants in the neotropics.* Washington, D.C.: U.S. Fish and Wildlife Service.

Rappole, J. H., M. A. Ramos, and K. Winker. 1989. Wintering wood thrush movements and mortality in southern Veracruz. *Auk* 106:402–10.

Şekercioğlu, C. H., P. R. Ehrlich, G. C. Daily, D. Aygen, D. Goehring, and R. F. Sandi. 2002. Disappearance of insectivorous birds from tropical forest fragments. *Proceedings of the National Academy of Sciences* 99:263–67.

Sherry, T. W., and R. T. Holmes. 1996. Winter habitat quality, population limitation, and conservation of neotropical-nearctic migrant birds. *Ecology* 77:36–48.

Sillet, T. S., and R. T. Holmes. 2002. Variation in survivorship of a migratory songbird throughout its annual cycle. *Journal of Animal Ecology* 71:296–308.

Strong, A. M., and T. W. Sherry. 2000. Habitat-specific effects of food abundance on the condition of ovenbirds wintering in Jamaica. *Journal of Animal Ecology* 69:883–95.

Strong, A. M., and T. W. Sherry. 2001. Body condition of Swainson's warblers wintering in Jamaica and the conservation value of Caribbean dry forest. *Wilson Bulletin* 113:410–18.

Studds, C. E., and P. P. Marra. 2005. Nonbreeding habitat occupancy and population processes: An upgrade experiment with a migratory bird. *Ecology* 86:2380–85.

Stutchbury, B. J. 1994. Competition for winter territories in a neotropical migrant: The role of age, sex and color. *Auk* 111:63–69.

Turner, I. M., and R. T. Corlett. 1996. The conservation value of small, isolated fragments of lowland tropical rain forest. *Trends in Ecology and Evolution* 11:330–33.

Van Bael, S. A., J. D. Brawn, and S. K. Robinson. 2003. Birds defend trees from herbivores in a neotropical forest canopy. *Proceedings of the National Academy of Sciences* 100: 8304–7.

Van Houtan, K. S., S. L. Pimm, R. O. Bierregaard, T. E. Lovejoy, and P. C. Stouffer. 2006. Local extinctions in flocking birds in Amazonian forest fragments. *Evolutionary Ecology Research* 8:129–48.

Van Laake, P. E., and A. Sánchez-Azofeifa. 2004. Focus on deforestation: Zooming in on hot spots in highly fragmented ecosystems in Costa Rica. *Agriculture Ecosystems and Environment* 102:3–15.

Warkentin, I. G., R. Greenberg, and J. Salgado Ortiz. 1995. Songbird use of gallery woodlands in recently cleared and older settled landscapes of the Selva Lacandona, Chiapas, Mexico. *Conservation Biology* 9:1095–106.

Wenny, D. G., and D. J. Levey. 1998. Directed seed dispersal by bellbirds in a tropical cloud forest. *Proceedings of the National Academy of Sciences* 95:6204–7.

Williams, M. 2003. *Deforesting the earth.* Chicago: University of Chicago Press.

Winker, K., J. H. Rappole, and M. A. Ramos. 1990. Population dynamics of the wood thrush in southern Veracruz, Mexico. *Condor* 92:444–60.

Wright, S. J. 2005. Tropical forests in a changing environment. *Trends in Ecology and Evolution* 20:553–60.

Wunderle, J. M., Jr. 1997. The role of animal seed dispersal in accelerating native forest regeneration on degraded tropical lands. *Forestry Ecology and Management* 99:223–35.

5: COFFEE WITH A CONSCIENCE

Betsell, J. 2004a. Coffee binds Bainbridge Island to Nicaragua Island. *Seattle Times,* September 21.

Betsell, J. 2004b. Cup by cup, coffee fuels world market. *Seattle Times,* September 19.

Brash, A. R. 1987. The history of avian extinction and forest conversion on Puerto Rico. *Biological Conservation* 39:97–111.

Cruz-Angon, A., and R. Greenberg. 2005. Are epiphytes important for birds in coffee plantations? An experimental assessment. *Journal of Applied Ecology* 42:150–59.

Daily, G. C., G. Ceballos, J. Pacheco, G. Suzán, and A. Sánchez-Azofeifa. 2003. Countryside biogeography of neotropical mammals: Conservation opportunities in agricultural landscapes of Costa Rica. *Conservation Biology* 17:1814–26.

Daugherty, H. E. 2005. Biodiversity conservation and rural sustainability: A case study of the Alexander Skutch Biological Corridor in southern Costa Rica. In

Ecosystems and sustainable development V, eds. E. Tiezzai, C. A. Brebbia, S. E. Jorgensen, and D. Almorza Gormar, 155–161. Southampton, UK: WIT Press.

Greenberg, R., P. Bichier, A. Cruz-Angon, and R. Reitsma. 1997. Bird populations in shade and sun coffee plantations in central Guatemala. *Conservation Biology* 11:448–59.

Greenberg, R., P. Bichier, and J. Sterling. 1997. Bird populations in rustic and planted shade-coffee plantations of eastern Chiapas, Mexico. *Biotropica* 29:501–14.

International Coffee Organization. 2005. *Trade statistics.* http://www.ico.org.

Luna, F. V., and H. S. Klein. 2003. *Slavery and the ecology of São Paulo 1750–1850.* Stanford, Calif.: Stanford University Press.

Mas, A. H., and T. V. Dietsch. 2004. Linking shade-coffee certification to biodiversity conservation: Butterflies and birds in Chiapas, Mexico. *Ecological Applications* 14:642–54.

Moguel, P., and V. M. Toledo. 1999. Biodiversity conservation in traditional coffee systems of Mexico. *Conservation Biology* 13:11–21.

Perfecto, I., A. Mas, T. Dietsch, and J. Vandermeer. 2003. Conservation of biodiversity in coffee agrosystems: A tri-taxa comparison in southern Mexico. *Biodiversity and Conservation* 12: 1239–52.

Petit, L. J., and D. R. Petit. Evaluating the importance of human-modified lands for neotropical bird conservation. *Conservation Biology* 17:687–94.

Pineda, E., C. Moreno, F. Escobar, and G. Halffter. 2005. Frog, bat, and dung beetle diversity in the cloud forest and coffee agrosystems of Veracruz, Mexico. *Conservation Biology* 19:400–10.

Rice, R.A, 1999. A place unbecoming: The coffee farm of northern Latin America. *Geographical Review* 89:554–79.

Rice, R.A. 2003. Coffee production in a time of crisis: Social and environmental connections. *SAIS Review* 23:221–45.

Rice, R.A., and J. Ward. 1996. *Coffee, conservation, and commerce in the Western Hemisphere.* Washington, D.C.: Smithsonian Migratory Bird Center and Natural Resources Defense Council.

Roberts, D. L., R. J. Cooper, and L. J. Petit. 2000. Flock characteristics of ant-following birds in premontane moist forest and coffee agroecosystems. *Ecological Applications* 10:1414–25.

Tejeda-Cruz, C. and W. J. Sutherland. 2004. Bird responses to shade-coffee production. *Animal Conservation* 7:169–79.

Tolme, P. 2004. Made in the shade. *Audubon Magazine* 108(3): 56–69.

Topik, S.C., and A. Wells. 1998. *The second conquest of Latin America: Coffee, henequen and oil during the export boom 1850–1930.* Austin: University of Texas Press.

Wagner, R. 2001. *The history of coffee in Guatemala.* Bogotá, Colombia: Benjamín Villegas and Assoc.

Wunderle, J. M., Jr., and S. M. Latta. 1996. Avian abundance in sun and shade-coffee plantations and remnant pine forest in the Cordillera Central, Dominican Republic. *Ornithologia Neotropical* 7:19–34.

Wunderle, J. M., Jr., and S. M. Latta. 1998. Avian resource use in Dominican shade-coffee plantations. *Wilson Bulletin* 110: 271–81.

Wunderle, J. M., Jr., and S. M. Latta. 2000. Winter site fidelity of nearctic migrants in shade-coffee plantations of different sizes in the Dominican Republic. *Auk* 117:596–614.

6: Falling from the Sky

Alegria, H. A., T. F. Bidleman, and T. J. Shaw. Organochlorine pesticides in ambient air of Belize, Central America. *Environmental Science Technology* 24:1953–58.

Arbona, S. I. 1998. Commercial agriculture and agrochemicals in Almolonga, Guatemala. *Geographical Review* 88:47–63.

Bartuszevige, A. M., A. P. Caparella, R. G. Harper, J. A. Frick, B. Criley, K. Doty, and E. Erhart. 2002. Organochlorine pesticide contamination in grassland-nesting passerines that breed in North America. *Environmental Pollution* 117:225–32.

Basili, G., and S. A. Temple. 1995. A perilous migration. *Natural History* 95(9): 40–47.

Basili, G., and S. A. Temple. 1999. Dickcissels and crop damage in Venezuela: Defining the problem with ecological models. *Ecology* 9:732–39.

Busby, D. G., P. A. Pearce, N. R. Garrity, and L. M. Reynolds. 1983. Effect of an organophosphorus insecticide on brain cholinesterase activity in white-throated sparrows exposed to aerial forest spraying. *Journal of Applied Ecology* 20:225–63.

Busby, D. G., L. M. White, and P. A. Pearce. 1990. Effects of aerial spraying of fenitrothion on breeding white-crowned sparrows. *Journal of Applied Ecology* 27:743–55.

Capparella, A. P., J. A. Klemens, R. G. Harper, and J. A. Frick. 2003. Lack of widespread contamination in South American resident passerines. *Bulletin of Environmental Contamination and Toxicology* 70:769–74.

Carson, R. 1962. *Silent spring.* Repr., New York: Houghton Mifflin Co., 2002.

Fildes, K., L. B. Astheimer, P. Story, W. A. Buttemer, and M. J. Hooper. 2006. Cholinesterase response in native birds exposed to fenitrothion during locust control operations in eastern Australia. *Environmental Toxicology and Chemistry* 25:2964–70.

Fleischli, M. A., J. C. Franson, N. J. Thomas, D. L. Finley, and W. Riley Jr. 2004. Avian mortality events in the United States caused by anticholinesterase pesticides: A retrospective summary of National Wildlife Health Center Records from 1980 to 2000. *Archives of Environmental Contamination and Toxicology* 46:542–50.

Frick, J. A., J. A. Klemens, R. G. Harper, and A. P. Capparella. 1998. Effect of skin removal on estimated levels of organochlorine pesticide contamination in passerine birds. *Bulletin of Environmental Contamination and Toxicology* 61:658–63.

Galvao, L. A., J. A. Escamilla, S. Henao, E. Loyola, C. Castillo, and P. Arbelaez. 2002. *Pesticides and health in the Central American Isthmus.* Washington, D.C.: Pan American Health Organization and World Health Organization.

Gard, N. W., and M. J. Hooper. 1995. An assessment of potential hazards of pesticides and environmental contaminants. In *Ecology and management of neotropical migratory birds,* eds. T. E. Martin and D. M. Finch, 294–310. New York: Oxford University Press.

Harper, R. G., J. A. Frick, A. P. Capparella, B. Borup, M. Nowak, D. Biesinger, and C. F. Thompson. 1996. Organochlorine pesticide contamination in neotropical migrant passerines. *Archives of Environmental Contamination and Toxicology* 31: 386–90.

Hooper, M., J. P. Mineau, M. E. Zaccagnini, and B. Woodbridge. 2002. Pesticides and international migratory bird conservation. In *Handbook of ecotoxicology,* 2nd ed., eds. D. J. Hoffman, B. A. Rattner, G. A. Burton Jr., and J. Cairns Jr., 737–54. New York: Lewis Publishers.

Jiménez, B., R. Rodríguez-Estrella, R. Merino, G. Gómez, L. Rivera, M. J. González, E. Abad, and J. Rivera. 2005. Results and evaluation of the first study of organochlorine contaminants (PCDDs, PCDFs, PCBs and DDTs), heavy metals and metalloids in birds from Baja California, México. *Environmental Pollution* 133:139–46.

Kalantzi, O. I., R. E. Alcock, P. A. Johnston, D. Santillo, R. L. Stringer, G. O. Thomas, and K. C. Jones. 2001. The global distribution of PCBs and organochlorine pesticides in butter. *Environmental Science Technology* 35:1013–18.

Klemens, J. A., R. G. Harper, J. A. Frick, A. P. Capparella, H. B. Richardson, and M .J. Coffey. 2000. Patterns of organochlorine pesticide contamination in neotropical migrant passerines in relation to diet and winter habitat. *Chemosphere* 41:1107–13.

Klemens, J. A., M. L. Wieland, V. J. Flanagin, J. A. Frick, and R. G. Harper. 2003. A cross-taxa survey of organochlorine pesticide contamination in a Costa Rica wildland. *Environmental Pollution* 122:245–51.

Mineau, P. 2003. Avian species. In *Encyclopedia of Agrochemicals,* eds. J. R. Plimmer, D. W. Gammon, and N. N. Ragsdale, 129–143. Hoboken, NJ: John Wiley and Sons, Inc.

Mineau, P. 2003. Direct losses of birds to pesticides—Beginnings of a quantification. In *Bird conservation implementation and integration in the Americas: Proceedings of the 3rd International Partners in Flight Conference 2002,* eds. C. J. Ralph and T. Rich, 1065–70. General Technical Report PSW-GTR-191. Albany, CA: U.S.D.A. Forest Service.

Mineau, P. 2004. Birds and pesticides: Are pesticide regulatory decisions consistent with the protection afforded migratory bird species under the Migratory Bird Treaty Act? *William and Mary Environmental Law Review* 28:313–38.

Mineau, P., C. M. Downes, D. A. Kirk, E. Bayne, and M. Csizy. 2005. Patterns of bird species abundance in relation to granular insecticide use in the Canadian prairies. *Ecoscience* 12:267–78.

Mineau, P., and M. Whiteside. 2006. Lethal risk to birds from insecticide use in the United States: A spatial and temporal analysis. *Environmental Toxicology and Chemistry* 25:1214–22.

Mora, J. A. 1997. Transboundary pollution: Persistent organochlorine pesticides in migrant birds of the southwestern United States and Mexico. *Environmental Toxicology and Chemistry* 16:3–11.

Murray, D. L. 1994. *Cultivating crisis. The human cost of pesticides in Latin America.* Austin: University of Texas Press.

Naylor, R. L., and P. R. Erlich. 1997. Natural pest control services and agriculture. In *Nature's services: Societal dependence on natural ecosystems,* ed. G. C. Daily, 151–74. Washington, D.C.: Island Press.

Schafer, K. S., M. Reeves, S. Spitzer, and S. E. Kegley. 2004. *Chemical trespass: Pesticides in our bodies and corporate accountability.* San Francisco, CA: Pesticide Action Network North America.

Seabloom, R. W., G. L. Pearson, L. W. Oring, and J. R. Reilly. 1973. An incident of fenthion mosquito control and subsequent avian mortality. *Journal of Wildlife Diseases* 9:18–20.

Sherwood, S., D. Cole, C. Crissman, and M. Paredes. 2005. From pesticides to people: Improving ecosystem health in the northern Andes. In *The pesticide detox: Towards a more sustainable agriculture,* ed. J. N. Pretty, 147–64. London: Earthscan.

Taylor, M. D., S. J. Kaine, F. P. Carvalho, D. Barcelo, and J. Everaarts. 2003. *Pesticide residues in coastal tropical ecosystems.* New York: Taylor and Francis.

U.N. Food and Agriculture Organization. 2005. Pesticide import statistics. http://faostat.fao.org/site/423/default.aspx

U.S. Food and Drug Administration. 2005. 2003 report and database. *FDA*

pesticide program residue monitoring 1999–2003. http://www.cfsan.fda.gov/
~dms/pesrpts.html

Vyas, N. B., W. J. Kuenzel, E. F. Hill, and J. R. Sauer. 1995. Acephate affects
migratory orientation of the white-throated sparrow *(Zonotrichia albicollis).*
Environmental Toxicology and Chemistry 14:1961–65.

Weidensaul, S. 1999. *Living on the wind: Across the hemisphere with migratory birds.*
New York: North Point Press.

Wesseling, C. 2001. Dangerous pesticide use in Central America—Wanted: A
new approach. *Pesticide News* 54:12–14.

Wolfe, M. F., and R. J. Kendall. 1998. Age-dependent toxicity of diazinon and
terbufos in European starlings *(Sturnus vulgaris)* and red-winged blackbirds
(Agelaius phoeniceus). Environmental Toxicology and Chemistry 17: 1300–12.

7: BRIGHT LIGHTS, BIG DANGER

Able, K. 1999. *Gathering of angels: Migrating birds and their ecology.* Ithaca, NY:
Cornell University Press.

Barrow, W. C., Jr., C. Chao-Chen, R. B. Hamilton, K. Ouchley, and T. J.
Spengler. 2000. Disruption and restoration of en route habitat, a case study:
The Chenier plain. *Studies in Avian Biology* 20:71–87.

Cochran, W. W., H. Mouritsen, and M. Wikelski. 2004. Migrating songbirds
recalibrate their magnetic compass daily from twilight cues. *Science* 304:405–8.

Cronin, W. 1983. *Changes in the land: Indians, colonists and the ecology of New
England.* New York: Hill and Wang.

Duncan, C. D., B. Abel, D. Ewert, M. L. Ford, S. Mabey, D. Mehlman, P.
Patterson, R. Sutter, and M. Woodrey. 2002. Protecting stopover sites for
forest-dwelling migratory landbirds. Unpublished report. Arlington, VA: The
Nature Conservancy.

Erickson, W. P., G. D. Johnson, M. D. Strickland, D. P. Young Jr., K. J. Sernka,
R. E. Good. 2001. Avian collisions with wind turbines: A summary of existing
studies and comparisons to other sources of avian collision mortality in the
U.S. Cheyenne, WY: Western Ecosystems Technology, Inc.

Evans, W. R., and K. V. Rosenberg. 2000. Acoustic monitoring of night-migrating
birds: A progress report. In *Strategies of bird conservation: The Partners in Flight
planning process,* eds. R. Bonney, D. N. Pashley, R. J. Cooper, and L. Niles, 151–
59. Proceedings of the 3rd Partners in Flight Workshop, October 1–5,1995,
Cape May, NJ. Proceedings RMRS-P-16. Ogden, UT: U.S.D.A. Forest Service,
Rocky Mountain Research Station.

Evans Ogden, L. 1996. *Collision course: The hazards of lighted structures and windows to migrating birds.* Toronto: World Wildlife Fund and Fatal Lights Awareness Program.

Farnsworth, A. 2005. Flight calls and their value for future ornithological studies and conservation research. *Auk* 122:733–46.

Gallagher, T. 1994. Night sounds. *Birdscope* 8(3): 1–2.

Gauthreaux, S., Jr. 1992. The use of weather radar to monitor long-term patterns of trans-Gulf migration in spring. In *Ecology and conservation of neotropical migrant landbirds,* eds. J. M. Hagan III and D. W. Johnston, 96–100. Washington, D.C.: Smithsonian Institution Press.

Gauthreaux, S., Jr., and C. G. Belser. 2003. Radar ornithology and biological conservation. *Auk* 120:266–77.

James, R. D., and G. Coady. 2003. *Exhibition Place wind turbine bird monitoring program in 2003.* Report to Toronto Hydro Energy Services Inc. and WindShare, December.

Kerlinger, P. 2000. *Avian mortality at communication towers: A review of recent literature, research and methodology.* Cape May Point, NJ: Office of Migratory Bird Management, U.S. Fish and Wildlife Service. www.fws.gov/migratorybirds/issues/towers/review.pdf

Klem, D., Jr. 1989. Bird-window collisions. *Wilson Bulletin* 101:606–20.

Libby, O. G. 1899. The nocturnal flight of migrating birds. *Auk* 16:140–45.

Manville, A. M., II. 2005. Bird strikes and electrocutions at power lines, communication towers and wind turbines: State of the art and state of the science—Next steps toward mitigation. *Bird conservation implementation and integration in the Americas: Proceedings of the 3rd International Partners in Flight Conference 2002,* eds. C. J. Ralph and T. Rich, 1051–64. General Technical Report PSW-GTR-191. Albany, CA: U.S.D.A. Forest Service.

Moore, F. R., and D. A. Aborn. 2000. Mechanisms of en route habitat selection: How do migrants make habitat decisions during stopover? *Studies in Avian Biology* 20:34–42.

Nijhuis, M. 2006. Selling the wind. *Audubon Magazine* 108(5):54–60.

Osborn, R. G., K. F. Higgins, R. E. Usgaard, and C. D. Dieter. 2000. Bird mortality associated with wind turbines at the Buffalo Ridge Wind Resource Area, Minnesota. *American Midland Naturalist* 143:41–52.

Shire, G. G., K. Brown, and G. Winegrad. 2000. *Communication towers: A deadly hazard to birds.* Report for the American Bird Conservancy, June. www.abcbirds.org/policy/towerkillweb.pdf

Simons, T. R., F. R. Moore, and S. A. Gauthreaux. 2004. Mist-netting trans-gulf migrants at coastal stopover sites: The influence of spatial and temporal variability on capture data. *Studies in Avian Biology* 29:135–43.

Simons, T. R., S. M. Pearson, and F. R. Moore. 2000. Application of spatial models to the stopover ecology of trans-gulf migrants. *Studies in Avian Biology* 20:4–14.

Weidensaul, S. 1999. *Living on the wind: Across the hemisphere with migratory birds.* New York: North Point Press.

Wikelski, M., E. M. Tarlow, A. Raim, R. H. Diehl, R. P. Larkin, and G. H. Visser. 2003. Costs of migration in free-flying songbirds. *Nature* 423:704.

8: Stalking the Songbirds

American Bird Conservancy. 2006. Domestic cat predation on birds and other wildlife. *Birds and cats—The Cats Indoors! campaign.* http://www.abcbirds.org/cats

Askins, R. A. 1999. History of grassland birds in eastern North America. *Studies in Avian Biology* 19:60–71.

Baker, P. J., A. J. Bentley, R. J. Ansell, and S. Harris. 2005. Impact of predation by domestic cats *Felis catus* in an urban area. *Mammal Review* 35:302–12.

Brawn, J. D., and S. K. Robinson. 1996. Source-sink population dynamics may complicate the interpretation of long-term census data. *Ecology* 77:3–12.

Brittingham, M. C., and S. A. Temple. 1983. Have cowbirds caused forest songbirds to decline? *BioScience* 33:31–35.

Brown, B. T. 1993. Bell's vireo. In *The birds of North America,* no. 35, eds. A. Poole, P. Stettenheim, and F. Gill, 1–20. Washington, D.C.: American Ornithologists' Union; and Philadelphia: Academy of Natural Sciences.

Burke, D. M., and E. Nol. 2000. Landscape and fragment size effects on reproductive success of forest-breeding birds in Ontario. *Ecological Applications* 10: 1749–61.

Caplan, J. 2005. Paper war: Environmentalists take on Victoria's Secret for mailing more than one million catalogs a day. *Time,* December 11.

Cavitt, J. F., and T. M. Martin. 2002. Effects of forest fragmentation on brood parasitism and nest predation in eastern and western landscapes. *Studies in Avian Biology* 25:73–80.

Coleman, J. S., and S. A. Temple. 1993. Rural residents' free-ranging domestic cats: A survey. *Wildlife Society Bulletin* 21:381–90.

Coleman, J. S., S. A. Temple, and S. R. Craven. 1997. *Cats and wildlife: A conservation dilemma.* Madison: University of Wisconsin-Extension. http://wildlife.wisc.edu/extension/catfly3.htm

Crawford, H. S., and D. T. Jennings. 1989. Predation by birds on spruce budworm *Choristoneura fumiferana:* Functional, numerical, and total responses. *Ecology* 70:152–63.

Decapita, M. E. 2000. Brown-headed cowbird control on Kirtland's warbler nesting areas in Michigan, 1972–1995. In *Ecology and management of cowbirds and their hosts,* eds. J. N. M. Smith, T. L. Cook, S. I. Rothstein, S. K. Robinson, and S. G. Sealy, 333–41. Austin: University of Texas Press.

Donovan, T. M., F. R. Thompson III, J. Faaborg, and J. R. Probst. 1995. Reproductive success of migratory birds in habitat sources and sinks. *Conservation Biology* 9:1380–95.

Fauth, P. T. 2001. Wood thrush populations are not all sinks in the agricultural Midwestern United States. *Conservation Biology* 15:523–27.

Fiore, C.A., and K. B. Sullivan. 2000. *Domestic cat* (Felis catus) *predation of birds in an urban environment.* http://www.geocities.com/the_srco/Article.html

Friesen, L., M. D. Cadman, and R. J. MacKay. 1999. Nesting success of neotropical migrant songbirds in a highly fragmented landscape. *Conservation Biology* 13:338–46.

Gale, G. A., L. A. Hanners, and S. R. Patton. 1997. Reproductive success of worm-eating warblers in a forested landscape. *Conservation Biology* 11:246–50.

George, T. L., and D. S. Dobkin. 2002. Introduction: Habitat fragmentation and western birds. *Avian Studies in Biology* 25:4–7.

Griffith, J. T., and J. C. Griffith. 2000. Cowbird control and the endangered Least Bell's Vireo: A management success story. In *Ecology and management of cowbirds and their hosts,* eds. J. N. M. Smith, T. L. Cook, S. I. Rothstein, S. K. Robinson, and S. G. Sealy, 342–56. Austin: University of Texas Press.

Hannon, S. J., and S. E. Cotterill. 1998. Nest predation in aspen woodlots in an agricultural area in Alberta: The enemy from within. *Auk* 115:16–25.

Harrison, R. B., F. K. A. Schmiegelow, and R. Naidoo. 2005. Stand-level response of breeding forest songbirds to multiple levels of partial-cut harvest in four boreal forest types. *Canadian Journal of Forest Research* 35: 1553–67.

Henry, J. D. 2002. *Canada's boreal forest.* Washington, D.C.: Smithsonian Institution Press.

Herkert, J. R., D. L. Reinking, D. A. Wiedenfeld, M. Winter, J. L. Zimmerman, W. E. Jensen, E. J. Finck, R. R. Koford, D. H. Wolfe, S. K. Sherrod, M. A. Jenkins, J. Faaborg, and S. K. Robinson. 2003. Effects of prairie fragmentation on the nest success of breeding birds in the midcontinental United States. *Conservation Biology* 17:587–94.

Holmes, R. T., J. C. Schultz, and P. Nothnagle. 1979. Bird predation on forest insects: An exclosure experiment. *Science* 206:462–63.

Hull, J. 2005. The final frontier. *Audubon Magazine* 107(5):46–71.

Humane Society of the United States. 2006. *Keep your cat safe at home: HSUS's Safe Cats campaign.* http://www.hsus.org

Lepczyk, C. A., A. G. Mertig, and J. Liu. 2003. Landowners and cat predation across rural-to-urban landscapes. *Biological Conservation* 115:191–201.

Marquis, R. J., and C. J. Whelan. 1994. Insectivorous birds increase growth of white oak through consumption of leaf-chewing insects. *Ecology* 75:2007–14.

Mayfield, H. F. 1977. Brown-headed cowbird: Agent of extermination? *American Birds* 31:107–33.

Morton, E. S. 1973. On the evolutionary advantages and disadvantages of fruit eating in tropical birds. *American Naturalist* 107:8–22.

Niemi, G., J. Hanowski, P. Helle, R. Howe, M. Mönkkönen, L. Venier, and D. Welsh. 1998. Ecology sustainability of birds in boreal forests. *Conservation Ecology* [online] 2(2): 17. http://www.ecologyandsociety.org/vol2/iss2.

Nogales, J., A. Martín, B. R. Tershy, C. J. Donlan, D. Veitch, N. Puerta, B. Wood, and J. Alonso. 2004. A review of feral cat eradication on islands. *Conservation Biology* 18:310–19.

Peterjohn, B. G., and J. R. Sauer. 1999. Population status of North American grassland birds from the North American Breeding Bird Survey, 1966–1996. *Studies in Avian Biology* 19:27–44.

Robinson, G. R., and S. N. Handel. 1993. Forest restoration on a closed landfill: Rapid addition of new species by bird dispersal. *Conservation Biology* 7:271–78.

Robinson, S. K., F. R. Thompson III, T. M. Donovan, D. R. Whitehead, and J. Faaborg. 1995. Regional forest fragmentation and the nesting success of migratory birds. *Science* 267:1987–90.

Schmiegelow, F. K. A., C. S. Machtans, and S. J. Hannon. 1997. Are boreal forest birds resilient to forest fragmentation? An experimental study of short-term community responses. *Ecology* 78:1914–32.

Simons, T. R., G. L. Farnsworth, and S. A. Shriner. 2000. Evaluating the Great Smoky Mountains National Park as a population source for the wood thrush. *Conservation Biology* 14:1133–44.

Tewksbury, J. J., S. J. Hejl, and T. E. Martin. 1998. Breeding productivity does not decline with increasing fragmentation in a western landscape. *Ecology* 79:2890–2903.

Weidensaul, S. 2006. Songs from the wood. *New York Times,* May 30.

Wilcove, D. S. 1985. Nest predation in forest tracts and the decline of migratory songbirds. *Ecology* 66:1211–14.

Winter, L., and G. E. Wallace. 2006. *Impacts of feral and free-ranging cats on bird species of conservation concern.* The Plains, VA: American Bird Conservancy. http://www.abcbirds.org/cats/NFWF.pdf

Winter, M., and J. Faaborg. 1999. Patterns of area sensitivity in grassland-nesting birds. *Conservation Biology* 13:1424–36.

9: Living on the Edge

Ahlering, M. A., and J. Faaborg. 2006. Avian habitat management meets conspecific attraction: If you build it, will they come? *Auk* 123:301–12.

Bielefeldt, J., and R. N. Rosenfield. 1997. Reexamination of cowbird parasitism and edge effects in Wisconsin forests. *Journal of Wildlife Management* 61: 1222–26.

Brittingham, M. C., and S. A. Temple. 1983. Have cowbirds caused forest songbirds to decline? *BioScience* 33:31–35.

Chalfoun, A. D., F. R. Thompson III, and M. J. Ratnaswamy. 2002. Nest predators and fragmentation: A review and metaanalysis. *Conservation Biology* 16:306–18.

Chiver, I., E. S. Morton, and B. J. M. Stutchbury. 2007. Incubation delays territory defence by male blue-headed vireos, *Vireo solitarius. Animal Behaviour* 73:143–48.

Donovan, T. M., P. W. Jones, E. M. Annand, and F. R. Thompson III. 1997. Variation in local-scale edge effects: Mechanisms and landscape context. *Ecology* 78:2064–75.

Dunford, W., and K. Freemark. 2004. Matrix matters: Effects of surrounding land uses on forest birds near Ottawa, Canada. *Landscape Ecology* 20:497–511.

Fraser, G., and B. J. M. Stutchbury. 2004. Area-sensitive birds move extensively among forest patches. *Biological Conservation* 118:377–87.

Gates, J. E., and L. W. Gysel. 1978. Avian nest dispersion and fledging success in field-forest ecotones. *Ecology* 59:871–83.

Hahn, D. C., and J. S. Hatfield. 2000. Host selection in the forest interior: Cowbirds target ground-nesting species. In *Ecology and management of cowbirds and their hosts,* eds. J. N. M. Smith, T. L. Cook, S. I. Rothstein, S. K. Robinson, and S. G. Sealy, 120–27. Austin: University of Texas Press.

Hahn, B. A., and E. D. Silverman. 2006. Social cues facilitate habitat selection: American redstarts establish breeding territories in response to song. *Biological Letters* 2:337–40.

Hames, R. S., K. V. Rosenberg, J. D. Lowe, S. E. Barker, and A. A. Dhondt. 2002. Effects of forest fragmentation on tanager and thrush species in eastern and western North America. *Studies in Avian Biology* 25:81–91.

Lahti, D. C. 2001. The "edge effect on nest predation" hypothesis after twenty years. *Biological Conservation* 99:365–74.

Marini, M. A., S. K. Robinson, and E. J. Heske. 1995. Edge effects on nest predation in the Shawnee National Forest, southern Illinois. *Biological Conservation* 74:203–13.

Morton, E. S. 2005. Predation and variation in breeding habitat use in the ovenbird, with special reference to breeding habitat selection in northwestern Pennsylvania. *Wilson Bulletin* 117:327–456.

Morton, E. S., L. Forman, and M. Braun. 1990. Extrapair fertilizations and the evolution of colonial breeding in purple martins. *Auk* 107:275–83.

Neudorf, D. L., B. J. M. Stutchbury, and W. H. Piper. 1997. Covert extra-territorial behavior of female hooded warblers. *Behavioral Ecology* 8: 595–600.

Norris, D. R., T. E. Pitcher, and B. J. M. Stutchbury. 2000. The spatial response of male hooded warblers to edges in isolated fragments. *Condor* 102:595–600.

Norris, D. R., and B. J. M. Stutchbury. 2001. Extraterritorial movements of a forest songbird in a fragmented landscape. *Conservation Biology* 15:729–36.

Norris, D. R., and B. J. M. Stutchbury. 2002. Sexual differences in gap crossing ability of a forest songbird revealed through radiotracking. *Auk* 119:528–32.

Parker, T. H., B. M. Stanbery, C. D. Becker, and P. S. Gipson. 2005. Edge and area effects on the occurrence of migrant forest songbirds. *Conservation Biology* 19:1157–17.

Paton, P. W. 1994. The effect of edge on avian nest success: How strong is the evidence? *Conservation Biology* 8:17–26.

Robbins, C. S., D. K. Dawson, and B. A. Dowell. 1989. Habitat area requirements of breeding forest birds of the middle Atlantic states. *Wildlife Monographs* 103:1–34.

Stutchbury, B. J. M. 1998. Extra-pair mating effort of male hooded warblers. *Animal Behavior* 55:553–61.

Tarof, S. A., L. M. Ratcliffe, M. M. Kasumovic, and P. T. Boag. 2005. Are least flycatcher (*Empidonax minimus*) clusters hidden leks? *Behavioural Ecology* 16:207–17.

Temple, S. A., and J. R. Cary. 1988. Modeling dynamics of habitat-interior bird populations in fragmented landscapes. *Conservation Biology* 2:340–47.

Thompson, F. R., III, S. K. Robinson, T. M. Donovan, J. R. Faaborg, D. R. Whitehead, and D. R. Larsen. 2000. Biogeographic, landscape and local factors affecting cowbird abundance. In *Ecology and management of cowbirds and their hosts,* eds. J. N. M. Smith, T. L. Cook, S. I. Rothstein, S. K. Robinson, and S. G. Sealy, 271–79. Austin: University of Texas Press.

Villard, M. A. 1998. On forest-interior species, edge avoidance, area sensitivity and dogmas in avian conservation. *Auk* 115:801–5.

Wagner, R. H. 1998. Hidden leks: Sexual selection and the clustering of avian territories. In *Female and male extra-pair mating tactics in birds*, eds. P. G. Parker and N. Burley. Ornithological Monographs 49:123–46.

Ward, M. P., and S. Schlossberg. 2004. Conspecific attraction and the conservation of territorial songbirds. *Conservation Biology* 18:519–25.

Winslow, D. E., D. R. Whitehead, C. F. Whyte, M. A. Koukal, G. M. Greenberg, and T. B. Ford. 2000. In *Ecology and management of cowbirds and their hosts,* eds. J. N. M. Smith, T. L. Cook, S. I. Rothstein, S. K. Robinson, and S. G. Sealy, 298–310. Austin: University of Texas Press.

Woolfenden, B. E., B. J. M. Stutchbury, and E. S. Morton. 2005. Extra-pair fertilizations in the Acadian flycatcher: Males obtain EPFs with distant females. *Animal Behavior* 69:921–29.

Epilogue

Dunn, P. O., and D. W. Winkler. 1999. Climate change has affected the breeding date of tree swallows throughout North America. *Proceedings of the Royal Society of London B* 266:2487–90.

Flannery, T. 2005. *The weather makers: How we are changing the climate and what it means for life on earth.* Toronto: HarperCollins.

Hill, G. E., D. J. Mennill, B. W. Rolek, T. L. Hicks, and K. A. Swiston. 2006. Evidence suggesting that ivory-billed woodpeckers (*Campephilus principalis*) exist in Florida. *Avian Conservation and Ecology* 1(3):2 [online]. http://www.ace.eco.org/vol1/iss3/art2/

Mazerolle, D. F., K. W. Dufour, K. A. Hobson, and H. E. den Haan. 2005. Effects of large-scale climatic fluctuations on survival and production of young in a neotropical migrant songbird, the yellow warbler *Dendroica petechia. Journal of Avian Biology* 36:155–63.

Myers, N. 1997. The world's forests and their ecosystem services. In *Nature's services: Societal dependence on natural ecosystems,* ed. G. C. Daily, 215–35. Washington, D.C.: Island Press.

Nott, M. P., D. F. DeSante, R. B. Siegel, and P. Pyle. 2002. Influences of the El Niño/Southern Oscillation and the North Atlantic Oscillation on avian productivity in forests of the Pacific Northwest of North America. *Global Ecology and Biogeography* 11:333–42.

Şekercioğlu, C. H., G. C. Daily, and P. R. Erlich. 2004. Ecosystem consequences of bird declines. *Proceedings of the National Academy of Sciences* 101:18042–47.

Sillet, T. S., R. T. Holmes, and T. W. Sherry. 2000. Impacts of a global climate cycle on population dynamics of a migratory songbird. *Science* 288:2040–42.

U.N. Millennium Ecosystem Assessment. 2005. *Ecosystems and human well-being: Synthesis.* Washington, D.C.: Island Press.

INDEX

Page numbers in **bold** refer to illustrations
and material discussed in figures and tables.